Intermediate Chinese

Yong Ho

Hippocrene Books, Inc.
New York

For information, address:
Hippocrene Books
171 Madison Avenue
New York, NY 10016

ISBN 0-7818-0992-4

Cataloging-in-Publication data is available from the
 Library of Congress.

Printed in the United States of America.

Contents

Acknowledgements

I wish to express my thanks to the following people
who helped with the various aspects of the book:

Jianping Zhao
*for assisting with preparing pinyin for the characters used in the
book and general formatting and technical issues;*

David Caso, Ernest Hernandez
for providing illustrations;

Youli Hu
for providing drawings and preparing the glossaries;

My daughter Adele
for general assistance as she did with Beginner's Chinese;

And You
for using the book in your study of Chinese.

Introduction

Intermediate Chinese is a continuation of my *Beginner's Chinese* published in 1997 by Hippocrene Books. After I wrote *Beginner's Chinese*, I didn't plan to write a follow-up book, although I did publish a number of other books on Chinese and Chinese history in the meantime. Since its publication, *Beginner's Chinese* has been very well received by students of Chinese. Since 1997, the book has undergone three printings, becoming a bestseller on Hippocrene's booklist. Both the publisher and I have received many encouraging letters from people, some of whom wrote from as far as China. Many of them have asked for a second book.

Part of the success of *Beginner's Chinese* lies in its organizational principles and manner of presentation, but I attribute a larger part to the upsurge in the interest in learning Chinese in the United States and elsewhere. The interest stems from a number of fronts. Recently, *The Washington Post* (May 28, 2002) carried the following dramatic chart showing the top ten languages spoken in the world (speakers in millions):

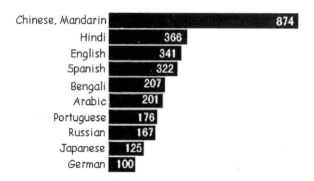

What was listed for Chinese are Mandarin speakers, but since Mandarin is the *lingua franca* in China, the actual number of people speaking and understanding Mandarin is much higher. The need to communicate with a quarter of the world's population and learn about its culture and society is certainly a stimulating factor. Another reason for the enhanced interest is certainly a stimulating factor. Another reason for the enhanced interest in Chinese is the strong growth of the Chinese population in the U.S. In September 2002, the U.S. Census Bureau published national statistics highlighting the prevalence of foreign languages spoken in U.S. households by persons age five years and over. While Spanish remains the most prevalent foreign language spoken in the U.S., Chinese is now ranked #2 in the nation, overtaking French and German since the last Census in 1990. 81% of Chinese-Americans now report that they speak Chinese at home.

Aside from these, Dr. Claudia Ross, President of the Chinese Language Teachers Association in the U.S., pointed out two notable sources that are spurring the interest in learning Chinese: the economic vitality of the Chinese speaking world and the well-publicized need by the U.S. government for personnel with Chinese language skills. Realizing the value and importance of learning Chinese, more and more schools in the U.S., particularly those at the pre-collegiate level, are now offering Chinese programs.

As teachers of Chinese, we are both excited and challenged. One of the challenges we face is to select and create good and effective textbooks for learners of Chinese, particularly for elementary and intermediary students because they rely more on the textbook than advanced students. *Intermediate Chinese*, together with *Beginner's Chinese*, is an effort in this direction. This book, like *Beginner's Chinese*, is based on the premise that less is more and it is still communication-oriented. It tries to present basic sentence patterns and vocabulary necessary for dealing with particular communicative topics. While the focus is still very much on conversation, attention is also paid to reading and writing.

One of the stumbling blocks for students of Chinese is writing the characters. With the advancement of computer technology, students can now avail themselves of a number of software programs to produce Chinese characters on the computer. My colleagues Dr. Ping Xu of Baruch College in New York City and Dr. Theresa Jen of Bryn Mawr College in Pennsylvania have designed a Penless Chinese Program to assist students learning to write characters using the computer. Their

program is available for free downloading at
http://www.penlesschinese.org. Another source of information about
character writing is the *Cheng & Tsui Chinese Character Dictionary* (by
Cheng & Tsui Company in Boston. Toll-free orders: (800) 554-1963),
which provides guidance to reading, understanding and writing two
thousand most frequently used characters in Chinese. I also strongly
recommend that every student of Chinese get a copy of the software
program *Clavis Sinica.* This software was developed by Dr. David Porter,
an English professor at University of Michigan, based on his own
experience learning Chinese. This innovative software combines a
versatile Chinese text reader with a comprehensive and richly cross-
referenced Chinese dictionary. With the help of *Clavis Sinica*, you can
make your way through any digitized Chinese document without the
need for a dictionary. Just click on an unknown character and you will
see its English definition, pinyin pronunciation, and the meaning of the
compound in which it is used. For detailed information about this
software, visit http://clavisinica.com.

To assist learners with making a smooth transition, this book also
provides a vocabulary list of words that appeared in *Beginner*'s *Chinese.*
The book also includes the following appendixes: Computing in Chinese,
and Internet Resources for Students of Chinese.

Happy learning!

Grammatical Terms Explained

Adverbial
A word, phrase or clause that functions to modify a verb, an adjective or another adverb, providing such information as time, place, manner, reason, condition and so on.

Aspect
Manner in which an action takes place. English distinguishes four aspects: indefinite, continuous, perfect and perfect continuous, whereas Chinese distinguishes indefinite, continuous and perfect. The indefinite aspect indicates the habitual or repeated action. The continuous aspect indicates the continuation or progression of the action. The perfect aspect indicates the completion of an action.

Classifier
A word used between a numeral and a noun to show a sub-class to which the noun belongs.

Complement
That part of the sentence that follows the verb and completes the verb. As such, they are also called verb complements. The most common complements in Chinese are those of direction, result and degree. Directional complements indicate the direction of the action in relation to the speaker and are not separated from the verb by any particle. Complements of result and degree indicate the result and the degree of the action expressed by the verb, and they are separated from the verb by the particle 得 de.

Object
A noun, pronoun, phrase or clause that is used after, and affected in some way by, a transitive verb. If it is affected in a direct way, it is called the direct object. If it is affected in an indirect way, it is called the indirect object. In the sentence *he gave me a book*, *a book* is the direct object and *me* is the indirect object.

Particle
A word that has only grammatical meaning, but no lexical meaning, such as 吗 ma, 呢 ne and 吧 ba in Chinese.

Predicate
The part of a sentence that states or asserts something about the subject. This role is only assumed by the verb in English, but can also be assumed by the adjective in Chinese.

Predicative adjective
An adjective used after the verb *to be* in English, as in *the book is interesting*, which is opposed to an attributive adjective used before a noun, as in *this is an interesting book.* The predicative adjective in Chinese is used without the verb *to be*, and functions as the predicate of the sentence.

Subject
Something about which a statement or assertion is made in the rest of the sentence.

Transitive and intransitive verb
A transitive verb is one that needs to take an object such as *we study Chinese.* An intransitive verb is one that does not take an object such as *walk, run* and *go.*

Abbreviations & Conventions

adjective	adj.
adverb	adv.
noun	n.
verb	v.
somebody	sb.
something	sth.

Italics used in the vocabulary list refers to explanations or descriptions of words rather than definitions.

1

PAST & FUTURE

A：玛莉，你 最近 怎么样？
　　Mǎlì, nǐ zuìjìn zěnmeyàng?

B：坐 下，我 要 告诉 你 一 件 事。
　　Zuò xià, wǒ yào gàosù nǐ yí jiàn shì.

A：什么 事？
　　Shénme shì?

B：我 快 结婚了。
　　Wǒ kuài jiéhūn le.

A：你 要 当 新娘 了？太 好 了。祝贺 你！
　　Nǐ yào dāng xīnniáng le? Tài hǎo le. Zhùhè nǐ!
　　新郎 是 谁？
　　Xīnláng shì shuí?

B: 是 大卫。
Shì Dàwèi.

A: 你是 什么 时候 认识 他 的?
Nǐ shì shénme shíhou rènshi tā de?

B: 我 是 去年 认识 他 的。
Wǒ shì qùnián rènshi tā de.

A: 你 是 在 哪儿 认识 他 的?
Nǐ shì zài nǎr rènshi tā de?

B: 我 是 在 北京 认识 他的。当时 我们 都 在 北京
Wǒ shì zài Běijīng rènshi tā de. Dāngshí wǒmen dōu zài Běijīng
学 中文。
xué Zhōngwén.

A: 你们 是 在 什么 学校 学 的 中文?
Nǐmen shì zài shénme xuéxiào xué de Zhōngwén?

B: 我们 是 在 北京 大学 学 的 中文。
Wǒmen shì zaì Běijīng Dàxué xué de Zhōngwén.

A: 你们 打算 什么 时候 结婚?
Nǐmen dǎsuan shénme shíhou jiéhūn?

B: 下 个 月 三 号。你 很 快 就 会 收 到 我们的 请帖。
Xià ge yuè sān hào. Nǐ hěn kuài jiù huì shōudào wǒmende qǐngtiě.
到时 你 一定 要 来 参加 我们的 婚礼。
Dàoshí nǐ yídìng yào lái cānjiā wǒmende hūnlǐ.

A: 我 一定 来。婚礼 以后,你们 要 去 哪儿度 蜜月?
Wǒ yídìng lái. Hūnlǐ yǐhòu, nǐmen yào qù nǎr dù mìyuè?

B：我们　要　去 香港。
Wǒmen yào qù Xiānggǎng.

A：你们　以前　去 过 香港　　吗？
Nǐmen yǐqián qù guo Xiānggǎng ma?

B：没有，　这　是 第一次。听说　　香港　　是 个 很 有意思
Méiyou, zhè shì dì yī cì. Tīngshuō Xiānggǎng shì ge hěn yǒuyìsī
的 地方。
de dìfang.

A：你 回 来 以后 告诉　我 是 不 是 这样。
Nǐ huí lái yǐhòu gàosù wǒ shì bu shì zhèyàng.

B：一 定。
Yídìng.

　　*　　　　*　　　　*　　　　*　　　　*

A：玛莉，你们　是 什么　　时候　从　香港　　回 来 的？
Mǎlì, nǐmen shì shénme shíhou cóng Xiānggǎng huí lai de?

B：我们　是 上　　星期 回 来 的。
Wǒmen shì shàng xīngqī huí lai de.

A：你们　在 香港　　玩儿 了 几 天？
Nǐmen zài Xiānggǎng wánr le jǐ tiān?

B：我们　　在 香港　　玩儿 了 一 个 星期。
Wǒmen zài Xiānggǎng wánr le yí ge xīngqī.

A：香港　　怎么样？
Xiānggǎng zěnmeyàng?

3

B：香港　　　很　好玩儿，风景　　也　很　美。
Xiānggǎng hěn hǎowánr, fēngjǐng yě hěn měi.

A：你们　在 香港　　的 时候，　住 在 哪儿？
Nǐmen zài Xiānggǎng de shíhou, zhù zài nǎr?

B：我们　　住 在 半岛　饭店。
Wǒmen zhù zài Bàndǎo Fàndiàn.

A：除了 香港，　　你们　还 去 了 哪儿？
Chúle Xiānggǎng, nǐmen hái qù le nǎr?

B：我们　　还 去 了 澳门。
Wǒmen hái qù le Àomén.

A：是 吗？你们　是 怎么 去 澳门　的？是 不 是 坐 飞机 去
Shì ma? Nǐmen shì zěnme qù Àomén de? Shì bu shì zuò fēijī qù
的？
de?

B：我们　　不 是 坐 飞机 去 的，我们　是 坐 船　去 的。
Wǒmen bú shì zuò fēijī qù de, wǒmen shì zuò chuán qù de.

A：从　香港　　坐 船　到 澳门 要 多 长　时间？
Cóng Xiānggǎng zuò chuán dào Àomén yào duō cháng shíjiān?

B：澳门　离 香港　　很 近, 坐 船　只 要 一 个 小时。
Àomén lí Xiānggǎng hěn jìn, zuò chuán zhǐ yào yí ge xiǎoshí.

　　　*　　　*　　　*　　　*　　　*

A：王　先生，　　我 想　问 你 一 件 私事。不 知道 你 会
Wáng Xiānsheng, wǒ xiǎng wèn nǐ yí jiàn sī shì. Bù zhīdào nǐ huì

不 会 介意?
bu huì jièyì?

B: 你 问 吧。
Nǐ wèn ba.

A: 你 有 没有 结婚?
Nǐ yǒu méiyou jiéhūn?

B: 我 结 了。
Wǒ jié le.

A: 你 是 什么 时候 结 的婚?
Nǐ shì shénme shíhou jié de hūn?

B: 我 是 三 年 前 结 的。你 呢, 李 先生? 你 有
Wǒ shì sān nián qián jié de. Nǐ ne, Lǐ Xiānsheng? Nǐ yǒu
没有 结婚?
méiyou jiéhūn?

A: 还 没有。
Hái méiyou.

B: 有 女朋友 吗?
Yǒu nǚpéngyou ma?

A: 有。她 和我 在 一 个 单位。
Yǒu. Tā hé wǒ zài yí ge dānwèi.

B: 你们 准备 什么 时候 结婚?
Nǐmén zhǔnbèi shénme shíhou jiéhūn?

A：现在　还　不 知道。可能　两　年　以后 吧。
Xiànzài hái bù zhīdào. Kěnéng liǎng nián yǐhòu bā.

Reading Passage

我的朋友大卫快结婚了。我下星期要参加他的婚礼。大卫的新娘是
玛莉。大卫和玛莉都是美国人。他们是去年在北京大学学中文的时
候认识的。来北京以前，大卫是银行职员，玛莉是小学老师。他们
要在中国结婚。他们的爸爸妈妈都要来北京参加他们的婚礼。大卫
和玛莉结婚后要去南京大学教英语。他们一年以后回美国。

Wǒde péngyou Dàwèi kuài jiéhūn le. Wǒ xià xīngqī yào cānjiā tāde hūnlǐ.
Dàwèi de xīnniáng shì Mǎlì.   Dàwèi hé Mǎlì dōu shì Měiguórén. Tāmen
shì qùnián zài Běijīng Dàxué xué Zhōngwén de shíhou rènshi de. Lái
Běijīng yǐqián, Dàwèi shì yínháng zhíyuán. Mǎlì shì xiǎoxué lǎoshī.
Tāmen yào zài Zhōngguó jiéhūn. Tāmen de bàba māma dōu yào lái
Běijīng cānjiā tāmende hūnlǐ. Dàwèi hé Mǎlì jiéhūn hòu yào qù Nánjīng
Dàxué jiāo Yīngyǔ. Tāmen yì nián yǐhòu huí Měiguó.

New Words and Expressions

最近	zuìjìn	recently; shortly; these days
事	shì	matter; thing (to do)
快 ...... 了	kuài ... le	about to
当	dāng	become; act as
新娘	xīnniáng	bride
祝贺	zhùhè	congratulate; congratulations
新郎	xīnláng	bridegroom

当时	dāngshí	at that time
打算	dǎsuan	plan (v & n)
结婚	jiéhūn	get married
就	jiù	right away
会	huì	will (modal verb)
收到	shōudào	receive
请帖	qǐngtiě	invitation card/letter
到时	dàoshí	at that (future) time
参加	cānjiā	participate (in); join; take part (in)
婚礼	hūnlǐ	wedding
以后	yǐhòu	after; later; in the future
以前	yǐqián	before; previously; in the past; ago
蜜月	mìyuè	honeymoon
有意思	yǒuyìsi	interesting
这样	zhèyàng	so; like this
半岛	bàndǎo	Peninsula
回	huí	return (to a place); reply
风景	fēngjǐng	scenery
美	měi	pretty; beautiful
除了	chúle	besides; in addition to
还	hái	also; additionally
澳门	Àomén	Macao
私	sī	private
介意	jièyì	mind (v)
举行	jǔxíng	hold
职员	zhíyuán	clerk

7

教	jiāo	teach

Supplementary Words and Expressions

订婚	dìnghūn	be engaged (to)
离婚	líhūn	divorce (v)
分居	fēnjū	separate (v)
再婚	zàihūn	remarry
未婚夫	wèihūnfū	fiancé
未婚妻	wèihūnqī	fiancée
爱	ài	love (v & n)
谈恋爱	tán liàn'ài	date (v)
礼物	lǐwù	gift; present
送	sòng	give as a present
漂亮	piàoliang	good-looking; pretty
宴会	yànhuì	banquet
亲戚	qīnqī	relatives

Language Points

Punctuation marks in Chinese

They are for the most part the same as those in English except that the period is in the form of a small circle 。instead of a dot, and the ellipsis consists of six dots (......) instead of three. An extra mark in Chinese is "、", which is variously translated as the enumerative comma, half-comma, listing comma and series comma. It is used after items in an enumeration:

我们　去了北京、上海、　西安　和香港。
Wǒmen qù le Běijīng, Shànghǎi, Xī'ān, hé Xiānggǎng.
We went to Beijing, Shanghai, Xi'an and Hong Kong.

Another mark unfamiliar to English speakers is the title mark: 《　》, used to bracket a book title, movie title, and so on. An example of it is 《中级中文》 zhōngjí Zhōngwén (*Intermediate Chinese*).

你最近怎么样 nǐ zuìjìn zěnmeyàng?

Unlike *recently* in English, 最近 zuìjìn can refer to future as well as past. Basically it refers to a point, past or future, that is closest to the present. So we can say both of the following:

我　最近　去了中国。
Wǒ zuìjìn qù le Zhōngguó.
I went to China recently.

我　最近　要　去中国。
Wǒ zuìjìn yào qù Zhōngguó.
I'm going to China soon.

Indication of the future

Chinese does not have a tense system. The following words and expressions are often used in conjunction with a verb to indicate future:

1. 要 ...... 了 yào ... le (be going to; be about to):

我　妈妈　要　来　美国　了。
Wǒ māma yào lái Měiguó le.
My mother is coming to America.

9

要 yào in this sense is often preceded by 就 jiù or 快 kuài for additional emphasis.

2. 快 ......了 kuài ... le (be about to; soon; before long):

火车　快　来了。
Huǒchē kuài lái le.
The train is about to arrive.

快　下课　了。
Kuài xiàkè le.
The class will be over soon.

快 ......了 kuài ... le can also be used with a noun in between to mean *almost*:

我　来美国　快　十　年　了。
Wǒ lái Měiguó kuài shí nián le.
It is almost ten years since I came to America.

快　三　点　了。
Kuài sān diǎn le.
It's almost three o'clock.

快　新年　了。
Kuài xīnnián le.
It is almost New Year.

3. 打算 dǎsuan (plan), both as a noun and a verb:

A: 你 毕业后　有　什么　　打算?
　　Nǐ bìyè hòu yǒu shénme dǎsuan?
　　What's your plan after you graduate?

B: 我　打算　工作。
　　Wǒ dǎsuan gōngzuò.
　　I plan to work.

4. 准备 zhǔnbèi (plan):

你 今年　准备　在 哪儿过 年？
Nǐ jīnnián zhǔnbèi zài nǎr　guò nián?
Where are you planning to spend your New Year this year?

While 打算 dǎsuan is more often used in spoken language, 准备 zhǔnbèi occurs more in written language.

5. 会 huì (will)
会 huì is a modal verb expressing a future possibility:

老师　明天　　会 来 吗？
Lǎoshī míngtiān huì lái ma?
Will the teacher come tomorrow?

今天 不会 下雨。
Jīntiān bú huì xiàyǔ.
It won't rain today.

Indication of the past

As mentioned above, Chinese does not have a tense system, so there is no specific verbal form that indicates a past event. Past events are usually indicated by time words such as 现在 xiànzài (now), 过去 guòqù (in the past), 三年前 sān nián qián (three years ago), etc. Please disassociate the particle 了 le from the English suffix -ed, which is used to indicate the past. In one of its many uses, 了 le serves as an aspect marker indicating the completion of an action. Although most completed actions took place in the past, they can also take place in the future such as when we say in English, *I will have finished reading the book by the end of this week.*

Additionally, 了 le is not to be used when the verb is cognitive in nature or when the verb indicates a past habitual action (see *Beginner's Chinese*, Lesson 10).

When asking questions about the time, place and manner of a past event, Chinese uses the 是 shì ...... 的 de construction, where the item following 是 shì is highlighted. Additionally, 是 shì can be omitted:

他 (是) 什么　时候　去 中国　　的?
Tā (shì) shénme shíhou qù Zhōngguó de?
When did he go to China?

你 (是) 在 哪儿认识 你 太太 的?
Nǐ shì zài nǎr rènshi nǐ tàitai de?
Where did you meet your wife?

你今天　(是) 怎么　来 的?
Nǐ jīntiān (shì) zěnme lái de?
How did you come today?

When the verb is a transitive one, 的 de is usually placed between the verb and the object:

你今天　(是) 在 哪儿吃 的中饭?
Nǐ jīntiān (shì) zài nǎr chī de zhōngfàn?
Where did you eat lunch today?

你 (是) 在 哪儿上　的 大学?
Nǐ (shì) zài nǎr shàng de dàxué?
Where did you go to college?

Note that the response to the questions above should take the same form. If the object is a pronoun or if it is a noun followed by a directional complement (see below), 的 de must be placed at the end of the sentence:

你 是 在 哪儿认识 他 的?
Nǐ shì zài nǎr rènshi tā de?
Where did you become acquainted with him?

他 是 昨天 回 上海 的。
Tā shì zuótiān huí Shànghǎi de.
He returned to Shanghai yesterday.

If the sentence takes the negative form, 不 bù is used before 是 shì, which cannot be omitted:

我 不 是 在 北京 大学 学 的 中文。
Wǒ bú shì zài Běijīng Dàxué xué de Zhōngwén.
I didn't study Chinese at Beijing University.

以后 yǐhòu and 以前 yǐqián

Unlike *after* and *before* in English, which are prepositions and conjunctions, 以后 yǐhòu and 以前 yǐqián are nouns used adverbially to indicate time.

When used by itself, 以后 yǐhòu means *later* or *in the future*. Since it is used to indicate time, it appears before the verb:

我 以后 要 当 老师。
Wǒ yǐhòu yào dāng lǎoshī.
I would like to become a teacher in the future.

你 还 小, 我 以后 告诉 你。
Nǐ hái xiǎo, wǒ yǐhòu gàosù nǐ.
You are still young. I'll tell you later.

When modified by a noun, a phrase or a sentence, 以后 yǐhòu means *after*. Additionally, the 以后 yǐhòu phrase or clause always appears before the main clause:

13

2000 年　以后
2000 nián yǐhòu
after 2000

下班　以后，他们　要　去　看　电影。
Xiàbān yǐhòu, tāmen yào qù kàn diànyǐng.
They are going to see a movie after work.

我　来美国　以后住　在　纽约。
Wǒ lái Měiguó yǐhòu zhù zài Niǔyuē.
I lived in New York after I came to America.

When used by itself, 以前 yǐqián means *before* or *previously*. Since it is used to indicate time, it appears before the verb:

我　以前没有　吃　过广东　　菜。
Wǒ yǐqián méiyou chī guo Guǎngdōng cài.
I have not had Cantonese food before.

When modified by a noun, a phrase or a sentence, 以前 yǐqián means *before a certain time* or *some time ago*. Additionally, the 以前 yǐqián phrase or sentence always appears before the main sentence:

三　天　以前
sān tiān yǐqián
three days ago

吃饭　以前要　先　洗手。
Chīfàn yǐqián yào xiān xǐ shǒu.
Wash your hands before eating.

你来美国　以前会不会说　英语?
Nǐ lái Měiguó yǐqián huì bu huì shuō Yīngyǔ?
Did you speak English before you came to America?

以 yǐ in 以前 yǐqián and 以后 yǐhòu can be left out when used at the end of a phrase or a clause:

三 天 前
Sān tiān qián
three days ago

来美国 前
lái Měiguó qián
before coming to America

一个月后
yí ge yuè hòu
a month later

结婚 后
jiéhūn hòu
after getting married

的 de used after an adjective

A monosyllabic adjective can directly modify a noun:

好 人
hǎo rén
good person

旧 车
jiù chē
old car

But 的 de is needed when the adjective is disyllabic or polysyllabic:

高兴 的事
gāoxìng de shì

happy event

有意思 的电影
yǒuyìsi de diànyǐng
interesting movie

A monosyllabic attributive adjective modified by an adverb also requires the use of 的 de before a noun:

很 好 的 人
hěn hǎo de rén
very good person

非常　热 的夏天
fēicháng rè de xiàtiān
extremely hot summer

你们是什么时候从香港回来的 nǐmen shì shénme shíhou cóng Xiānggǎng huí lái de?

When used after a verb, 来 lái indicates the direction of the action in relation to the speaker. As such, it is usually used after certain verbs such as 到 dào (go to), 带 dài (bring, carry), 寄 jì (mail), 上 shàng (go up), 下 xià (go down), 进 jìn (enter), 出 chū (exit), 回 huí (return). This use of 来 lái is opposed to 去 qù. Compare: 进来 jìn lai (*come in*—in the direction of the speaker) and 进去 jìn qu (*go in*—away from the speaker), 上来 shàng lai (*come up*—the speaker is up) and 上去 shàng qu (*go up*— away from the speaker). This use of 来 lái and 去 qù is referred to in grammar as the directional complement. When used as a directional complement, 来 lái and 去 qù are pronounced in the neutral tone.

香港很好玩儿 Xiānggǎng hěn hǎowánr

好 hǎo is often used with certain verbs to form adjectives. Examples are: 好吃 hǎochī (delicious), 好喝 hǎohē (good to drink), 好听 hǎotīng (ear-pleasing; good to listen to), 好看 hǎokàn (pretty, good-looking) and 好玩儿 hǎowánr (fun).

除了 chúle

When used in the sense of *besides*, the preposition 除了 chúle is usually used in conjunction with the adverb 还 hái or 也 yě. The phrase introduced by 除了 chúle always comes at the beginning of a sentence:

除了 中文, 他还 会 说 日语。
Chúle Zhōngwén, tā hái huì shuō Rìyǔ.
Besides Chinese, he also speaks Japanese.

除了 星期一，我们 星期三 也 有 英语 课。
Chúle xīngqīyī, wǒmen xīngqīsān yě yǒu Yīngyǔ kè.
Besides Monday, we also have English class on Wednesday.

的时候 de shíhou

In the sense of *time when*, 的时候 de shíhou is always modified by a phrase or a sentence. Additionally, the phrase or clause with 的时候 de shíhou always appears before the main clause:

吃饭 的 时候, 不要 说话。
Chīfàn de shíhou, búyào shuōhuà.
Don't talk while eating.

我 在 中国 的 时候, 去 过 青岛。
Wǒ zài Zhōngguó de shíhou, qù guo Qīngdǎo.
I visited Qingdao when I was in China.

你们在香港玩儿了几天 nǐmen zài Xiānggǎng wánr le jǐ tiān?

In *Beginner's Chinese*, mention was made that adverbials of time should precede verbs in Chinese, but we should also know that this rule only applies to a point of time. If the time refers to a duration or period that the action expressed by the verb experienced, it should follow the verb in the sentence:

他 在 那 个公司　工作　　了 三　年。
Tā zài nà ge gōngsi gōngzuò le sān nián.
He worked at that company for three years.

雨 下 了五　个 小时。
Yǔ xià le wǔ ge xiǎoshí.
It rained for five hours.

可能两年以后吧 kěnéng liǎng nián yǐhòu ba

吧 ba is a sentence-final particle, used to indicate:

1. A supposition or guess as in the sentence cited: *probably in two years.*

2. Suggestion, request or command:

我们　　开始 学习 吧。
Wǒmen kāishǐ xuéxí ba.
Let's begin our study.

3. Confirmation:

你 是 中国人　　吧。
Nǐ shì Zhōngguórén ba.
You are Chinese, aren't you?

Exercises

I. Answer the following questions:

1. 你 是 什么　 时候　开始　学　中文　　 的?
   Nǐ shì shénme shíhou kāishǐ xué zhōngwén de?

2. 你 在 这儿 住 了几年?
   Nǐ zài zhèr　zhù le jǐ nián?

3. 你 今天　吃 了中饭　　 吗? 你 是 在 哪儿吃 的 中饭?
   Nǐ jīntiān chī le zhōngfàn ma? Nǐ shì zài nǎr　 chī de zhōngfàn?

4. 你 今天　是 怎么　来　学校　　 的?
   Nǐ jīntiān shì zěnme lái xuéxiào de?

5. 你 今天　怎么 回　家? 你 回　家 以后 要 作 什么?
   Nǐ jīntiān zěnme huí jiā?　Nǐ huí jiā yǐhòu yào zuò shénme?

6. 你 今年　夏天　打算　作 什么?
   Nǐ jīnnián xiàtiān dǎsuan zuò shénme?

7. 你 现在　住 哪儿? 你 以前　住 哪儿?
   Nǐ xiànzài zhù nǎr?　 Nǐ yǐqián zhù nǎr?

8. 你 以前 去 过 中国　　 吗? 你 以后 会 去 中国　　 吗?
   Nǐ yǐqián qù guo Zhōngguó ma? Nǐ yǐhòu huì qù Zhōngguó ma?

9. 你 学习 的 时候, 喜欢　听 音乐 吗?
   Nǐ xuéxí de shíhou, xǐhuan tīng yīnyuè ma?

10. 除了 今天, 这星期　 你 还 有 中文　　 课 吗?
    Chúle jīntiān,　zhè xīngqī nǐ hái yǒu Zhōngwén kè ma?

II. How do you say the following:

1. married for thirty years
2. divorced for five years
3. attend a friend's wedding
4. go to Hawaii (夏威夷 Xiàwēiyí) for honeymoon
5. let's go
6. bride and groom
7. ten years ago; in ten years
8. before going to work; after getting off work
9. when they got married
10. return from America

III. Fill in the blanks with the following words and expressions:

最近 zuìjìn; 要 yào; 以前 yǐqián; 以后 yǐhòu; 是 ...... 的 shì ... de;
快 ......了 kuài ... le; ...... 的时候 de shíhou

1. 我 下班 _____ 要 去看 一个 朋友。
   Wǒ xiàbān _____ yào qù kàn yí ge péngyou.

2. 你 今天 _____ 几点 起床 _____?
   Nǐ jīntiān _____ jǐ diǎn qǐchuáng _____?

3. 我的 老师 _____ 去 了香港。
   Wǒde lǎoshī _____ qù le Xiānggǎng.

4. 他 在 北京 _____ 常 去 博物馆。
   Tā zài Běijīng _____ cháng qù bówùguǎn.

5. 一 百 年 _____ 没 有 飞机。
   Yì bǎi nián _____ méi yǒu fēijī.

6. 我 哥哥 下 个 月 _____ 去 电话　公司　工作。
   Wǒ gēge xià ge yuè _____ qù diànhuà gōngsī gōngzuò.

7. _____ 中国　没 有 美国　银行。 现在　有。
   _____ Zhōngguó méi yǒu Měiguó yínháng. Xiànzài yǒu.

8. 我 _____ 告诉 你 这 件 事。
   Wǒ _____ gàosù nǐ zhè jiàn shì.

9. 她 吃饭 _____ 喜欢　看　电视。
   Tā chīfàn _____ xǐhuān kàn diànshì.

10. 电影 _____ 几点　开始 _____?
    Diànyǐng _____ jǐ diǎn kāishǐ _____?

IV. Insert the time expressions in the parentheses in the proper place in the following sentences:

1. 老师们　每 天　上班。　　　　　　(七点)
   Lǎoshīmen měi tiān shàngbān.　　　(qī diǎn)

2. 老师们　每 天　工作。　　　　　　(七个小时)
   Lǎoshīmen měi tiān gōngzuò.　　　(qī ge xiǎoshí)

3. 我的　美国　朋友　在 广州　住 了。 (三 年)
   Wǒde Měiguó péngyou zài Guǎngzhōu zhù le.　(sān nián)

4. 大卫　和 玛丽 结婚。　　　　　　(下 个 月)
   Dàwèi hé Mǎlì jiéhūn.　　　　　　(xià ge yuè)

5. 你 在 澳门　玩儿 了?　　　　　　(几天)
   Nǐ zài Àomén wánr le?　　　　　　(jǐ tiān)

V. Fill in the blanks with the following expressions:

好玩儿 hǎowánr, 好看 hǎokàn, 好听 hǎotīng, 好吃 hǎochī, 好喝 hǎohē

1. 中国　菜 很 _____ 。
   Zhōngguó cài hěn _____ .

2. 美国　音乐 很 _____ 。
   Měiguó yīnyuè hěn _____ .

3. 青岛　啤酒很 _____ 。
   Qīngdǎo píjiǔ hěn _____ .

4. 这 本 书 不 _____ 。
   Zhè běn shū bù _____ .

5. 香港　不 _____ 。
   Xiānggǎng bù _____ .

VI. Decide which of the following adjectives must be followed by 的 de when modifying a noun:

新 _____ 汽车	好吃 _____ 菜	短_____ 大衣
xīn _____ qìchē	hǎochī _____ cài	duǎn _____ dàyī

不 老 _____ 人	高兴_____ 事	热 _____ 茶
bù lǎo _____ rén	gāoxìng _____ shì	rè _____ chá

VII. Translate the following into Chinese:

1. I didn't go to the bank today.
2. Before she came to America, she was a teacher. After she came to America, she was a student.

3. My parents were not home ten days ago.
4. What time did you have lunch today?
5. They have worked for the company for twenty years.
6. What are you planning to do tonight?
7. My younger sister is about to be married.
8. Besides France, we also went to England and Germany.
9. Children like to ask a lot of questions when they are at the movies.
10. She said that she would tell me later.

VIII. Translate the following into English:

1. 我 姐姐 结婚 以前 住 在 加州。
   Wǒ jiějie jiéhūn yǐqián zhù zài Jiāzhōu.

2. 上海   以前 没 有 地铁。
   Shànghǎi yǐqián méi yǒu dìtiě.

3. 现在   有 很 多 人 不 打算 结婚。
   Xiànzài yǒu hěn duō rén bù dǎsuan jiéhūn.

4. 快 下雨 了。
   Kuài xiàyǔ le.

5. 她 是 三 个星期 以前 从 中国   回 来 的。
   Tā shì sān ge xīngqī yǐqián cóng Zhōngguó huí lái de.

6. 除了 英语,   我的 老师 还 会 说 法语 和西班牙语。
   Chúle Yīngyǔ, wǒde lǎoshī hái huì shuō Fǎyǔ hé Xībānyáyǔ.

7. 我 最近 很 忙,   没 有 时间 学 中文,   但是 以后 我
   Wǒ zuìjìn hěn máng, méi yǒu shíjiān xué Zhōngwén, dànshì yǐhòu wǒ
   会 学。
   huì xué.

23

8. 他们 是 坐 飞机去 华盛顿 的。
 Tāmen shì zuò fēijī qù Huáshèngdùn de.

9. 你 不 工作 的 时候，喜欢 做 什么?
 Nǐ bù gōngzuò de shíhou, xǐhuān zuò shénme?

10. 雪 下 了 两 天。
 Xuě xià le liǎng tiān.

IX. Writing

Write five sentences for things you did in the past and five sentences for things you will do in the future.

English Translation of the Text

Conversations

A: Mary, how have you been recently?
B: Sit down. I have something to tell you.
A: What is it?
B: I'm getting married.
A: You will be a bride? Great. Congratulations! Who is the bridegroom?
B: It's David.
A: When did you meet him?
B: I met him last year.
A: Where did you meet him?
B: I met him in Beijing. At that time, we were both studying Chinese in Beijing.
A: What school did you study Chinese at?
B: We studied Chinese at Beijing University.
A: When are you planning to get married?
B: The third of next month. You will soon receive our invitation. You must come to our wedding.

A: I'll definitely come. Where are you going to spend your honeymoon after the wedding?

B: We'll go to Hong Kong.

A: Have you been there before?

B: No. This is the first time. I heard that Hong Kong is an interesting place.

A: Tell me if it is the case after you come back.

B: Sure.

        *   *   *   *   *

A: Mary, when did you come back from Hong Kong?

B: We came back last week.

A: How many days did you spend in Hong Kong?

B: We spent a week in Hong Kong.

A: How is Hong Kong?

B: Hong Kong is a fun place. The scenery is also beautiful.

A: Where did you stay when you were in Hong Kong?

B: We stayed at the Peninsular Hotel.

A: Besides Hong Kong, where else did you go?

B: We also went to Macao.

A: Is that so? How did you go to Macao? Did you fly there?

B: We didn't fly. We went there by boat.

A: How long does it take to go from Hong Kong to Macao by boat?

B: Macao is very close to Hong Kong. It takes only an hour by boat.

        *   *   *   *   *

A: Mr. Wang, I'd like to ask you a question about a private matter. I wonder if you would mind.

B: Go ahead.

A: Are you married?

B: Yes, I am.

A: When did you get married?

B: I got married three years ago. How about you, Mr. Li? Are you married?

A: Not yet.

B: Do you have a girlfriend?
A: Yes. She and I are in the same workplace.
B: When are you planning to get married?
A: Don't know now. Maybe in two years.

Reading Passage

My friend David is getting married soon. I'll be attending his wedding
next week. David's bride is Mary. Both David and Mary are Americans.
They met when they were studying Chinese at Beijing University last
year. Before they came to Beijing, David was a bank clerk and Mary was
an elementary school teacher. They would like to get married in China.
Their parents are coming to Beijing to attend their wedding. After the
wedding, David and Mary are going to teach English at Nanjing
University. They will return to America in a year.

2

CHINESE & ENGLISH

Conversations

A：马丁， 听说　 你在学 中文?
Mǎdīng, tīngshuō nǐ zài xué Zhōngwén?

B：对，我很 喜欢 中文。
Duì, wǒ hěn xǐhuan Zhōngwén.

A：你学了多 长　 时间 了?
Nǐ xué le duō cháng shíjiān le?

B：我 学 了一年 多 了。
Wǒ xué le yì nián duō le.

A：你学 得 怎么样?
Nǐ xué de zěnmeyàng?

B：我 想　 我学 得还 可以。我 现在　 已经 能　 认 五百
Wǒ xiǎng wǒ xué de hái kěyǐ. Wǒ xiànzài yǐjīng néng rèn wǔbǎi

个字，会 写 三百个字了。
ge zì, huì xiě sānbǎi ge zì le.

A：真 了不起。你 说 中文 说 得也很 好。
Zhēn liǎobuqǐ. Nǐ shuō Zhōngwén shuō de yě hěn hǎo.

B：哪里，我 说 中文 说 得还不太 流利。
Nǎlǐ, wǒ shuō Zhōngwén shuō de hái bú tài liúlì.

A：你 觉得中文 难 不难?
Nǐ juéde Zhōngwén nán bu nán?

B：有的 地方 难，有的 地方 不 难。比如说 语法和 发音 不
Yǒude dìfang nán, yǒude dìfang bù nán. Bǐrúshuō yǔfǎ hé fāyīn bù
难，但是 写 字 难 一些。
nán, dànshì xiě zì nán yìxiē.

A：你 每 天 写汉字 吗?
Nǐ měi tiān xiě hànzì ma?

B：我 想 每 天 写，但是 有时 工作 忙， 没 有
Wǒ xiǎng měi tiān xiě, dànshì yǒushí gōngzuò máng, méi yǒu
时间 练习。
shíjiān liànxí.

A：你 觉得什么 是学 中文 的 最好 的 办法?
Nǐ juéde shénme shì xué Zhōngwén de zuì hǎo de bànfǎ?

B：我 觉得最 好 的办法是 去中国 学。你想 去 吗?
Wǒ juéde zuì hǎo de bànfǎ shì qù Zhōngguó xué. Nǐ xiǎng qù ma?

A：当然 想。 语言 环境 很 重要。 可是 我在
Dāngrán xiǎng. Yǔyán huánjìng hěn zhòngyào. Kěshì wǒ zài

工作， 不能 在 中国 住 很 长 时间。
gōngzuò, bù néng zài Zhōngguó zhù hěn cháng shíjiān.

B：你 可以 夏天 去。中国 的 很 多 学校 有 暑期
Nǐ kěyǐ xiàtiān qù. Zhōngguó de hěn duō xuéxiào yǒu shǔqī
中文 班。
Zhōngwén bān.

A：我 如果 去 中国 学 中文， 你 想 我 应该 去 哪
Wǒ rúguǒ qù Zhōngguó xué Zhōngwén, nǐ xiǎng wǒ yīnggāi qù nǎ
个 城市？
ge chéngshì?

B：我 想 你 应该 去 北京。 北京 人 都 说 普通话。
Wǒ xiǎng nǐ yīnggāi qù Běijīng. Běijīng rén dōu shuō pǔtōnghuà.

*   *   *   *   *

A：小 王， 你的 英语 最近 有 很 大 的 进步。
Xiǎo Wáng, nǐde Yīngyǔ zuìjìn yǒu hěn dà de jìnbù.

B：谢谢。 我的 英语 还 很 差。
Xièxie. Wǒde Yīngyǔ hái hěn chà.

A：你 学 英语 学 了 几年 了？
Nǐ xué Yīngyǔ xué le jǐ nián le?

B：我 学 英语 已经 学了 两 年 多 了。但是 我 想
Wǒ xué Yīngyǔ yǐjīng xué le liǎng nián duō le. Dànshì wǒ xiǎng
我的 英语 还 不够 好。
wǒde Yīngyǔ hái bú gòu hǎo.

A：你 为什么 要 学 英语？
Nǐ wèishénme yào xué Yīngyǔ?

B：我 想　以后 去 英国　　上学。　　懂　英语，工作　机会
Wǒ xiǎng yǐhòu qù Yīngguó shàngxué. Dǒng Yīngyǔ, gōngzuò jīhuì
也 会 多 一些。
yě huì duō yìxiē.

A：你 觉得 学 英语　什么　最 难?
Nǐ juéde xué Yīngyǔ shénme zuì nán?

B：我 觉得 说　最 难。主要　是 我 没 有 机会 练 口语。
Wǒ juéde shuō zuì nán. Zhǔyào shì wǒ méi yǒu jīhuì liàn kǒuyǔ.

A：我们　可以 互相　帮助。　你 跟 我 练 中文，　　我 跟
Wǒmen kěyǐ hùxiāng bāngzhù. Nǐ gēn wǒ liàn Zhōngwén, wǒ gēn
你 练 英语。
nǐ liàn Yīngyǔ.

B：这 是 一个 好　主意。
Zhè shì yí ge hǎo zhǔyì.

Reading Passage

小王在北京的中国银行工作，她在那儿已经工作了五年。小王的家
离单位很远，每天她起得很早，五点半就起床了。她要坐一个小时
的地铁才能到公司。小王每天工作八个小时，下班后她还去英语学
校学英语。她学英语已经学了两年多了。她学得很好，已经能用英
语和外国客户交谈了。

Xiǎo Wáng zài Běijīng de Zhōngguó Yínháng gōngzuò, tā zài nàr yǐjīng
gōngzuò le wǔ nián. Xiǎo Wáng de jiā lí dānwèi hěn yuǎn, měi tiān tā qǐ
de hěn zǎo, wǔ diǎn bàn jiù qǐchuáng le. Tā yào zuò yí ge xiǎoshi de dìtiě
cái néng dào gōngsī. Xiǎo Wáng měi tiān gōngzuò bā ge xiǎoshi, xiàbān
hòu tā hái qù Yīngyǔ xuéxiào xué Yīngyǔ. Tā xué Yīngyǔ yǐjīng xué le

iǎng nián duō le. Tā xué de hěn hǎo, yǐjīng néng yòng Yīngyǔ hé wàiguó
ɛèhù jiāotán le.

New Words and Expressions

在	zài	*progressive aspect marker*
得	de	*verb complement marker*
还	hái	fairly; passably; still
可以	kěyǐ	pretty good; not bad
已经	yǐjīng	already
认	rèn	recognize
真	zhēn	really; truly
了不起	liǎobuqǐ	amazing; remarkable
哪里	nǎlǐ	*polite response to a compliment*
流利	liúlì	fluent
难	nán	hard; difficult
比如说	bǐrúshuō	for example
发音	fāyīn	pronounce; pronunciation
一些	yìxiē	somewhat; a little
汉字	hànzì	Chinese characters
练习	liànxí	practice (n & v)
办法	bànfǎ	way; means; method
环境	huánjìng	environment
重要	zhòngyào	important
暑期	shǔqī	summertime; summer vacation
班	bān	class
如果	rúguǒ	if

31

应该	yīnggāi	should; ought to
城市	chéngshì	city
进步	jìnbù	progress (n & v)
差	chà	not good; poor
够	gòu	enough
上学	shàngxué	attend school; go to school
主要	zhǔyào	main; primary; mainly; primarily
机会	jīhuì	opportunity
练	liàn	practice (v)
口语	kǒuyǔ	spoken language
互相	hùxiāng	each other; mutually
帮助	bāngzhù	help; assist
跟	gēn	with; and
主意	zhǔyì	idea
就	jiù	as early as; already; then
才	cái	as late as; not until
到	dào	arrive; reach
客户	kèhù	client
交谈	jiāotán	converse; chat

Supplementary Words and Expressions

阅读	yuèdú	reading
作文	zuòwén	composition
考试	kǎoshì	examination; examine
句子	jùzi	sentence

忘	wàng	forget
复习	fùxí	review (n & v)
光盘	guāngpán	CD-ROM
录音	lùyīn	record (voice); recording
生词	shēngcí	new words
课文	kèwén	text
声调	shēngdiào	tone
念	niàn	read aloud
录音带	lùyīndài	audiotape
录像带	lùxiàngdài	videotape

Language Points

Indication of the progressive aspect

To indicate the progressive or continuous aspect of an action, Chinese uses the aspect marker 在 zài before the verb. The particle 呢 ne can be used optionally at the end of the sentence:

经理 在 打 电话　 (呢)。
Jīnglǐ zài dǎ diànhuà (ne).
The manager is making a phone call.

我 先生　 在 睡觉 (呢)。
Wǒ xiānsheng zài shuìjiào (ne).
My husband is sleeping.

For emphasis, 在 zài can be preceded by the adverb 正 zhèng (right then; just):

33

他 来 的 时候， 我 正　 在 学习。
Tā lái de shíhou, wǒ zhèng zài xuéxí.
When he came, I was studying.

When either 正 zhèng or 呢 ne appears in the sentence, 在 zài can be omitted:

他 正　 看书 (呢)。
Tā zhèng kànshū (ne).
He is reading.

他们 吃饭 呢。
Tāmen chīfàn ne.
They are eating.

The negative word for the progressive aspect marker is 没有 méiyou instead of 不 bù:

孩子们 没有　 在 玩儿。
Háizimen méiyou zài wánr.
The children are not playing.

你学了多长时间的中文了 nǐ xué le duō cháng shíjiān de Zhōngwén le?

Questions may arise as to why there are two 了 le in the sentence. The first 了 le is what we have learned—an aspect marker indicating the completion of an action. As explained earlier, the completion of an action can be in the future as well as the past. We should also note that this completion generally has no bearing on the present, i.e., it does not say anything about the status of the action at the point of speaking. To indicate the relevance, a second 了 le is used at the end of the sentence. This 了 le is grammatically referred to as a modal particle. The distinction is best demonstrated by the following graphs:

34

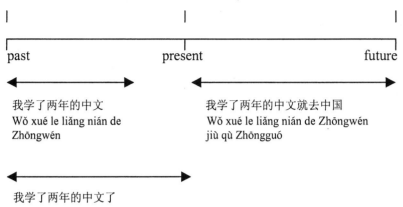

我学了两年的中文
Wǒ xué le liǎng nián de Zhōngwén

我学了两年的中文就去中国
Wǒ xué le liǎng nián de Zhōngwén jiù qù Zhōngguó

我学了两年的中文了
Wǒ xué le liǎng nián de Zhōngwén le

Now let's compare some sentences:

我 学 了 一 年 多 的 中文。
Wǒ xué le yì nián duō de Zhōngwén.
I studied Chinese for one year—*sometime in the past, having no bearing on the present.*

我 学 了 一 年 多 的 中文 了。
Wǒ xué le yì nián duō de Zhōngwén le.
I have been studying Chinese for more than one year—*up to the point of speaking.*

他 在 纽约 住 了十年。
Tā zài Niǔyuē zhù le shí nián.
He lived in New York for ten years—*sometime in the past, having no bearing on the present.*

他 在 纽约 住 了十年 了。
Tā zài Niǔyuē zhù le shí nián le.
He has lived in New York for ten years—*up to the point of speaking.*

我们　吃了饭 就 去 看　电影。

Wǒmen chī le fàn jiù qù kàn diànyǐng.

We'll go to see a movie right after we eat dinner—*event (seeing a movie) has not started yet.*

我们　吃了饭 就 去看　电影　　了。

Wǒmen chī le fàn jiù qù kàn diànyǐng le.

We went to see a movie right after we ate dinner—*event (seeing a movie) has taken place.*

Verb complements

The degree or result of a verb in Chinese is indicated for the most part by an adjective, which follows the verb and is marked by the particle 得 de. This part of the sentence is commonly referred to in grammar as the verb complement. This contrasts with English in that the degree or result of a verb is usually indicated by an adverb or an adverbial phrase. Examples of verb complements are:

他 写 得 好。

Tā xiě de hǎo.

He writes well.

火车　今天　到 得 早。

Huǒchē jīntiān dào de zǎo.

The train arrived early today.

When the sentence takes the negative form, 不 bù is placed after 得 de instead of before the verb:

他 写 得 不 好。

Tā xiě de bù hǎo.

He doesn't write well.

火车　今天　到　得不早。
Huǒchē jīntiān dào de bù zǎo.
The train did not arrive early today.

If the verb takes an object, the object needs to be placed immediately after the verb, thus creating a conflict with the complement marker 得 de, which should also be placed immediately after the verb. To satisfy both conditions, the object is placed after the verb, but the verb needs to be repeated after the object so that it can immediately precede 得 de:

他说　中文　　说　得很　流利。
Tā shuō Zhōngwén shuō de hěn liúlì.
He speaks Chinese fluently.

There are two ways commonly used in Chinese to avoid the repetitiveness:

a)　Leave out the initial verb:

他中文　　说　得很　流利。
Tā Zhōngwén shuō de hěn liúlì.

b)　Shift the object to the beginning of the sentence:

中文　　他说　得很　流利。
Zhōngwén tā shuō de hěn liúlì.

There are two ways to ask a question about the verb complement: 1) using 怎么样 zěnmèyang, and 2) using one of the two Yes/No question formats. For example, *how does he speak Chinese* can be expressed in one of the following ways:

他说　中文　　说　得怎么样?
Tā shuō Zhōngwén shuō de zěnmèyang?

37

他 说　中文　　说　得 流利 吗?
Tā shuō Zhōngwén shuō de liúlì　ma?

他 说　中文　　说　得 流利不 流利?
Tā shuō Zhōngwén shuō de liúlì　bu liúlì?

我现在已经能认五百个字，会写三百个字了 wǒ xiànzài yǐjīng néng rèn wǔbǎi ge zì, huì xiě sānbǎi ge zì le

When the adverb 已经 yǐjīng appears in the sentence, the modal particle 了 le must be used at the end of the sentence to indicate that the event has taken place.

你学英语学了几年了 nǐ xué Yīngyǔ xué le jǐ nián le

It was mentioned in Lesson 1 that words and expressions that indicate a duration of time should follow the verb instead of preceding it:

我　在北京　　住 了 五 年 了。
Wǒ zài Běijīng zhù le wǔ nián le .
I have lived in Beijing for five years.

However, there is a complication when the verb takes an object. The verb needs to be repeated after the object, just as the verb needs to be repeated after the object before it precedes a verb complement of degree or result (see above):

学生们　　　看　书 看 了一个 小时。
Xuéshengmen kàn shū kàn le yí ge xiǎoshi.
The students read (books) for an hour.

他 学 中文　　学 了 两 年 了。
Tā xué Zhōngwén xué le liáng nián le.
He has been studying Chinese for two years.

To avoid the repetition of the verb, Chinese often turns the duration of time into an attribute of the object:

学生们　　　看 了一个 小时　　的 书。
Xuéshengmen kàn le yí ge xiǎoshi de shū.

他 学 了 两　　年　　的 中文　　　了。
Tā xué le liǎng nián de Zhōngwén le.

This is quite comparable to the convertibility of the following sentences in English:

I can commit to teaching for one year.

I can commit to one year of teaching.

Response to compliments in Chinese

There is a propensity among the Chinese to respond to a compliment not by acknowledging it in the form of a *thank-you*, but by declining it. It is considered in Chinese culture too presumptuous to readily accept a compliment. The most commonly used expression in responding to a compliment is 哪里 nǎlǐ, which literally means *where*, used here with the implied meaning of *where is the connection between what I did and what you complimented*. Alternatively, speakers of Chinese would simply deny by saying that the compliment is not true and couple the denial with a self-effacing statement:

A: 你的 中文　　　很　　流利。
　　Nǐde Zhōngwén hěn liúlì.
　　Your Chinese is very fluent.

B: 哪里，我的 中文　　　不 流利，我的 中文　　　很　差。
　　Nǎlǐ, wǒde Zhōngwén bù liúlì, wǒde Zhōngwén hěn chà.
　　No, my Chinese is not fluent. My Chinese is very poor.

This propensity is also reflected in other aspects of Chinese social life. For example, it is not proper for a Chinese to open a gift in the presence of the giver. To do so would reveal that the recipient is too greedy. In receiving a present, one should never say, "this is exactly what I want." If anything, he or she probably should show disinterest and say, "this is something that I don't need." The idea is that one feels guilty for causing someone to spend money or time. So don't be offended when you give your Chinese friend a gift, but he or she shows little interest. Your Chinese friend is probably feeling guilty for causing you the trouble.

一些 yìxiē

Unlike most other verb modifiers, 一些 yìxiē in the sense of *somewhat, a few* or *a little* follows the verb instead of preceding it. This is also true of expressions such as 一点儿 yìdiǎn (a little), 极了 jíle (extremely).

两年多了 liǎng nián duō le and 十多年 shí duō nián

To indicate the idea of *over* (a certain amount) or *more than*, Chinese uses 多 duō. Note that the positioning of 多 duō is different depending on the actual number. If the number is less than ten, 多 duō is placed after the classifier, whereas if the number is greater than ten, 多 duō is placed before the classifier. Compare:

五 个 多 星期
wǔ ge duō xīngqī
more than five weeks

二十 多 个 小时
èrshí duō ge xiǎoshi
more than twenty hours

学中文的最好的办法 xué Zhōngwén de zuì hǎo de bànfǎ

It is time for us to remember the modifier-preceding-modified principle in Chinese. The verbal phrase 学中文 xué Zhōngwén (to learn Chinese)

40

modifies 办法 bànfǎ (method). As such, it is placed before 办法 bànfǎ. The modifier-modified relationship is marked by the particle 的 de. Similar examples are:

练习 口语 的 机会
liànxí kǒuyǔ de jīhuì
opportunity to practice spoken language

要 参加 的 婚礼
yào cānjiā de hūnlǐ
wedding to attend

去 过 的 地方
qù guo de dìfang
places visited

能 认识 的 汉字
néng rènshi de hànzì
Chinese characters that (one) can recognize

学习 的 时间
xuéxí de shíjiān
time to study

五点半就起床了 wǔ diǎn bàn jiù qǐchuáng le and 坐一个小时的 地铁才能到公司 zuò yí ge xiǎoshí de dìtiě cái néng dào gōngsī

就 jiù in the first sentence means *earlier than expected* or *better than expected*: get up as early as 5:30. In this sense 就 jiù is often opposed to 才 cái, which means *later than expected* or *worse than expected*: take the subway for as long as an hour before getting to work. Compare:

九 点 上课， 他八 点 就 来了。
Jiǔ diǎn shàngkè, tā bā diǎn jiù lái le.

Class started at 9, but he came as early as 8.

九 点　上课，他 十 点　才 来。
Jiǔ diǎn shàngkè, tā shí diǎn cái lái.
Class started at 9, but he didn't come until 10.

Note that the aspect marker 了 le cannot be used with 才 cái.

Exercises

I. Answer the following questions:

1. 你 在 我们的　城市　住 了几 年　了？
   Nǐ zài wǒmende chéngshì zhù le jǐ nián le?

2. 你 学 中文　　学 了几年　了？
   Nǐ xué Zhōngwén xué le jǐ nián le?

3. 你 写 汉字 写 得 怎么样？
   Nǐ xiě hànzì xiě de zěnmeyàng?

4. 你 做 饭　做 得 怎么样？
   Nǐ zuò fàn zuò de zěnmeyàng?

5. 你 工作　　吗？你 工作　　了几年　了？
   Nǐ gōngzuò ma? Nǐ gōngzuò le jǐ nián le?

6. 你 每 天 学 多 长　　时间　的 中文？
   Nǐ měi tiān xué duō cháng shíjiān de Zhōngwén?

7. 你 每　天 起 得 早 不 早？睡 得 晚 不 晚？
   Nǐ měi tiān qǐ de zǎo bu zǎo? Shuì de wǎn bu wǎn?

8. 你 现在　能　认 多少　汉字？能　写　多少　汉字？
   Nǐ xiànzài néng rèn duōshǎo hànzì? Néng xié duōshǎo hànzì?

9. 别人　说　你的 中文　　好，你 应该　怎么　回答？
   Biérén shuō nǐde Zhōngwén hǎo, nǐ yīnggāi zěnme huídá?

10. 你 昨天　晚上　　八 点 在 作 什么？
    Nǐ zuótiān wǎnshang bā diǎn zài zuò shénme?

II. Describe what people are doing in the following pictures, using one of the following indicators:

在 zài, 正在 zhèng zài, 在 zài …… 呢 ne

1. ＿＿＿＿＿＿＿＿＿＿＿＿＿＿＿＿。

2. ＿＿＿＿＿＿＿＿＿＿＿＿＿＿＿＿。

3. ＿＿＿＿＿＿＿＿＿＿＿＿＿＿＿＿。

4. _____。

5. _____。

6. _____。

III. Complete the following sentences:

1. 你 法语 说　得 _____。
   Nǐ Fǎyǔ shuō de _____.

2. 汽车　开 得 _____。
   Qìchē kāi de _____.

3. 我　太太 起床　　起 得 _____。
   Wǒ tàitai qǐchuáng qǐ de _____.

4. 外国　　学生　　写 字 写 得 _____?
   Wàiguó xuésheng xiě zì xiě de _____?

5. 雨 下 得 _____?
   Yǔ xià de _____?

IV. Change the following into negative sentences:

1. 老师 来 得 很 早。
   Lāoshī lái de hěn zǎo.

2. 我 妈妈 做 饭 做 得 很 好。
   Wǒ māma zuò fàn zuò de hěn hǎo.

3. 他 开 车 开 得 很 快。
   Tā kāi chē kāi de hěn kuài.

4. 那 个 老 人 走 得 很 慢。
   Nà ge lǎo rén zǒu de hěn màn.

5. 他们 在 北京 玩 得 很 高兴。
   Tāmen zài Běijīng wánr de hěn gāoxìng.

V. How do you say the following:

1. more than five days; more than twenty people
2. long enough, not high enough
3. easy in some respects and difficult in other respects
4. the best way to learn a foreign language
5. opportunity to practice spoken language
6. learn from each other
7. study Chinese with a Chinese friend
8. know a few Chinese characters
9. remarkable progress
10. talk with foreign clients in English

VI. Fill in the blanks with 就 jiù or 才 cài:

1. 她 从 大学 毕业 以后 _____ 结婚 了。
   Tā cóng dàxué bìyì yǐhòu _____ jiéhūn le.

2. 电影 已经 开始 了半 个 小时 他 _____ 来。
   Diànyǐng yǐjīng kāishǐ le bàn ge xiǎoshí tā _____ lái.

3. 我 爸爸 每 天 五 点_____ 起床 了。
   Wǒ bàba měi tiān wǔ diǎn _____ qǐchuáng le.

4. 我们 坐 了两 个 小时 的汽车 _____ 到 飞机场。
   Wǒmen zuò le liǎng ge xiǎoshí de qìchē _____ dào fēijīchǎng.

5. 马丁 来 中国 _____ 一 个 星期。
   Mǎdīng lái Zhōngguó _____ yí ge xīngqī.

6. 一个星期 后，暑假 _____ 开始 了。
   Yí ge xīngqī hòu, shǔjià _____ kāishǐ le.

VII. Translate the following into Chinese:

1. We ate for two hours.
2. He has been driving for more than five hours.
3. Students are attending a class.
4. What was your mother doing when you went home yesterday?
5. The American teacher made a thirty-minute phone call to America.
6. Did you sleep well last night?
7. My American friend speaks many languages, for example, Spanish, French and German.
8. I have been learning English for more than ten years, but my English is not good enough.
9. It snowed heavily.
10. She goes to bed late, but gets up early.

VIII. Translate the following into English:

1. 这 本 书 你 只 能 看 三 天。
   Zhè běn shū nǐ zhǐ néng kàn sān tiān.

2. 我 太太 在 中学 工作 了二十 年。
   Wǒ tàitai zài zhōngxué gōngzuò le èrshí nián.

3. 他 开 车 开了 三十 多 个 小时 才 开 到 加州。
   Tā kāi chē kāi le sānshí duō ge xiǎoshí cái kāi dào Jiāzhōu.

4. 我 每 天 坐 一个小时 的 汽车 去 上班。
   Wǒ měi tiān zuò yí ge xiǎoshí de qìchē qù shàngbān.

5. 学生们 写 了三十 分钟 的字。
   Xuéshengmen xiě le sānshí fēnzhōng de zì.

6. 老师 说 得很 慢。
   Lǎoshī shuō de hěn màn.

7. 美国 朋友 在 北京 玩儿 得 很 高兴。
   Měiguó péngyou zài Běijīng wánr de hěn gāoxìng.

8. 孩子们 看 电视 看 了两 个 小时。
   Háizimen kàn diànshì kàn le liǎng ge xiǎoshí.

9. 没 有 人 跟 我 练 中文。
   Méi yǒu rén gēn wǒ liàn Zhōngwén.

10. 我们 只 坐 了一个小时 的 火车 就 从 上海 到 了
    Wǒmen zhǐ zuò le yí ge xiǎoshí de huǒchē jiù cóng Shànghǎi dào le
    苏州。
    Sūzhōu.

IX. Topics for discussion and writing:

1. 你 觉得 中文　　难 不 难？什么　　地方　难？什么　　　地方
   Nǐ juéde Zhōngwén nán bu nán? Shénme dìfang nán? Shénme dìfang
   不 难？
   bù nán?

2. 你 是 怎么　学　汉字、语法、发音和 生词　　的？
   Nǐ shì zěnme xué hànzì, yǔfǎ, fāyīn hé shēngcí de?

3. 你 觉得 什么　　是 学　中文　　　的 最 好 的 方法？
   Nǐ juéde shénme shì xué Zhōngwén de zuì hǎo de fāngfǎ?

English Translation of the Text

Conversations:

A: Martin, I heard that you are learning Chinese?

B: Yes. I like Chinese very much.

A: How long have you been studying it?

B: I have been studying it for more than a year.

A: How have you been doing?

B: I think I'm fine. By now, I can recognize five hundred characters and write three hundred.

A: That's great. You also speak Chinese very well.

B: I'm not sure about that. I don't speak Chinese very fluently.

A: Do you think Chinese is difficult?

B: In some aspects, it is; in other aspects, it is not. For example, grammar and pronunciation are not difficult, but writing characters is a little hard.

A: Do you write characters every day?

B: I would like to, but sometimes I just don't have time to practice because of my work.

A: What do you think is the best way to learn Chinese?

B: I think the best way is to study it in China. Would you like to go?

A: Of course I would. Language environment is very important. But I'm working, so I can't spend a long time in China.

B: You can go there during the summer. Many schools in China have summer Chinese language classes.

A: If I go to China to study Chinese, which city do you think I should go to?

B: I think you should go to Beijing. People in Beijing all speak Mandarin.

*   *   *   *   *

A: Xiao Wang, you have made a lot of progress in English recently.

B: Thank you, but my English is still very poor.

A: How many years have you studied English?

B: I have studied English for more than two years, but I don't think my English is good enough.

A: Why do you want to study English?

B: I would like to study in England in the future. Besides, there will be more work opportunities if I know English.

A: What do you think is the most difficult thing in learning English?

B: I found that speaking is the most difficult, primarily because I don't have opportunities to practice spoken English.

A: We can help each other. You practice Chinese with me and I will practice English with you.

B: This is a good idea.

Reading Passages

Xiao Wang works at the Bank of China in Beijing. She has worked there for five years. Xiao Wang's home is far from her work. She gets up very early every day. She gets up as early as 5:30. She needs to take the subway for an hour before she can get to work. Xiao Wang works for eight hours every day. She also goes to an English school after work to study English. She has been learning English for more than two years. She is doing well in her study and can already conduct conversations in English with her foreign clients.

3

CALLING & ANSWERING

Conversations

A：喂！
Wèi!

B：您 找 谁?
Nín zhǎo shuí?

A：我 找 你们的 经理。他 在 不 在?
Wǒ zhǎo nǐmende jīnglǐ. Tā zài bu zài?

B：请 等 一下儿，我 去 看看 …… 对 不 起，他 在 开
Qǐng děng yíxiàr， wǒ qù kànkan …… Duìbuqǐ， tā zài kāi
会。你过 一会儿打来，好 吗?
huì. Nǐ guò yíhuìr dǎ lai, hǎo ma?

A：我 能 不 能 给 他 留 个 话?
Wǒ néng bu néng gěi tā liú ge huà?

B：当然 可以。您 贵 姓?
Dāngrán kěyǐ. Nín guì xìng?

A：我 姓 张。
Wǒ xìng Zhāng.

B：您的 电话 号码 是 多少?
Nínde diànhuà hàomǎ shì duōshǎo?

A：我的 号码 是 212－734－8659。
Wǒde hàomǎ shì 212－734－8659.

B：请问, 您 要 留 什么 话?
Qǐngwèn, nín yào liú shénme huà?

A：你们的 经理 回 来 后, 请 他 给 我 打 电 话。
Nǐmende jīnglǐ huí lai hòu, qǐng tā gěi wǒ dǎ diànhuà.

B：好, 张 先生。 我 一定 让 他 尽快 给您 回 话。
Hǎo, Zhāng Xiānsheng. Wǒ yídìng ràng tā jìnkuài gěi nín huí huà.

   *   *   *   *   *

A：我 昨天 晚上 给 你 打 电话, 没 有 人 接。你去
Wǒ zuótiān wǎnshang gěi nǐ dǎ diànhuà, méi yǒu rén jiē. Nǐ qù
哪儿了?
nǎr le?

B：我 哪儿 也 没 去。你 是 几点 给 我 打 的 电话?
Wǒ nǎr yě méi qù. Ni shì jǐ diǎn gěi wǒ dǎ de diànhuà?

A：我 是 八点 给 你 打的 电话。
Wǒ shì bā diǎn gěi nǐ dǎ de diànhuà.

B：我 八点 在 用 电脑 上 网。 我 上 网 的
Wǒ bā diǎn zài yòng diànnǎo shàng wǎng. Wǒ shàng wǎng de

51

时候，电话　就 打不 进 来。对不起，你 有 事 吗？
shíhou, diànhuà jiù dǎ bú jìn lai. Duìbuqǐ, nǐ yǒu shì ma?

A：没 有 大 事，只 是 想　和 你 聊聊。
Méi yǒu dà shì, zhǐ shì xiǎng hé nǐ liáoliao.

B：你 星期六　能　来 我 这儿 坐坐　吗？
Nǐ xīngqīliù néng lái wǒ zhèr zuòzuo ma?

A：可以，星期六　什么　时间　对 你 方便？
Kěyǐ, xīngqīliù shénme shíjiān duì nǐ fāngbiàn?

B：我 一 天 都　在 家。你 什么　时间　来 都 可以。
Wǒ yì tiān dōu zài jiā. Nǐ shénme shíjiān lái dōu kěyǐ.

　＊　　　　＊　　　　＊　　　　＊　　　　＊

A：中国　　餐馆　吗？
Zhōngguó cānguǎn ma?

B：是，这　是 中国　　餐馆。
Shì, zhè shì Zhōngguó cānguǎn.

A：你们　送　不 送　饭？
Nǐmen sòng bu sòng fàn?

B：送，您 要 什么　饭？
Sòng, nín yào shénme fàn?

A：请　给 我 送　一 个 炒饭　和 一个 豆腐。
Qǐng gěi wǒ sòng yí ge chǎofàn hé yí ge dòufu.

B：什么　时候 要 送　到？
Shénme shíhou yào sòng dào?

52

A: 请 在 七 点 前 送 到。

Qǐng zài qī diǎn qián sòng dào.

B: 没 问题。请 告诉 我 你的 地址。

Méi wèntí. Qǐng gàosu wǒ nǐde dìzhǐ.

A: 我的 地址 是 公园 大道 530 号 四楼 432 室。

Wǒde dìzhǐ shì Gōngyuán Dàdào 530 hào sì lóu 432 shì .

B: 你的 电话 号码 是 多少?

Nǐde diànhuà hàomǎ shì duōshǎo?

A: 我的 电话 号码 是 754－3698。

Wǒde diànhuà hàomǎ shì 754－3698.

B: 好, 一会儿 见。

Hǎo, yíhuìr jiàn.

A: 谢 谢。

Xièxie.

Reading Passage

现在手机越来越普遍。好象什么人都有一部。有的人甚至只有手机,没有普通的电话。手机给我们带来很多方便,别人可以随时跟我们联系,我们也可以随时跟别人联系。在用手机的时候,我们要尊重别人。有的人在电影院和上课的时候也不关掉手机,这是很讨厌的。还有的人一边开车一边用手机打电话,这样是不安全的。人们说得对,有一利就有一弊。

Xiànzài shǒujī yuèláiyuè pǔbiàn. Hǎoxiàng shénme rén dōu yǒu yí bù. Yǒude rén shènzhì zhǐ yǒu shǒujī, méi yǒu pǔtōng de diànhuà. Shǒujī gěi

53

wǒmen dài lái hěn duō fāngbiàn, biérén kěyǐ suíshí gēn wǒmen liánxì, wǒmen yě kěyǐ suíshí gēn biérén liánxì. Zài yòng shǒujī de shíhou, wǒmen yào zūnzhòng biérén. Yǒude rén zài diànyǐngyuàn hé shàngkè de shíhou yě bù guān diào shǒujī, zhè shì hěn tǎoyàn de. Hái yǒude rén yìbiān kāichē yìbiān yòng shǒujī dǎ diànhuà, zhèyàng shì hěn bù ānquán de. Rénmen shuō de duì, yǒu yí lì jiù yǒu yí bì.

New Words and Expressions

喂	wéi; wèi	hello
开会	kāi huì	attend a meeting
一会儿	yíhuìr	a little while
打	dǎ	make (a phone call); hit
给	gěi	to; give
留	liú	leave (a message)
号码	hàomǎ	(telephone) number
让	ràng	ask (sb. to do sth.); let
尽快	jìnkuài	as soon as possible
接	jiē	pick up; answer (a phone call)
电脑	diànnǎo	computer
上网	shàng wǎng	get on the internet
进	jìn	enter; come in
只是	zhǐshì	merely; only; just
聊	liáo	chat
对	duì	to; for; regarding
方便	fāngbiàn	convenient; convenience

送	sòng	deliver; take sb. or sth. to
份	fèn	classifier
炒饭	chǎofàn	fried rice
豆腐	dòufu	tofu
地址	dìzhǐ	address
大道	dàdào	avenue
室	shì	room; suite
手机	shǒujī	cell phone
越来越	yuèláiyuè	more and more; increasingly
普遍	pǔbiàn	popular
部	bù	classifier
甚至	shènzhì	even
普通	pǔtōng	common; ordinary
带	dài	bring; take; carry
别人	biérén	other people
随时	suíshí	any time
联系	liánxì	contact (v & n)
尊重	zūnzhòng	respect
关掉	guān diào	turn off (a device)
讨厌	tǎoyàn	annoying; be annoyed by
一边 ...... 一边	yìbiān … yìbiān	simultaneously; at the same time
安全	ānquán	safe
利	lì	benefit; advantage
弊	bì	drawback; disadvantage

Supplementary Words and Expressions

占线	zhànxiàn	busy line
公用电话	gōngyòng diànhuà	public phone
国际电话	guójì diànhuà	international call
国内电话	guónèi diànhuà	domestic call
长途电话	chángtú diànhuà	long distance call
投币电话	tóubì diànhuà	coin-operated phone
区号	qūhào	area code
电话号码本	diànhuà hàomǎ běn	phone book
总机	zǒngjī	switchboard
分机	fēnjī	(phone) extension
呼机	hūjī	beeper; pager
忙音	mángyīn	busy signal
电话卡	diànhuà kǎ	telephone card
拨	bō	dial

Language Points

喂 wéi, wèi

The word is pronounced in two ways in a telephone conversation depending on who is the caller and who is the answerer. The person who answers the phone would greet the caller by saying 喂 wéi, whereas the caller would pronounce it as 喂 wèi to attract attention. Additionally, the greeting convention in a telephone conversation in China is such that

callers would have to identify themselves first even if their calls are
made to a business.

一会儿 yíhuìr, 一下儿 yíxiàr and 一点儿 yìdiǎnr

These are often confused. Let's compare them:

一会儿 yíhuìr—*a little while*; it is often used with the verb 过 guò to
form a set phrase: 过一会儿 guò yíhuìr, meaning *in a little while*:

老师　现在　很　忙，　你过　一会儿　再问　他吧。
Lǎoshī xiànzài hěn máng. Nǐ guò yíhuìr　zài wèn tā ba.
The teacher is busy now. Please ask him in a little while.

一下儿 yíxiàr—used after a verb to suggest that the action is brief,
tentative or informal (see *Beginner's Chinese*, Lesson 7):

我　能　不能　看　一下儿你的 中文　　书？
Wǒ néng bu néng kàn yíxiàr　nǐde Zhōngwén shū?
Can I take a look at your Chinese book?

一点儿 yìdiǎnr—*a little bit*; used both as an adjective and adverb, e.g.

A：你会说　法语吗？
　　Nǐ huì shuō Fǎyǔ ma?
　　Do you speak French?
B：会　一点儿。
　　Huì yìdiǎnr.
　　A little.

A：你会说　什么　语言？
　　Nǐ huì shuō shénme yǔyán?
　　What languages do you speak?
B：我会说　英语、西班牙语 和 一点儿中文。
　　Wǒ huì shuō Yīngyǔ, Xībānyáyǔ hé yìdiǎnr Zhōngwén.

I speak English, Spanish and a little Chinese.

给 gěi

给 gěi can be used as a verb as well as a preposition. As a verb, it means *to give* and is usually followed by two objects:

我 妈妈 给 我 一 百 块 钱。
Wǒ māma gěi wǒ yì bǎi kuài qián.
My mother gave me $100.

学校 给 我们 班 一台电脑。
Xuéxiào gěi wǒmen bān yì tái diànnǎo.
The school gave our class a computer.

As a preposition, it is used with a noun to mean *to* or *for*. Since it is used to modify the verb of the sentence, the phrase is placed before the verb:

给 电话 公司 工作
gěi diànhuà gōngsī gōngzuò
work for a telephone company

给 学校 买 书
gěi xuéxiào mǎi shū
buy books for the school

给 我 妈妈 打 电话
gěi wǒ māma dǎ diànhuà
call my mother

给 我 朋友 写 信
gěi wǒ péngyou xiě xìn
write a letter to my friend

请他给我打电话 qǐng tā gěi wǒ dǎ diànhuà and 让他尽快给你回话 ràng tā jìnkuài gěi nǐ huí huà

Both 让 ràng and 请 qǐng can be used to mean *ask sb. to do sth.* Whether to use 让 ràng or 请 qǐng depends on who makes the request. If you ask someone to do something for you, you should generally use 请 qǐng, which is more polite. If someone asks you to do something, you should generally use 让 ràng. Compare:

我　请　他 给 我 买　报纸。
Wǒ qǐng tā gěi wǒ mǎi bàozhǐ.
I asked him to buy me a newspaper.

他 让　我　给 他买　报纸。
Tā ràng wǒ gěi tā mǎi bàozhǐ.
He asked me to buy him a newspaper.

哪儿也没有去 nǎr yě méiyou qù

This structure emphasizes that what is stated applies to any situation. It takes one of the following forms:

S + Wh-Q Word + 也 yě/都 dōu (+ neg) + V or
S + Wh-Q Word + V + S 也 yě /都 dōu + V

The difference between them is that the second structure involves two sentences.

The following examples illustrate the use of these two structures:

我们的　 老师　什么　 都 知道。
Wǒmende lǎoshī shénme dōu zhīdào.
Our teacher knows everything.

她 妈妈 什么　菜 都 会 作。
Tā māma shénme cài dōu huì zuò.
Her mother knows how to cook any dish.

汽车 哪儿都 不 能　停。
Qìchē nǎr　dōu bù néng tíng.
The car can't be parked anywhere.

我 怎么　说　她也 不 听。
Wǒ zěnme shuō tā yě bù tīng.
No matter what I say, she won't listen.

在 上海　他谁　都 不 认识。
Zài Shànghǎi tā shuí dōu bú rènshi.
He doesn't know anyone in Shanghai.

我　今天 什么　电话　也 没有　打。
Wǒ jīntiān shénme diànhuà yě méiyou dǎ.
I didn't make any phone calls today.

我 什么　时候　给 他 打 电话　他 都 不 在。
Wǒ shénme shíhou gěi tā dǎ diànhuà tā dōu bú zài.
He is never home whenever I call him.

用电脑上网 yòng diànnǎo shàng wǎng

Internet is expressed in Chinese in a number of forms. Basically it is translated as 因特网 yīntèwǎng (因特 yīntè being the transliteration of *inter*), or 互联网 hùliánwǎng (互 hù means *inter* or *mutual* and 联 lián means *link* or *connect*) or simply 网 wǎng (net).

用 yòng in the sentence is a preposition indicating instrument. Since the prepositional phrase modifies the verb, it is therefore placed before the verb. Other examples are:

用　中文　　说
yòng Zhōngwén shuō
say in Chinese

用　笔　写
yòng bǐ xiě
write in pen

用　手　作
yòng shǒu zuò
do by hand

我上网的时候，电话就打不进来 wǒ shàng wǎng de shíhou, diànhuà jiù dǎ bú jìn lai

In Lesson 1, we saw that 来 lai and 去 qu can serve as a directional complement after a verb to show the direction of the action in relation to the speaker. Furthermore, 来 lai and 去 qu can form a complex directional complement with certain verbs. These verbs include 上 shàng (go up), 下 xià (go down), 进 jìn (enter), 出 chū (exit), 回 huí (return), 过 guò (pass), 起 qǐ (rise) and so on. The complex directional complement indicates both a motion and the direction of the motion in relation to the location of the speaker. Compare: 走出来 zǒu chū lai (walk out—in the direction of the speaker) and 走出去 zǒu chū qu (walk out—away from the speaker). If the verb takes an object that indicates a location, the object must be placed before 来 lai: 学生们走进教室来了 xuéshengmen zǒu jìn jiàoshì lai le (the students walked into the classroom). If the object does not indicate a location, it can be placed either before or after 来 lái. Compare: 我爸爸带回很多书来 wǒ bàba dài huí hěn duō shū lai (my father brought back many books) and 我爸爸带回来很多书 wǒ bàba dài huí lai hěn duō shū. In the sentence cited from this lesson, 进来 jìn lai is used to indicate a motion (进 jìn) associated with the action (打 dǎ) and the direction of the action (来 lai). If the sentence takes the negative form, the negative word appears between the verb and the complex complement as in the sentence cited.

In the sentence, 就 jiù is used as an adverb, meaning *then*:

如果　天气 不 好，　我　就 不去 公园。
Rúguǒ tiānqì bù hǎo,　wǒ jiù bú qù gōngyuán.
If the weather is not good, then I won't go to the park.

他看　到 老师，就 走 了 过 去。
Tā kàn dào lǎoshī, jiù zǒu le guò qu.
When he saw the teacher, he walked over.

Note that 就 jiù occurs before the verb and after the subject. This is different from *then* in English, where it is placed before the subject.

来我这儿坐坐 lái wǒ zhèr zuòzuo

The object to 来 lái or 去 qù, if there is any, must be a place word. Ideas such as *please come to me* or *go to your mother* are expressed in Chinese by using either 这儿 zhèr or 那儿 nàr after the verb:

请　来 我 这儿。
Qǐng lái wǒ zhèr.

去 你妈妈　那儿。
Qù nǐ māma nàr.

这儿 zhèr is used when the referent is away from the speaker (e.g. 你妈妈 nǐ māma) and 那儿 nàr is used when the referent is close to the speaker (e.g. 我 wǒ) .

星期六什么时间对你方便 xīngqīliù shénme shíjiān duì nǐ fāngbiàn?

对 duì is used as a preposition meaning *to*, *regarding*, or *concerning*. Since the phrase modifies the verb or the predicate adjective of the sentence, it is placed before it. The 对 duì-phrase is often used with the following verbs and predicate adjectives:

他 对 我 说。
Tā duì wó shuō.
He said to me.

英语 对 我的 帮助 很 大。
Yīngyǔ duì wǒde bāngzhù hěn dà.
English is a great help to me.

他 对 音乐 没 有 兴趣。
Tā duì yīnyuè méi yǒu xìngqù.
He is not interested in music.

他们 对 我 很 好。
Tāmen duì wǒ hěn hǎo.
They are very nice to me.

一天都在家 yì tiān dōu zài jiā

Used in certain expressions, 一 yī means *all*, *entire*, or *whole* (for the tonal variations of the word, please refer to *Beginner's Chinese*, p. 40):

我们 一 家人 昨天 去 了博物馆。
Wǒmen yì jiā rén zuótiān qù le bówùguǎn.
Our whole family went to the museum yesterday.

他 有 一房子 的书。
Tā yǒu yì fángzi de shū.

He has a roomful of books.

As an adverb, 都 dōu is often used after such words as 每 měi (every), 全 quán (entire), 各 gè (each) and 任何 rènhé (any) to emphasize non-exclusiveness:

他们　全　家 都　去了博物馆。
Tāmen quán jiā dōu qù le bówùguǎn.
Their whole family went to the museum.

各 个 大学　都　给　外国人　　开 中文　　课。
Gè ge dàxué dōu gěi wàiguórén kāi Zhōngwén kè.
Each (every) university offers Chinese classes to foreigners.

你 每　天　都　看　报 吗?
Nǐ měi tiān dōu kàn bào ma?
Do you read newspapers every day?

Another example in this lesson is:

好象　　什么　人 都 有 一部 手机。
Hǎoxiàng shénme rén dōu yǒu yí bù shǒujī.
It seems that everyone has a cell phone.

什么时候要送到 shénme shíhou yào sòng dào

到 dào in the sense of *arrive* or *reach* is used after another verb as a complement to indicate a place or a time that the action extends to: 寄到中国 jì dào Zhōngguó (mail to China); 玩到十点 wán dào shí diǎn (play till ten o'clock); 走到学校 zǒu dào xuéxiào (walk to school).

Indicating an address

To state an address in Chinese, be mindful of one of the cardinal principles of word order in the language: larger units preceding smaller units. The order in this regard is completely the reverse of that in English. For example, the Chinese for the address:

509 West 121st Street, New York, NY

is

纽约　州　　　纽约　市　　　西 121 街 509 号
Niǔyuē Zhōu (State) Niǔyuē Shì (City) Xī 121 jiē 509 hào

部 bù as a classifier

As a classifier, 部 bù is used for such machinery or devices as cars, telephones, and machines.

别人 biérén

别 bié in 别人 biérén means *other*, however other than in 别人 biérén and a few other set expressions, it takes the form of 别的 biéde: 别的学校 biéde xuéxiào (other schools), 别的国家 biéde guójiā (other countries), 别的公司 biéde gōngsī (other companies).

还有的人一边开车一边用手机打电话 hái yǒude rén yìbiān kāichē yìbiān yòng shǒujī dǎ diànhuà

Used in pairs, 一边 …… 一边 …… yìbiān … yìbiān … indicates that two actions are taking place simultaneously:

他喜欢　一边　看书　　一边　听　音乐。
Tā xǐhuan yìbiān kànshū yìbiān tīng yīnyuè.
He likes to listen to music while reading.

很　多　大学生　　　一边　工作，　一边　上学。
Hěn duō dàxuéshēng yìbiān gōngzuò, yìbiān shàngxué.
Many college students go to school while they work.

65

Exercises

I. Answer the following questions:

1. 你的 电话 号码 是 多少?
   Nǐde diànhuà hàomǎ shì duōshao?

2. 你的 地址 是 什么?
   Nǐde dìzhǐ shì shénme?

3. 你 今天 有 没有 打 电话? 给 谁 打 了电话?
   Nǐ jīntiān yǒu méiyou dǎ diànhuà? Gěi shuí dǎ le diànhuà?

4. 手机 很 方便, 你 觉得 手机 有 没 有 不 好 的 地方?
   Shǒujī hěn fāngbiàn, nǐ juéde shǒujī yǒu méi yǒu bù hǎo de dìfang?

5. 有 人 给 你 妈妈 打电话, 但是 她不 在 家。你 应该
   Yǒu rén gěi nǐ māma dǎ diànhuà, dànshì tā bú zài jiā. Nǐ yīnggāi
   怎么 说?
   zěnme shuō?

6. 你去过 中国 吗? 你 在 中国 的 时候 有 没有
   Nǐ qù guo Zhōngguó ma? Nǐ zài Zhōngguó de shíhou yǒu méiyou
   用 过 公用 电话? 你会 用 吗?
   yòng guo gōngyòng diànhuà? Nǐ huì yòng ma?

7. 你知道 怎么 用 电脑 给别人 打电话 吗?
   Nǐ zhīdào zěnme yòng diànnǎo gěi biérén dǎ diànhuà ma?

8. 在 你的 城市 开 汽车 的 时候 能 不 能 用 手机 打
   Zài nǐde chéngshì kāi qìchē de shíhou néng bu néng yòng shǒujī dǎ

电话?
diànhuà?

9. 在 纽约　打 公用　　电话　要 多少　　钱?
Zài Niǔyuē dǎ gōngyòng diànhuà yào duōshao qián?

10. 你常常　　让 中国　　餐馆　给 你 送 饭 吗?
Nǐ chángchang ràng Zhōngguó cānguǎn gěi nǐ sòng fàn ma?

II. How do you say the following:

1. She is very nice to me.
2. What did he say to you?
3. 7 pm is not good for me.
4. Can I leave a message for her?
5. She wants to start work as soon as possible.
6. I'll take someone to the airport this afternoon.
7. Our whole family was home last night.
8. Our manager is at a meeting.
9. Please come to me if you have questions.
10. More and more people are learning Chinese.

III. Fill in the blanks with the following words and expressions:

一会儿 yíhuìr　　　一下儿 yíxiàr　　　一点儿 yìdiǎnr

1. 老师　现在　很 忙，你 过 _____　再 来 吧。
Lǎoshī xiànzài hěn máng, nǐ guò _____zài lái ba.

2. 我 能　不 能　试 _____ 这 件 衣服?
Wǒ néng bu néng shì _____ zhè jiàn yīfu?

67

3. 昨天　只下了 _____ 雨。
   Zuótiān zhī xià le _____ yǔ.

4. 我 不 饿，我 吃了 _____ 东西。
   Wǒ bú è,　wǒ chī le _____ dōngxi.

5. 他 每 天 中午　都 要 睡 _____。
   Tā měi tiān zhōngwǔ dōu yào shuì _____.

6. 我 能　不 能　用 _____ 你的电话？
   Wǒ néng bu néng yòng _____ nǐde diànhuà?

IV. Make sentences using the following expressions:

| 买 回 来 | 走　进去 | 跑 (run) 出 来 |
| mǎi huí lai | zǒu jìn qu | pǎo　chū lai |

| 开 上　去 | 带 回 去 | 爬 (climb)下 来 |
| kāi shàng qu | dài huí qu | pá　xià lai |

V. Translate the following into Chinese, using the patterns:

S + Wh-Q Word + 也 yě/都 dōu　(+ neg) + V or
S + Wh-Q Word + V + S 也 yě/都 dōu + V

1. You can buy a phone card in any store.
2. I didn't see any movies this year.
3. She didn't eat anything yesterday. Today, she doesn't want to eat anything either.
4. Whenever I call her, her phone is always busy.
5. The child wouldn't listen however her father talked to her.

VI. Translate the following into Chinese:

1. It is not safe to use the cell phone while driving.
2. Sorry, our manager is not in yet. Would you like to leave a message?
3. If you can't make it to school tomorrow, please give me a call.
4. Someone from Peking University called you this afternoon. She left a message asking you to call her back.
5. If you have anything important, please call my cell phone.
6. The teacher asked me to tell you that there is no class tomorrow.
7. I asked the teacher to take a look at my homework.
8. It is not good to study while watching TV at the same time.
9. Excuse me, could you tell me where I can find a pay phone?
10. Can you call me a little later on?

VII. Translate the following into English:

1. 她 让 我 给 她打电话， 可是 忘 了告诉 我 她的电话
   Tā ràng wǒ gěi tā dǎ diànhuà, kěshì wàng le gàosù wǒ tāde diànhuà
   号码。
   hàomǎ.

2. 我 最 不 喜欢 别人 在 我 吃饭 的 时候 给 我 打 电话。
   Wǒ zuì bù xǐhuan biérén zài wǒ chīfàn de shíhou gěi wǒ dǎ diànhuà.

3. 现在 晚上 给 很 多 人 打电话 都 打 不 进 去。我
   Xiànzài wǎnshang gěi hěn duō rén dǎ diànhuà dōu dǎ bú jìn qu. Wǒ
   想 他们 是 在 用 电脑 上 网。
   xiǎng tāmen shì zài yòng diànnǎo shàng wǎng.

4. 以前， 中国 的大学生 只 学习， 不 工作， 现在
   Yǐqián, Zhōngguó de dàxuéshēng zhǐ xuéxí, bù gōngzuò, xiànzài
   越来越 多 的大学生 一边 学习，一边 工作。
   yuèláiyuè duō de dàxuéshēng yìbiān xuéxí, yìbiān gōngzuò.

5. 二十年前, 大多数 (most) 中国人的家里都没有电话, 很不方便。
去看朋友不能先约 (set up; appoint) 时间。有时走很远的路去看
一个朋友，到了他家才知道他不在家。今天大多数中国人的家
里都有了电话，很多人还有了呼机 (pager) 和手机，很方便。
Èrshí nián qián, dàduōshù Zhōngguórén de jiā lǐ dōu méi yǒu
diànhuà, hěn bù fāngbiàn. Qù kàn péngyou bù néng xiān yuē (set up;
appoint) shíjiān. Yǒushí zǒu hěn yuǎn de lù qù kàn yí ge péngyou,
dào le tā jiā cái zhīdào tā bú zài jiā. Jīntiān dàduōshù Zhōngguórén
de jiā lǐ dōu yǒu le diànhuà, hěn duō rén hái yǒu le hūjī hé shǒujī,
hěn fāngbiàn.

VIII. Write and say your address in Chinese.

IX. Make a phone call to a Chinese restaurant to order food.

English Translation of the Text

Conversations

A: Hello!
B: Who would you like to speak to?
A: I'd like to speak to your manager. Is he there?
B: Just a minute. Let me check ... Sorry, he is at a meeting. Could you
call back a little later on?
A: Can I leave him a message?
B: Sure. What's your family name?
A: My family name is Wang.
B: What's your telephone number?
A: My number is 212-734-8659.
B: What's your message?
A: Please ask your manger to give me a call when he is back.

B: Sure, Mr. Wang. I'll definitely ask him to return your call as soon as possible.

* * * * *

A: I called you last night, but no one answered the phone. Where were you?
B: I didn't go anywhere. What time did you call me?
A: I called at 8.
B: I was on the internet at 8. When I'm online, calls won't get through. Sorry about that. Was there something you needed to talk to me about?
A: Nothing major. I only wanted to have a chat with you.
B: Could you stop by my place this Saturday?
A: Sure. What time on Saturday is good for you?
B: I'll be home the whole day. You can come anytime.

* * * * *

A: Is this the Chinese restaurant?
B: Yes, this is the Chinese restaurant.
A: Do you deliver?
B: Yes, we do. What would you like?
A: Please deliver ten dumplings and a tofu dish.
B: When would you like to have them?
A: Please have the food delivered by 7.
B: No problem. Please tell me your address.
A: My address is 530 Park Avenue, 4th Floor, Suite 432.
B: What's your phone number?
A: My number is 754-3698.
B: Okay, see you in a little while.
A: Thank you.

Reading Passages

Cell phones are getting more and more popular. It seems that everyone has one. Some people even just have a cell phone and no regular phone.

The cell phone brings us a lot of convenience. People can get in touch with us at any time and we can get in touch with people at any time. When using the cell phone, we should respect other people. There are people who don't even turn off their cell phones in movie theaters and in class. This is very annoying. There are also people who make calls on their cell phones while driving. This is very dangerous. It is well said that a benefit always comes with a drawback.

4

HERE & THERE

Conversations

A：词典 在 哪儿?
Cídiǎn zài nǎr?

B：词典 在 书架 的 上边。
Cídiǎn zài shūjià de shàngbian.

A：报纸 在 哪儿?
Bàozhǐ zài nǎr?

B：报纸 在 手表 的下边。
Bàozhǐ zài shǒubiǎo de xiàbian.

A：汽车 在 哪儿?
Qìchē zài nǎr?

B：汽车 在 学校 的 前边。
Qìchē zài xuéxiào de qiánbian.

A: 椅子 在 哪儿?
   Yǐzi zài nǎr?

B: 椅子 在 桌子 的 后边。
   Yǐzi zài zhuōzi de hòubian.

A: 猪 在 哪儿?
   Zhū zài nǎr?

B: 猪 在 牛 的 旁边。
   Zhū zài niú de pángbiān.

A: 刀 在 哪儿?
   Dāo zài nǎr?

B: 刀 在 盘子 的 右边。
   Dāo zài pánzi de yòubian.

A: 叉子 在 哪儿?
   Chāzi zài nǎr?

B: 叉子 在 盘子 的 左边。
   Chāzi zài pánzi de zuǒbian.

A: 中文 书 在 哪儿?
   Zhōngwén shū zài nǎr ?

B: 中文 书 在 书包 的 里面。
   Zhōngwén shū zài shūbāo de lǐmiàn.

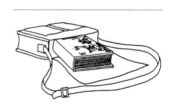

A：自行车　　在 哪儿？
Zìxíngchē zài nǎr?

B：自行车　　在 门 的 外边。
Zìxíngchē zài mén de wàibian.

A：餐馆　　在 哪儿？
Cānguǎn zài nǎr?

B：餐馆　　在 银行　　的 对面。
Cānguǎn zài yínháng de duìmiàn.

A：船　　在 哪儿？
Chuán zài nǎr?

B：船　　在 河 的 中间。
Chuán zài hé de zhōngjiān.

A：书店　　在 哪儿？
Shūdiàn zài nǎr?

B：书店　　在 银行　　和 餐馆　　的
Shūdiàn zài yínháng hé cānguǎn de
中间。
zhōngjiān.

A：左边　　是 什么？　右边　　是
Zuǒbian shì shénme? Yòubian shì
什么？
shénme?

B：左边　　是 汽车。右边　　是
Zuǒbian shì qìchē.　Yòubian shì

火车。
huǒchē.

A：对面 有 什么？
Duìmiàn yǒu shénme?

B：对面 有 电影院 和 面包店。
Duìmiàn yǒu diànyǐngyuàn hé miànbāodiàn.

A：日本 在 哪儿？
Rìběn zài nǎr?

B：日本 在 中国 的 东边。
Rìběn zài Zhōngguó de dōngbian.

A：韩国 在 哪儿？
Hánguó zài nǎr?

B：韩国 在 中国 的 东北边。
Hánguó zài Zhōngguó de dōngběibian.

A：中国 的 北边 有 什么
Zhōngguó de běibian yǒu shénme
国家？
guójiā?

B：中国 的 北边 有 蒙古 和
Zhōngguó de běibian yǒu Měnggǔ hé
俄国。
Éguó.

A：上海 在 中国 的 哪儿？
Shànghǎi zài Zhōngguó de nǎr?

B： 上海　　 在 中国　　 的 东部。
Shànghǎi zài Zhōngguó de dōngbù.

*　　　　*　　　　*　　　　*　　　　*

老师： 今天　是 新 学期 的 第一 天。我们　　 把 教室
Lǎoshī: Jīntiān shì xīn xuéqī de dì yī tiān. Wǒmen bǎ jiàoshì
重新　　 布置 一下儿，　好 不 好？
chóngxīn bùzhì yíxiàr,　 hǎo bu hǎo?

学 生： 好，老师。请 告诉 我们　　 怎么 做。
Xuésheng: Hǎo, lǎoshī. Qǐng gàosù wǒmen zěnme zuò.

老师： 先　把 这 些 新 书 放 在 书架 上。
Lǎoshī: Xiān bǎ zhè xiē xīn shū fàng zài shūjià shang.

学 生： 书架 还 放 在 老 地方　吗？
Xuésheng: Shūjià hái fàng zài lǎo dìfang ma?

老师： 我们　 把 书架 换 个 地方，把 它 放 在 两　个
Lǎoshī: Wǒmen bǎ shūjià huàn ge dìfang, bǎ tā fàng zài liǎng ge
窗子　　 的 中间，　　你们　觉得 好 不 好？
chuāngzi de zhōngjiān, nǐmen juéde hǎo bu hǎo?

学 生： 我 觉得 很 好。
Xuésheng: Wǒ juéde hěn hǎo.

老师： 我 买 了 一 张　中国　　 地图。请 把 它 挂 在
Lǎoshī: Wǒ mǎi le yì zhāng Zhōngguó dìtú.　 Qǐng bǎ tā guà zài
教室 后面　　 的 墙　上。
jiàoshì hòumiàn de qiáng shang.

学 生： 我 有 一 张　世界 地图，我 能 不 能　把 它 挂
Xuésheng: Wǒ yǒu yì zhāng shìjiè dìtú,　 wǒ néng bu néng bǎ tā guà

在 中国　　地图 的 旁边？
zài Zhōngguó dìtú　de pángbiān?

老师：　　好　主意。
Lǎoshī:　　Hǎo zhǔyì.

学生：　　老师，电脑　放 在哪儿？ 放　在你的桌子　上
Xuésheng:　Lǎoshī, diànnǎo fàng zài nǎr?　Fàng zài nǐde zhuōzi shang
　　　　　吗？
　　　　　ma?

老师：　　不，学校　给我们　买了一张　　电脑　桌子。
Lǎoshī:　　Bù, xuéxiào gěi wǒmen mǎi le yì zhāng diànnǎo zhuōzi.
　　　　　我们　可以把电脑　放　在电脑　桌子　上。
　　　　　Wǒmen kěyǐ bǎ diànnǎo fàng zài diànnǎo zhuōzi shang.

学生：　　太 好 了。电脑　桌子 在哪儿？
Xuésheng:　Tài hǎo le. Diànnǎo zhuōzi zài nǎr?

老师：　　在 教室 外面。　请　把它拿进来。
Lǎoshī:　　Zài jiàoshì wàimiàn. Qǐng bǎ tā ná jìn lai.

学生：　　电脑　桌子 拿进来了。你要　我把它放　在哪
　　　　　儿？
Xuésheng:　Diànnǎo zhuōzi ná jìn lai le.　Nǐ yào wǒ bǎ tā fàng zài
　　　　　nǎr?

老师：　　请　把它放 在教室　的后面。
Lǎoshī:　　Qǐng bǎ tā fàng zài jiàoshì de hòumiàn.

Reading Passage

家在中国东部的一个城市。我们的城市不大，城外有山，山下就
是长江。我们的城市在上海的西边。坐火车去那儿只要一个小时。
我每天坐汽车上班，汽车站就在我家的前边。我家的左边有银行和
商店，右边有餐馆和电影院。我们的城市很宁静。我很喜欢住在这
儿。

Wǒ jiā zài Zhōngguó dōngbù de yí ge chéngshì. Wǒmende chéngshì bú
dà, chéngwài yǒu shān, shān xià jiù shì Chángjiāng. Wǒmende chéngshì
zài Shànghǎi de xībian. Zuò huǒchē qù nàr zhǐ yào yí ge xiǎoshí. Wǒ měi
tiān zuò qìchē shàngbān, qìchēzhàn jiù zài wǒ jiā de qiánbian. Wǒ jiā de
zuǒbian yǒu yínháng hé shāngdiàn, yòubian yǒu cānguǎn hé
diànyǐngyuàn. Wǒmende chéngshì hěn níngjìng. Wǒ hěn xǐhuan zhù zài
zhèr.

New Words and Expressions

书架	shūjià	bookshelf
椅子	yǐzi	chair
桌子	zhuōzi	table; desk
书包	shūbāo	book bag
门	mén	door; gate
沙发	shāfā	sofa
韩国	Hánguó	(South) Korea
国家	guójiā	country
蒙古	Ménggǔ	Mongolia
俄国	Éguó	Russia

部	bù	part; section
学期	xuéqī	semester
把	bǎ	*preposition*
教室	jiàoshì	classroom
重新	chóngxīn	again; anew
布置	bùzhì	arrange (furniture); decorate
先	xiān	first
放	fàng	put; lay
窗子	chuāngzi	window
地图	dìtú	map
挂	guà	hang
墙	qiáng	wall
世界	shìjiè	world
拿	ná	take; hold
长江	Chángjiāng	Yangtze River
宁静	níngjìn	quiet; tranquil

Supplementary Words and Expressions

附近	fùjìn	nearby; vicinity
房间	fángjiān	room
公寓	gōngyù	apartment
卧室	wòshì	bedroom
厨房	chúfáng	kitchen
客厅	kètīng	living room

饭厅	fàntīng	dining room
卫生间	wèishēngjiān	bathroom
车库	chēkù	garage
楼上	lóushàng	upstairs
楼下	lóuxià	downstairs
黑板	hēibǎn	blackboard
加拿大	Jiā'nádà	Canada
墨西哥	Mòxīgē	Mexico
太平洋	Tàipíngyáng	Pacific Ocean
大西洋	Dàxīyáng	Atlantic Ocean

Language Points

Indication of locations

To indicate relative locations or positions, Chinese uses position words. These words differ from English prepositions *in, on* and so on. They are nouns used in conjunction with the preposition 在 zài. Since these position words are used after nouns to indicate locations, they are often referred to as "postpositions."

The following is a complete list of nouns used to indicate locations or positions:

上边	shàngbian	on; over; above
下边	xiàbian	under; below; underneath
前边	qiánbian	in front of; ahead of
后边	hòubian	behind; at the back of
旁边	pángbiān	beside; next to
里边	lǐbian	in; inside

外边	wàibian	outside
左边	zuǒbian	left of; on the left
右边	yòubian	right of; on the right
对面	duìmiàn	across from; opposite
中间	zhōngjiān	in the middle of; between; among
东边	dōngbian	east of; in the east
南边	nánbian	south of; in the south
西边	xībian	west of; in the west
北边	běibian	north of; in the north

Alternatively, 边 biān in 上边 shàngbian, 下边 xiàbian, 前边 qiánbian, 后边 hòubian, 里边 lǐbian and 外边 wàibian can be replaced by 面 miàn or 头 tóu, and 边 biān in 左边 zuǒbian, 右边 yòubian, 东边 dōngbian, 南边 nánbian, 西边 xībian and 北边 běibian can be replaced by 面 miàn. Additionally, 边 biān (or 面 miàn or 头 tóu) is often left out altogether in 里边 lǐbian and 上边 shàngbian.

Similar to the patterns we learned in Lesson 3 in *Beginner's Chinese* that indicate locations, the position words introduced in this lesson are used in the following three patterns:

1. S + 在 zài (N) + (的 de) + position word

书 在 桌子 的 上边。
Shū zài zhuōzi de shàngbian.
The book is on the table.

船 在 桥 的 下边。
Chuán zài qiáo de xiàbian.
The boat is under the bridge.

中国 在 日本 的 西边。
Zhōngguó zài Rìběn de xībian.
China is west of Japan.

学生们　　　在　外边。
Xuéshengmen zài wàibian.
The students are outside.

Note that the subject in the pattern must be definite or specified. Also when a noun is present after 在 zài, it can be optionally followed by 的 de to indicate the attributive relationship. Note also that when 边 biān is left out from the position word, 的 de cannot be used. Compare:

学校　　(的)　里边　有　商店。
Xuéxiào de　lǐbian yǒu shāngdiàn.
There is a store in the school.

学校　　　里有　商店。
Xuéxiào lǐ yǒu shāngdiàn.

2. (N) + (的 de) + position word + 有 yǒu + S

桌子　　上　　有　书。
Zhuōzi shang yǒu shū.
There is a book on the table.

乔　　下　有　　船。
Qiáo xià yǒu chuán.
There is a boat under the bridge.

美国　　的 北边　　有　一个 国家。
Měiguó de běibian yǒu yí ge guójiā.
There is a country north of the United States.

里边　有　商店。
Lǐbian yǒu shāngdiàn.
There is a store inside.

These are so-called existential or presentational sentences, where the subject is indefinite or unspecified. If the subject is definite or specified, 是 shì should generally be used instead of 有 yǒu:

香港　　 的 北边　 是 广州。
Xiānggǎng de běibian shì Guǎngzhōu.
North of Hong Kong is Guangzhou.

张　　先生　　 的 左边　 是 张　　太太。
Zhāng Xiānsheng de zuǒbian shì Zhāng Tàitai.
Left of Mr. Zhang is Mrs. Zhang.

There is supposed to be a 在 zài before N + position word, but it is invariably left out when it appears at the beginning of an existential sentence.

Please note that position words are not necessary after nouns that indicate a place:

曼哈顿　　 在 纽约。
Mànhādùn zài Niǔyuē.
Manhattan is in New York.

我 在 学校　 工作。
Wǒ zài xuéxiào gōngzuò.
I work in a school.

教室后面的墙 上 jiàoshì hòumiàn de qiáng shang

Mention was made in *Beginner's Chinese* that modifiers always precede modified in Chinese, whether they are individual words or phrases or sentences. In this case, 教室后面 jiàoshì hòumiàn (at the back of the classroom) modifies or defines 墙 qiáng (wall) to mean *wall at the back of the classroom*. It is therefore placed before 墙 qiáng. When the modifier is a phrase or a sentence, it is always marked at the end by the article 的 de to indicate the attributive relationship. Similar examples ᵣe:

桌子　上　　的 电脑
huōzi shang de diànnǎo
ᵣe computer on the table

图书馆　　里 的 书
ᵣshūguǎn lǐ de shū
ᵣooks in the library

公园　　　外 的 河
ōngyuán wài de hé
ᵣe river outside the park

边 biān 和 部 bù

ᵣ indicating the relative position of two locations, directional words 东 ōng, 南 nán, 西 xī, and 北 běi used with 边 biān (东边 dōngbian, 西边 ᵣibiān, etc.) suggest that the two locations are outside of each other, ᵣhereas those used with 部 bù (东部 dōngbù, 西部 xībù, etc.) suggest ᵣat one location is part of the other. Compare:

日本 在 中国　　的东边。
ᵣiběn zài Zhōngguó de dōngbian.
ᵣapan is to the east of China.

上海　　在 中国　　的 东部。
ᵣànghǎi zài Zhōngguó de dōngbù.
ᵣhanghai is in the eastern part of China.

ᵣoints of the compass

ᵣhen we enumerate the four points of the compass (north, south, east ᵣnd west) in Chinese, the conventional order is to follow the clockwise

85

direction starting from the east: 东 dōng (east), 南 nán (south), 西 xī (west), and 北 běi (north).

Additionally, 东 dōng (east) and 西 xī (west) serve as the cardinal points when we indicate points such as northeast, northwest, southeast and southwest, which is exactly the reverse of the order in English: 东南 dōngnán (southeast), 东北 dōngběi (northeast), 西南 xīnán (southwest) and 西北 xīběi (northwest). See the illustration of the following graph:

The 把 bǎ-construction

Frequently used in Chinese, 把 bǎ is a grammatical device used to shift the object before the verb. The 把 bǎ-construction takes the following form:

S + 把 bǎ + O + V + other elements

Several conditions must be met in using the 把 bǎ-construction:

1. For an object to be shifted to the front, it must be a definite or specified one. We can say 把这本书看完了 bǎ zhè běn shū kàn wán le (finish reading the book), but we can't say 把一本书看完了 bǎ yì běn shū kàn wán le (finish reading a book).

2. The verb must be one that can produce a tangible result in the object, such as causing it to change hands, location, form, state, or to disappear and so on. We can say 把书放在桌上 bǎ shū fàng zài zhuō shang (put the book on the table), but we can't say 把这件事知道 bǎ zhè jiàn shì zhīdào (to know the matter). Verbs that cannot be used in the 把 bǎ-construction include 认识 rènshi (know), 喜欢 xǐhuan (like), 开始 kāishǐ (begin), 来 lái (come), 回 huí (go back to), 坐 zuò (sit), 进 jìn (enter), 有 yǒu (have), 是 shì (be) and so on.

3. The verb must be a complex one, i.e. it must be followed by another element. This element can be a verb complement such as 完 wán or a particle such as 了 le.

When there is a choice, the sentence that uses the 把 bǎ-construction differs in meaning from the one that doesn't. Although both 他吃了饭 tā chī le fàn and 他把饭吃了 tā bǎ fàn chī le can be translated as *he ate the food*, the foci of the sentences are different. 他吃了饭 tā chī le fàn answers the question *what did he do*, whereas 他把饭吃了 tā bǎ fàn chī le answers the question *what did he do to the food*.

With certain verbs, the use of the 把 bǎ-construction is obligatory. These verbs include 放 fàng (put), 摆 bǎi (lay), and 留 liú (leave behind). These verbs share a common feature in that they cause the object to move from one place to another.

If the 把 bǎ-construction takes the negative form, the negative word should precede 把 bǎ:

老师　没有　把 电脑　放 在 她的 桌子　上。
Lǎoshī méiyou bǎ diànnǎo fàng zài tāde zhuōzi shang.
The teacher didn't put the computer on her desk.

有的　学生　　上课　的 时候 也 不 把 手机 关　　掉。
Yǒude xuésheng shàngkè de shíhou yě bù bǎ shǒujī guān diào.
Some students don't even turn off their cell phones in class.

Exercises

I. Answer the following questions:

(For questions 1-6, please refer to the pictures given.)

1. 狗　在 哪儿?
   Gǒu zài nǎr?

2. 刀　在 哪儿?
   Dāo zài nǎr?

3. 盘子 在 哪儿?
   Pánzi zài nǎr?

4. 电脑　在 哪儿?
   Diànnǎo zài nǎr?

5. 教室　里 有 什么?
   Jiàoshì lǐ yǒu shénme?

6. 餐馆　在 银行　的左边 吗?
   Cānguǎn zài yínháng de zuǒbian ma?

7. 你的 书包　里有 什么?
   Nǐde shūbāo lǐ yǒu shénme?

8. 你家 附近 有 中国　餐馆　吗?
   Nǐ jiā fùjìn yǒu Zhōngguó cānguǎn ma?

9. 俄国 在 中国　的南边　吗?
   Éguó zài Zhōngguó de nánbian ma?

10. 美国　的北边　是 加拿大 吗?
    Měiguó de běibian shì Jiā'nádà ma?

II. How do you say the following?

East Asia	Southeast Asia	South America
North America	North Africa	South Africa
Central Africa	Central Asia	Western Europe
Eastern Europe	Northern Europe	Southern Europe

III. Fill in the blanks with 在 (zài), 是 (shì) or 有 (yǒu):

1. 医院 ＿＿＿＿ 我们 公司　的 对面。
   Yīyuàn ＿＿＿＿wǒmen gōngsī de duìmiàn.

2. 学校　里 ＿＿＿＿ 老师 和 学生。
   Xuéxiào lǐ ＿＿＿＿ lǎoshī hé xuésheng.

89

3. 我 家 的 东边 _____ 中国 银行。
   Wǒ jiā de dōngbian _____ Zhōngguó Yínháng.

4. 加拿大 _____ 美国 的北边。
   Jiā'nádà _____ Měiguó de běibian.

5. 中国 的 北边 _____ 俄国 和 蒙古。
   Zhōngguó de běibian _____ Éguó hé Ménggǔ.

6. 电影院 _____ 学校 和 银行 的中间。
   Diànyǐngyuàn _____ xuéxiào hé yínháng de zhōngjiān.

7. 桌子 上 _____ 书 和 词典。
   Zhuōzi shang _____ shū hé cídiǎn.

8. 南边 _____ 北京 火车站。
   Nánbian _____ Běijīng Huǒchēzhàn.

9. 他的 女朋友 坐 _____ 他 左边。
   Tāde nǚpéngyou zuò _____ tā zuǒbian.

10. 冰箱 里 _____ 很 多 菜。
    Bīngxiāng lǐ _____ hěn duō cài.

IV. Tell the differences between the following pairs:

汽车 的后面	后面 的 汽车
qìchē de hòumiàn	hòumiàn de qìchē

学校 的 前面	前面 的学校
xuéxiào de qiánmiàn	qiánmiàn de xuéxiào

书 的 上边	上边 的书
shū de shàngbian	shàngbian de shū

商店　　的 东边　　　　东边　　　的 商店
shāngdiàn de dōngbian　　　dōngbian de shāngdiàn

银行　　的 对面　　　　对面　　　的 银行
yínháng de duìmiàn　　　　duìmiàn de yínháng

V. Say where the following countries are in relation to those in the brackets:

英国 Yīngguó (法国 Fǎguó)　　　　印度 Yìndù (中国 Zhōngguó)
墨西哥 Mòxīgē (美国 Měiguó)　　　日本 Rìběn (韩国 Hánguó)
波兰 Bōlán (俄国 Éguó)　　　　　埃及 Āijí (苏丹 Sūdān)

VI. The 把 ba-construction.

A. Change the following sentences using the 把 ba-construction:

1. 他 卖　了他的 汽车。
   Tā mài le tāde qìchē.

2. 我　关　　掉　了我的 手机。
   Wǒ guān diào le wǒde shǒujī.

3. 他们　　喝 了茶。
   Tāmen hē le chá.

4. 妈妈　洗了 那 件　毛衣。
   Māma xǐ le nà jiàn máoyī.

5. 公司　换　　了我的 工作。
   Gōngsī huàn le wǒde gōngzuò.

B. How do you say the following:

1. put your book in your book bag

2. forgot my wallet at home
3. deliver the food to the school
4. bring your friend home
5. write your name on the paper

VII. Translate the following into Chinese:

1. The cat (猫 māo) is under the bed.
2. The Atlantic Ocean is to the east of the United States.
3. Our school is between the hospital and the bank.
4. The map is behind the door.
5. My home is next to a store.
6. There are three bookshelves in the classroom.
7. Children are playing outside the building.
8. The liquor store is across from the restaurant.
9. There are two countries north of China.
10. California is in the western part of the United States.

VIII. Translate the following into English:

美国在北美洲，是世界第四大国家（第一大国家是俄国，第二大国家是加拿大，第三大国家是中国）。美国的北边是加拿大，南边是墨西哥，东边和西边没有国家。东边是大西洋，西边是太平洋。

Měiguó zài Běi Měizhōu, shì shìjiè dì sì dà guójiā (dì yī dà guójiā shì Éguó, dì èr dà guójiā shì Jiā'nádà, dì sān dà guójiā shì Zhōngguó). Měiguó de běibian shì Jiā'nádà, nánbian shì Mòxīgē, dōngbian hé xībian méi yǒu guójiā. Dōngbian shì Dàxīyáng, xībian shì Tàipíngyáng.

IX. Discussion and writing topics:

1. Describe your home or apartment.
2. Describe your community.
3. Describe a geographical area.

English Translation of the Text

Conversations

A: Where is the dictionary?
B: The dictionary is on the bookshelf.
A: Where is the newspaper?
B: The newspaper is under the watch.
A: Where is the car?
B: The car is in front of the school.
A: Where is the chair?
B: The chair is behind the desk.
A: Where is the pig?
B: The pig is next to the cow.
A: Where is the knife?
B: The knife is to the right of the plate.
A: Where is the fork?
B: The fork is to the left of the plate.
A: Where is the Chinese book?
B: The Chinese book is in the book bag.
A: Where is the bike?
B: The bike is outside the door.
A: Where is the restaurant?
B: The restaurant is across from the bank.
A: Where is the boat?
B: The boat is in the middle of the river.
A: Where is the bookstore?
B: The bookstore is between the bank and the restaurant.
A: What is on the left? What is on the right?
B: The bus is on the left and the train is on the right.
A: What's opposite here?
B: Opposite here are a movie theater and a bakery.
A: Where is Japan?
B: Japan is to the east of China.
A: Where is Korea?
B: Korea is to the northeast of China.
A: What countries lie to the north of China?

B: Mongolia and Russia are to the north of China.
A: What part of China is Shanghai in?
B: Shanghai is in the eastern part of China.

        *   *   *   *   *

Teacher:	Today is the first day of the new semester. Let's rearrange the classroom, shall we?
Student:	Good, teacher. Please tell us what to do.
Teacher:	First put these new books on the bookshelf.
Student:	Shall we put the bookshelf in the old place?
Teacher:	Let's put the bookshelf in a different place. Put it between the two windows. What do you think?
Student:	I think it is good.
Teacher:	I bought a map of China. Please hang it up on the wall at the back of the classroom.
Student:	I have a map of the world. Can I hang it next to the map of China?
Teacher:	Good idea.
Student:	Teacher, where should the computer go? Shall I put it on your desk?
Teacher:	No. The school bought a computer table for us. We can put the computer on the computer table.
Student:	That's great. Where is the computer table?
Teacher:	It's outside the classroom. Please bring it in.
Student:	I got it in. Where should I put it?
Teacher:	Please put it at the back of the classroom.

Reading Passage

I live in a city in the eastern part of China. Our city is not big. There is a mountain outside the city. Below the mountain is the Yangtze River. Our city is to the west of Shanghai. It takes only an hour to get to Shanghai from our place. I go to work by bus every day. The bus stop is right in front of my house. There are a bank and a store to the left of my house, and there are a restaurant and a movie theater to the right of my house. Our city is very quiet. I like living here very much.

5

SCHOOL & SCHOOL LIFE

Conversations

A: 你 在 哪儿上学?
Nǐ zài nǎr shàngxué?

B: 我 在 第 五 中学 上学。
Wǒ zài Dì Wǔ Zhōngxué shàngxué.

A: 你 上 初中 还是 高中?
Nǐ shàng chūzhōng háishi gāozhōng?

B: 我 上 高中。
Wǒ shàng gāozhōng.

A: 你 现在 是 几年级?
Nǐ xiànzài shì jǐ niánjí?

B: 我 现在 是 高中 一 年级。
Wǒ xiànzài shì gāozhōng yì niánjí.

A：你们 班 有 多少 学生？
Nǐmen bān yǒu duōshao xuésheng?

B：我们 班 有 四十个学生。
Wǒmen bān yǒu sìshí ge xuésheng.

A：你们 每 天 有 几节课？
Nǐmen měi tiān yǒu jǐ jié kè?

B：我们 每 天 有 七节 课，上午 四节，下午 三 节。
Wǒmen měi tiān yǒu qī jié kè, shàngwǔ sì jié, xiàwǔ sān jié.

A：你们 有 些 什么 课？
Nǐmen yǒu xiē shénme kè?

B：我们 有 语文、数学、外语、历史、体育、音乐、 自然
Wǒmen yǒu yǔwén, shùxué, wàiyǔ, lìshǐ, tǐyù, yīnyuè, zìrán
科学 和 美术 等等。
kēxué hé měishù děngdeng.

A：你们 有 什么 外语 课？
Nǐmen yǒu shénme wàiyǔ kè?

B：我们 有 英语、 法语和日语，但是 大多数 学生 都
Wǒmen yǒu Yīngyǔ, Fǎyǔ hé Rìyǔ, dànshì dàduōshù xuésheng dōu
选 英语。
xuǎn Yīngyǔ.

A：你们 有 没 有 外国 老师？
Nǐmen yǒu méi yǒu wàiguó lǎoshī?

B：有，我们 有 两 个外国 老师，一个是 英国人， 一个
Yǒu, wǒmen yǒu liǎng ge wàiguó lǎoshī, yí ge shì Yīngguórén, yí ge

是 日本人。 他们 教 我们 英语 和 日语。
shì Rìběnrén. Tāmen jiāo wǒmen Yīngyǔ hé Rìyǔ.

*   *   *   *   *

A： 你 在 哪儿上学?
Nǐ zài nǎr shàngxué?

B： 我 不 上学 了。我 毕业了。
Wǒ bú shàngxué le. Wǒ bìyè le.

A： 你 已经 毕业了? 真 快。你 有 没有 找 到 工作?
Nǐ yǐjīng bìyè le? Zhēn kuài. Nǐ yǒu méiyou zhǎo dào gōngzuò?

B： 我 没有 找 工作, 我 想 读 研究生。
Wǒ méiyou zhǎo gōngzuò, wǒ xiǎng dú yánjiūshēng.

A： 你 想 读 什么 专业?
Nǐ xiǎng dú shénme zhuānyè?

B： 我 想 读 文学。
Wǒ xiǎng dú wénxué.

A： 读 研究生 要 几年?
Dú yánjiūshēng yào jǐ nián?

B： 读 硕士 要 两 年, 读 博士 一般 要 五年。
Dú shuòshì yào liǎng nián, dú bóshì yìbān yào wǔ nián.

A： 你 要 读 硕士 还是 博士?
Nǐ yào dú shuòshì háishi bóshì?

B： 我 现在 还 不 知道。我 想 先 读 硕士, 以后 再
Wǒ xiànzài hái bù zhīdào. Wǒ xiǎng xiān dú shuòshì, yǐhòu zài

决定 要 不 要 读 博士。你 呢? 你 还 在 上学 吗?
juédìng yào bu yào dú bóshì. Nǐ ne? Nǐ hái zài shàngxué ma?

A: 不, 我 也 毕业了, 正 在 找 工作。
Bù, wǒ yě bìyè le, zhèng zài zhǎo gōngzuò.

B: 你 想 作 什么?
Nǐ xiǎng zuò shénme?

A: 我 学 的是 英语, 我 想 当 英语 老师。
Wǒ xué de shì Yīngyǔ, wǒ xiǎng dāng Yīngyǔ lǎoshī.

B: 听说 很 多 学校 现在 要 老师, 你 一定 能 找
Tīngshuō hěn duō xuéxiào xiànzài yào lǎoshī, nǐ yídìng néng zhǎo
到 老师 的 工作。
dào lǎoshī de gōngzuò.

A: 但愿 如此。
Dànyuàn rú cǐ.

　　　　*　　　　*　　　　*　　　　*　　　　*

A: 小 王, 有 人 说 在 中国 进 大学 难, 出 大学
Xiǎo Wáng, yǒu rén shuō zài Zhōngguó jìn dàxué nán, chū dàxué
容易, 在 美国 进大学 容易, 出 大学 难。你 觉得 是
róngyì, zài Měiguó jìn dàxué róngyì, chū dàxué nán. Nǐ juéde shì
这样 吗?
zhèyang ma?

B: 是 这样。 中国 每 年 有 很 多 高中 毕业生,
Shì zhèyang. Zhōngguó měi nián yǒu hěn duō gāozhōng bìyèshēng,
但是 没 有 足够 的大学, 所以 不是 每 个 高中
dànshi méi yǒu zúgòu de dàxué, suǒyǐ bú shì měi ge gāozhōng

毕业生　都　能　　上　　大学。
bìyèshēng dōu néng shàng dàxué.

A：那么　怎么　才　能　　进　大学　呢？
Nàme zěnme cái néng jìn dàxué ne?

B：你　要　通过　　很　严格　的　考试。如果　成绩　　不　好，就　不
Nǐ yào tōngguò hěn yángé de kǎoshì. Rúguǒ chéngjī bù hǎo, jiù bù

能　进　大学　或　不　能　　进　很　好　的　大学。
néng jìn dàxué huò bù néng jìn hěn hǎo de dàxué.

A：在　美国　　上　　大学　不　要　通过　　考试，但是　　要　进　好
Zài Měiguó shàng dàxué bú yào tōngguò kǎoshì, dànshì yào jìn hǎo
的　大学　也　不　容易。
de dàxué yě bù róngyì.

Reading Passage

中国的学校分小学，中学和大学。孩子们一般在六岁或七岁开始上小学。中学又分初中和高中。小学六年，初中三年，高中三年，大学四年。每个孩子必须上小学和初中，大多数人也上高中和大学。大学毕业后，大多数人开始工作，也有人继续学习，读研究生。以前，学生一个星期要上六天的课，现在一个星期上五天的课，星期六和星期天不上学。中国的小学生和中学生很辛苦，他们每天要作很多作业，很少有时间玩儿。

Zhōngguó de xuéxiào fēn xiǎoxué, zhōngxué hé dàxué. Háizimen yìbān
zài liù suì huò qī suì kāishǐ shàng xiǎoxué. Zhōngxué yòu fēn chūzhōng
hé gāozhōng. Xiǎoxué liù nián, chūzhōng sān nián, gāozhōng sān nián,
dàxué sì nián. Měi ge háizi bìxū shàng xiǎoxué hé chūzhōng, dàduōshù
rén yě shàng gāozhōng hé dàxué. Dàxué bìyè hòu, dàduōshù rén kāishǐ

gōngzuò, yě yǒu rén jìxù xuéxí, dú yánjiūshēng. Yǐqián, xuésheng yí ge xīngqī yào shàng liù tiān de kè, xiànzài yí ge xīngqī shàng wǔ tiān de kè, xīngqīliù hé xīngqītiān bú shàngxué. Zhōngguó de xiǎoxuéshēng hé zhōngxuéshēng hěn xīnkǔ, tāmen měi tiān yào zuò hěn duō zuòyè, hěn shǎo yǒu shíjiān wánr.

New Words and Expressions

初	chū	beginning (of a time period); primary
高	gāo	high; tall
年级	niánjí	(of school) grade; year
节	jié	period (of a class)
语文	yǔwén	language arts
数学	shùxué	mathematics
外语	wàiyǔ	foreign language
体育	tǐyù	physical education
自然科学	zìrán kēxué	natural science
美术	měishù	fine art
等等	děngdeng	so on
大多数	dàduōshù	majority; most of
选	xuǎn	select; choose
毕业	bìyè	graduate (v)
毕业生	bìyèshēng	graduate (n)
研究生	yánjiūshēng	graduate student
读	dú	study; read aloud
文学	wénxué	literature

硕士	shuòshì	master's degree; master's degree holder
博士	bóshì	doctoral degree; doctoral degree holder
先 ...... 再	xiān ... zài	first ... then
决定	juédìng	decide; decision
专业	zhuānyè	major; profession; specialty
但愿如此	dànyuàn rú cǐ	hope so
出	chū	go out; exit
容易	róngyì	easy
足够	zúgòu	enough; adequate
所以	suǒyǐ	therefore
那么	nàme	in that case; like that; so
通过	tōngguò	pass
严格	yángé	rigorous; strict; tough
考试	kǎoshì	exam (v); examination
成绩	chéngjī	grade; result; achievement
或	huò	or
分	fēn	divide; separate; distinguish
又	yòu	further
必须	bìxū	must
继续	jìxù	continue
辛苦	xīnkǔ	hard (adj.); toilsome

Supplementary Words and Expressions

| 教育 | jiàoyù | educate; education |

学士	xuéshì	bachelor's degree; bachelor's degree holder
幼儿园	yòu'éryuán	kindergarten
本科生	běnkēshēng	undergraduate student
暑假	shǔjià	summer vacation
寒假	hánjià	winter vacation
课外活动	kèwài huódòng	extracurricular activity
回答	huídá	answer (n. & v.)
翻译	fānyì	translate; translation
作业	zuòyè	(of school) assignment
交	jiāo	submit; hand in
作文	zuòwén	composition
测验	cèyàn	test; quiz
词汇	cíhuì	vocabulary

Language Points

Classifiers for 课 kè and 班 bān

Two classifiers can be used for 课 kè: 节 jié and 门 mén, but there is a difference. 节 jié is used to indicate a period of class such as 我们每天有七节课 wǒmen měi tiān yǒu qī jié kè (we have seven periods of classes every day), whereas 门 mén is used to indicate a course such as 我们这学期学四门课 wǒmen zhè xuéqī xué sì mén kè (we take four courses this semester).

你们有些什么课 nǐmen yǒu xiē shénme kè?

些 xiē in the sentence is short for 一些 yì xiē. It is a suffix used after 一 yī and demonstrative pronouns 这 zhè, 那 nà, and 哪 nǎ to indicate an indeterminate or unspecified amount: 一些 yìxiē (some); 这些 zhèxiē (these), 那些 nàxiē (those) and 哪些 nǎxiē (which ones). Note that 些 xiē is not a plural suffix. If what follows 这 zhè or 那 nà is a specific number, 些 xiē cannot be used:

这 三 本 书
zhè sān běn shū
these three books

那 五 个 人
nà wǔ ge rén
those five people

初 chū

初 chū in the sense of *beginning* or *primary* is only used in certain set expressions such as 初中 chūzhōng (junior high school), 年初 niánchū (beginning of the year) and 月初 yuèchū (beginning of the month).

我不上学了 wǒ bú shàngxué le

This 了 le is different from the aspect particle 了 le we discussed in *Beginner's Chinese* (Lesson 10). Instead of indicating the completion of an action, it indicates a change of condition, suggesting a contrast to the previous state or action:

天 冷 了。
Tiān lěng le.
It is getting cold—implying that it is no longer warm.

103

他 有　工作　了。
Tā yǒu gōngzuò le.
He has a job now—implying that he didn't have a job before.

Compare the following two sentences:

我　没　有　钱。
Wǒ méi yǒu qián.
I don't have money—a statement of fact.

我 没　有　钱　了。
Wǒ méi yǒu qián le.
I don't have money now—a new situation implying that I had money
before.

In this usage, 了 le can be used with cognitive and non-action verbs such
as 喜欢 xǐhuan (like) and 是 shì (to be):

我　太太 现在　喜欢　吃　豆腐 了。
Wǒ tàitai xiànzài xǐhuan chī dòufu le.
My wife likes to eat tofu now—implying that she didn't like it before.

我们　是 公民　了。
Wǒmen shì gōngmín le.
We are now citizens—implying that we were not before.

The negative form of this usage of 了 le is 不 bù instead of 没有 méiyou
unless the verb is 有 yǒu, when 没 méi should be used:

我　不 吸烟 了。
Wǒ bù xīyān le.
I no longer smoke.

他 没　有　汽车 了。
Tā méi yǒu qìchē le.

He no longer has a car.

This use of 了 le can also suggest the emergence of a new situation:

现在　　四点　了, 我们　　上　　课 吧。
Xiànzài sì diǎn le, wǒmen shàng kè ba.
It's four o'clock now; let's begin our class.

我　三十　岁了。
Wǒ sānshí suì le.
I'm thirty years old now.

你有没有找到工作 nǐ yǒu méiyou zhǎo dào gōngzuò?

Used after a verb as a complement, 到 dào suggests the successful accomplishment of an action that involves a certain amount of difficulty and effort. Compare:

买　了电影　　票
mǎi le diànyǐng piào
bought the movie ticket—no difficulty or effort suggested.

买　到　了电影　票
mǎi dào le diànyǐng piào
succeeded in buying the movie ticket—difficulty or effort suggested.

吃　了北京　烤鸭。
chī le Běijīng kǎoyā
ate Peking Duck—no difficulty suggested; it was easily available.

吃　到　了北京　烤鸭。
chī dào le Běijīng kǎoyā
managed to eat Peking Duck—difficulty suggested; there may have been many people waiting in line.

There are two negative forms for this use of 到 dào: 1) 没有 měiyou + V + 到 dào for the unsuccessful completion of an action and 2) V + 不到 bú dào for a projected failure to succeed:

现在　是 冬天，　吃 不 到　西瓜。
Xiànzài shì dōngtiān, chī bú dào xīguā.
It is winter now. We can't find watermelons to eat.

我　去 晚　了，没有　看　到 他。
Wǒ qù wǎn le,　méiyou kàn dào tā.
I got there late, so I didn't get to see him.

我学的是英语 wǒ xué de shì Yīngyǔ

The noun modified by a sentence is often left out, as in this instance, resulting in a nominal construction. This often happens when the noun has occurred in the prior speech context or is understood. The missing noun in the sentence cited is 专业 zhuānyè (major or subject). Other examples are:

好的 (人) 多 hǎo de (rén) duō, 坏的 (人) 少 huài de (rén) shǎo (there are more good people than bad people); 我说的 (话), 你懂不懂 Wǒ shuō de (huà), nǐ dǒng bu dǒng (do you understand what I say?).

那么怎么才能进大学呢 nàme zěnme cái néng jìn dàxué ne?

那么 nǎme is a discourse connector used at the beginning of a sentence referring to the prior discourse with the meaning of *in that case*.

才 cái in the sentence indicates that one situation is conditional upon another. The above sentence means *what conditions must be met before one can get into a university*. For this reason, it is often translated as *not ... until ...* or *must do ... before ...* Other examples are:

他 来 了以后 你 才 能　去。
Tā lái le yǐhòu nǐ cái néng qù.
You can't go until he comes.

你 作 完　作业 才 能　 看　电视。
Nǐ zuò wán zuòyè cái néng kàn diànshì.
You need to finish your homework before you can watch TV.

如果 rúguǒ …… 就 jiù ……

There are three major differences between 如果 rúguǒ (if) …… 就 jiù
(then) …… in Chinese and *if* …, *(then)* … in English:

1. The 如果 rúguǒ (if) clause always precedes the 就 jiù (then) clause.

2. The subject in the 如果 rúguǒ (if) clause can either precede 如果
rúguǒ or follow it. We can say both of the following:

如果　你 不 来，我　就 不 去。
Rúguǒ nǐ bù lái,　wǒ jiù bú qù.

你 如果 不 来，我　就 不 去。
Nǐ rúguǒ bù lái,　wǒ jiù bú qù.
If you don't come, I won't go.

3. 就 jiù is an adverb. As such, it occurs before the verb and after the
subject. This is different from *then* in English, where it is placed before
the subject.

或 huò and 还是 háishi

Although both are translated as *or*, they differ significantly in usage.
While 或 huò is used between two alternatives in declarative sentences,

还是 háishi is used between two alternatives in interrogative sentences. For example:

你 今天 来 或 明天 　 来 都 可以。
Nǐ jīntiān lái huò míngtiān lái dōu kěyǐ.
It's okay whether you come today or tomorrow.

你 今天 来 还是 明天 　 来?
Nǐ jīntiān lái háishi míngtiān lái?
Are you coming today or tomorrow?

你 喜欢 　 米饭 还是 面条?
Nǐ xǐhuan mǐfàn háishi miàntiáo?
Do you like rice or noodles?

如果 　 成绩 　 不好，就不能 　 进 大学 或 不能 　 进 很 好 的
Rúguǒ chéngjī bù hǎo, jiù bù néng jìn dàxué huò bù néng jìn hěn hǎo de
大学。
dàxué.
If your grades are not good, you can't get into a college or you can't get into a good college.

或 huò can alternatively be expressed as 或者 huòzhě.

Exercises

I. Answer the following questions:

1. 你 是 学生 　 吗? 你 在 哪儿上学?
   Nǐ shì xuésheng ma? Nǐ zài nǎr shàngxué?

2. 你 是 在 哪儿上 　 的 大学?
   Nǐ shì zài nǎr shàng de dàxué?

3. 你 在 大学 时，读 的 是 什么　专业？
Nǐ zài dàxué shí, dú de shì shénme zhuānyè?

4. 你上　　大学 时，每 天 有 几节课？是什么　课？
Nǐ shàng dàxué shí, měi tiān yǒu jǐ jié kè? Shì shénme kè?

5. 你们　学校　有 没 有 外国　老师？他们　教 什么　课？
Nǐmen xuéxiào yǒu méi yǒu wàiguó lǎoshī? Tāmen jiāo shénme kè?

6. 你们　上　星期 有 没 有 中文　　作业？有 什么
Nǐmen shàng xīngqī yǒu méi yǒu Zhōngwén zuòyè? Yǒu shénme
作业？
zuòyè?

7. 你们的 中文　　课要不要 考试？什么　　时候 考？
Nǐmende Zhōngwén kè yào bu yào kǎoshì? Shénme shíhou kǎo?

8. 这 学期 什么　　时候　结束？
Zhè xuéqī shénme shíhou jiéshù?

9. 你 在 大学 的时候，最 喜欢 什么　课？最不喜欢
Nǐ zài dàxué de shíhou, zuì xǐhuan shénme kè? Zuì bù xǐhuan
什么　课？
shénme kè?

10. 现在　什么　工作　好 找？什么　工作　不 好 找？
Xiànzài shénme gōngzuò hǎo zhǎo? Shénme gōngzuò bù hǎo zhǎo?

II. How do you say the following, using 了 le?

1. We have become teachers.
2. It's getting hot.
3. She can drive a car now.
4. My father no longer works.

5. Students in this class have a computer now.

III. How do you say the following, using the nominal contruction?

1. what our teacher said
2. what we read
3. what the company did
4. what you want
5. what they can't do

IV. Fill in the blanks with one of the verbs listed below with the complement 到 dào:

看　　找　　买　　吃
kàn　　zhǎo　　mǎi　　chī

1. 孩子们　去博物馆 ＿＿＿＿＿＿ 了很 多 有意思 的 东西。
   Háizimen qù bówùguǎn ＿＿＿＿＿＿ le hěn duō yǒuyìsī de dōngxī.

2. 我 去 了很 多 书店，但是 没有＿＿＿＿＿＿ 这 本 书。
   Wǒ qù le hěn duō shūdiàn, dànshì méiyǒu ＿＿＿＿＿＿ zhè běn shū.

3. 街 上 的 餐馆 都 关门 了。他们 没有＿＿＿＿＿＿
   Jiē shang de cānguǎn dōu guānmén le. Tāmen méiyou ＿＿＿＿＿＿
   饭。
   fàn.

4. 他 刚 毕业 就 ＿＿＿＿＿＿ 了工作。
   Tā gāng bìyè jiù ＿＿＿＿＿＿ le gōngzuò.

. 很 多 人 想 看 这 个 电影， 我 没有＿＿＿＿＿ 票。
Hěn duō rén xiǎng kàn zhè ge diànyǐng, wǒ méiyou ＿＿＿＿＿
piào.

/. Fill in the blanks with either 或 (者) huò (zhě) or 还是 háishi:

. 你 在 家 吃 中饭＿＿＿＿＿ 在 公司 吃 中饭？
Nǐ zài jiā chī zhōngfàn ＿＿＿＿＿ zài gōngsī chī zhōngfàn?

. 我 想 请 你＿＿＿＿＿ 你的 朋友 作 这 件 事。
Wǒ xiǎng qǐng nǐ ＿＿＿＿＿ nǐde péngyou zuò zhè jiàn shì.

. 大卫 和 他太太 想 去香港＿＿＿＿＿ 澳门 度 蜜月。
Dàwèi hé tā tàitai xiǎng qù Xiānggǎng ＿＿＿＿＿ Àomén dù mìyuè.

. 学生们 问 老师 这 星期 有 考试＿＿＿＿＿ 下 星期
Xuéshengmen wèn lǎoshī zhè xīngqī yǒu kǎoshì ＿＿＿＿＿ xià
xīngqī
有 考试。
yǒu kǎoshì.

. 日本 在 中国 的东边 ＿＿＿＿＿ 西边？
Rìběn zài Zhōngguó de dōngbian ＿＿＿＿＿ xībian?

/I. Each sentence below contains an error. Find it and correct t:

1. 这些 五 本 书 都 是 我的。
Zhèxiē wǔ běn shū dōu shì wǒde.

2. 我 想 星期六 还是 星期天 去 看 电影。
Wǒ xiǎng xīngqīliù háishi xīngqītiān qù kàn diànyǐng.

3. 今年　夏天　很　多　人　去 中国　　旅行，我　不 买　到
   Jīnnián xiàtiān hěn duō rén qù Zhōngguó lǚxíng, wǒ bú mǎi dào
   飞机票。
   fēijīpiào.

4. 如果　不 能　去 英国，　　就　我们　去　法国。
   Rúguǒ bù néng qù Yīngguó, jiù wǒmen qù Fǎguó.

5. 我　爸爸 妈妈　四 十 年　结婚　了。
   Wǒ bàba māma sìshí nián jiéhūn le.

6. 汽车　在 前面　　的 房子。
   Qìchē zài qiánmiàn de fángzi.

7. 老师　很　好　对 我们。
   Lǎoshī hěn hǎo duì wǒmen.

8. 你的　美国　朋友　说　中文　　很　好。
   Nǐde Měiguó péngyou shuō Zhōngwén hěn hǎo.

9. 你　昨天　怎么　来 学校？
   Nǐ zuótiān zěnme lái xuéxiào?

10. 他 学　中文　　学 了 两　多　年　了。
    Tā xué Zhōngwén xué le liǎng duō nián le.

VII. Translate the following into Chinese:

1. I didn't go to college after I graduated from high school.
2. There are twenty-eight students in my son's class.
3. The students were very happy because the teacher said that there wa
   no homework.
4. I'm sorry I can't go to see the movie with you tonight. I need to
   study because there is a test tomorrow.

5. Many parents want their children to be lawyers and doctors after they graduate from college.
6. Our summer vacation starts at the beginning of July.
7. The teacher asked the students to hand in their homework the following Monday.
8. Students must pass these exams before they can be admitted to college.
9. Many college students don't want to go to graduate school.
10. Have you found a job?

VIII. Translate the following into English:

1. 这 个 学校　从 小学　到 高中　　有 十二 个 年级。
   Zhè ge xuéxiào cóng xiǎoxué dào gāozhōng yǒu shíèr ge niánjí.

2. 研究生　　每 个 学期 要 上　四 门 或 五 门 课。
   Yánjiūshēng měi ge xuéqī yào shàng sì mén huò wǔ mén kè.

3. 高中　　毕业生　必须 通过 (pass) 外语 考试 才 能　上
   Gāozhōng bìyèshēng bìxū tōngguò wàiyǔ kǎoshì cái néng shàng
   大学。
   dàxué.

4. 现在　美国　越来越 多 的 中学　开 中文　　课。
   Xiànzài Měiguó yuèláiyuè duō de zhōngxué kāi Zhōngwén kè.

5. 他 能　找 到 工作，　但是 他 没有　找。
   Tā néng zhǎo dào gōngzuò, dànshì tā méiyou zhǎo.

6. 英语　专业　又 分 英国　语言 和 英国　文学。
   Yīngyǔ zhuānyè yòu fēn Yīngguó yǔyán hé Yīngguó wénxué.

7. 在 中国，　学生　必须 先 读 硕士 才 能　读博士。
   Zài Zhōngguó, xuésheng bìxū xiān dú shuòshì cái néng dú bóshì.

113

在 美国， 读博士不 一定 先 读 硕士。
Zài Měiguó, dú bóshì bù yídìng xiān dú shuòshì.

8. 很 多 大学 毕业生 如果 找 不 到 工作 就去读
Hěn duō dàxué bìyèshēng rúguǒ zhǎo bú dào gōngzuò jiù qù dú
研究生。
yánjiūshēng.

9. 我 觉得 在 美国 进 大学 和 出 大学 都 不 容易。
Wǒ juéde zài Měiguó jìn dàxué hé chū dàxué dōu bù róngyì.

10. 大多数 外国 学生 来美国 上 大学 或 读
Dàduōshù wàiguó xuésheng lái Měiguó shàng dàxué huò dú
研究生 都 要 先 通过 英语 考试。
yánjiūshēng dōu yào xiān tōngguò Yīngyǔ kǎoshì.

IX. Discussion and writing topics:

1. 有 人 说 在 美国 进大学 容易， 出 大学 难， 你 同意
Yǒu rén shuō zài Měiguó jìn dàxué róngyì, chū dàxué nán, nǐ tóngyì
不 同意？
bu tóngyì?

2. 你 觉得 学生 在 进 大学 以前 应该 不 应该 通过
Nǐ juéde xuésheng zài jìn dàxué yǐqián yīnggāi bu yīnggāi tōngguò
严格 的 考试？
yángé de kǎoshì?

3. 谈谈 你的 国家 的 教育 制度 (system)。
Tántan nǐde guójiā de jiàoyù zhìdù.

English Translation of the Text

onversations

.: What school do you go to?

: I go to Middle School Number Five.

: Are you in junior middle school or senior middle school?

: I'm in senior middle school.

: What year are you in?

: I'm in the first year.

: How many students are there in your class?

: There are forty students in my class.

: How many periods of classes do you have every day?

: We have seven periods every day, four in the morning and three in the afternoon.

: What classes do you have?

: We have language arts, mathematics, foreign language, history, physical education, music, natural sciences, fine arts and so on.

: What foreign languages do you have?

: We have English, French and Japanese, but most students choose English.

: Do you have foreign teachers?

: Yes, we do. We have two foreign teachers, one British and one Japanese. They teach us English and Japanese.

*   *   *   *   *

: What school are you attending?

: I don't go to school any more. I graduated.

: You already graduated? It was so fast. Have you found a job?

: I didn't look for one. I want to go to graduate school.

: What subject would you like to major in?

: I would like to major in literature.

: How many years will your graduate study take?

: It takes two years to get an M.A. It usually takes five years to get a Ph.D.

A: Are you going to get an M.A. or Ph.D.?
B: I don't know yet. I would like to get an M.A. first and then decide i I should go for a Ph.D. How about you? Are you still in school?
A: No, I also graduated. I'm looking for a job.
B: What would you like to do?
A: I studied English and I would like to become an English teacher.
B: I heard that many schools are now looking for teachers. You can definitely find a teaching job.
A: I hope so.

*   *   *   *   *

A: Xiao Wang, I heard that it is difficult to get into a college, but it is easy to get out of it in China. Do you think so?
B: I do. There are many students who graduate from high schools ever year, but there are not enough colleges. So not every high school graduate can go to college.
A: So what does one need to do in order to get into college?
B: You need to pass very tough exams. If your grades are not good, yc can't get into a college or you can't get into a good college.
A: You don't have to pass an exam to get into a college in America, bu it is not easy to get into a good one either.

Reading Passage

Schools in China are divided into elementary schools, middle schools and universities. Children usually start elementary school at 6 or 7. Middle school is further divided into junior middle school and senior middle school. Elementary school is six years, junior middle school is three years, senior middle school is three years and college is four years Every child must attend elementary school and junior middle school, bu most people also attend senior middle school and college. After college, most people start working, but there are also people who continue their study by going to graduate school. In the past, students went to school six days a week, but now they go to school five days a week. There is n school on Saturday and Sunday. Elementary and middle school students

China live a very hard life because they have to do a lot of homework
d don't have much time to enjoy themselves.

6

HEALTH & FITNESS

Conversations

A：你 是 不 是 不 舒服？你的 脸色 不 太 好。
　　Nǐ shì bu shì bù shūfu? Nǐde liǎnsè bú tài hǎo.

B：我 是 有点儿 不 舒服。
　　Wǒ shì yǒudiǎnr bù shūfu.

A：你 有 什么 感觉？
　　Nǐ yǒu shénme gǎnjué?

B：我 头 疼。我 想 我 今天 不能 去 上班 了。
　　Wǒ tóu téng. Wǒ xiǎng wǒ jīntiān bù néng qù shàngbān le.

A：你 是 不 应该 去 上班。 你 应该 去 看 医生。
　　Nǐ shì bù yìnggāi qù shàngbān. Nǐ yìnggāi qù kàn yīshēng.

*　　　　*　　　　*　　　　*　　　　*

A：你 哪儿不 舒服？
Nǐ nǎr bù shūfu?

B：医生， 我 有点儿 头 疼。我 想 我 是 感冒 了。
Yīshēng, wǒ yǒudiǎnr tóu téng. Wǒ xiǎng wǒ shì gǎnmào le.

A：你 是什么 时候 开始 头 疼 的？
Nǐ shì shénme shíhou kāishǐ tóu téng de?

B：昨天 晚上。
Zuótiān wǎnshang.

A：发 不 发烧？
Fā bu fāshāo?

B：我 想 不 发烧，但是 我 咳嗽。
Wǒ xiǎng bù fāshāo, dànshì wǒ késòu.

A：我 给你 检查 一下儿吧。
Wǒ gěi nǐ jiǎnchá yíxiàr ba.

*   *   *   *   *

A：医生 怎么 说？
Yīshēng zěnme shuō?

B：他 说 我 有 炎症。
Tā shuō wǒ yǒu yánzhèng.

A：他 有 没有 说 怎么 治？
Tā yǒu méiyou shuō zěnme zhì?

B：他 给 我 作 了检查， 说 不 要紧。
Tā gěi wǒ zuò le jiǎnchá, shuō bú yàojǐn.

119

A： 他 有 没有 给 你 开 药?
Tā yǒu méiyou gěi nǐ kāi yào?

B： 开 了。医生 说 我 吃 一个星期 的 药 就 会 好 的。
Kāi le. Yīshēng shuō wǒ chī yí ge xīngqī de yào jiù huì hǎo de.
如果 药 吃 完 后 病 还 不好,他 要 我 去看 他。
Rúguǒ yào chī wán hòu bìng hái bù hǎo, tā yào wǒ qù kàn tā.

A： 这 种 药 怎么 吃?
Zhè zhǒng yào zěnme chī?

B： 一天 三 次, 一次两 片。
Yì tiān sān cì, yí cì liǎng piàn.

* * * * *

A： 你 昨天 怎么 没 来上课?
Nǐ zuótiān zěnme méi lái shàngkè?

B： 我 病 了。
Wǒ bìng le.

A： 你 怎么 了?
Nǐ zěnme le?

B： 我 有点儿 发烧。
Wǒ yǒudiǎnr fāshāo.

A： 你的病 现在 有 没有 好?
Nǐde bìng xiànzài yǒu méiyou hǎo?

B： 今天 比 昨天 好 多 了, 但是 还 没有 全 好。
Jīntiān bǐ zuótiān hǎo duō le, dànshì hái méiyou quán hǎo.

A：你 有 没有　去 看　医生？
Nǐ yǒu méiyou qù kàn yīshēng?

B：没有，　我　想　　是小　病，不 要紧。
Méiyou, wǒ xiǎng shì xiǎo bìng, bú yàojǐn.

A：你 要　注意 休息。
Nǐ yào zhùyì xiūxi.

B：我　会　的。
Wǒ huì de.

　　*　　　　*　　　　*　　　　*　　　　*

A：听说　　你 最近 身体 不 好，常常　　去 看 医生。　你
Tīngshuō nǐ zuìjìn shēntǐ bù hǎo, chángcháng qù kàn yīshēng. Nǐ
怎么　了？
zěnme le?

B：我　过敏。
Wǒ guòmǐn.

A：你 对 什么　　过敏？
Nǐ duì shénme guòmǐn?

B：我　不 知道，医生们　　也 不 知道，所以 谁　都 治 不 好
Wǒ bù zhīdào, yīshēngmen yě bù zhīdào, suǒyǐ shuí dōu zhì bù hǎo
我的　病。
wǒde bìng.

A：你 可以试试　中医。
Nǐ kěyǐ shìshi zhōngyī.

B: 你 觉得 中医　能　治 好 西医治不好　的病　吗?
Nǐ juéde zhōngyī néng zhì hǎo xīyī zhì bù hǎo de bìng ma?

A: 有　可能。
Yǒu kěnéng.

B: 这　是 好　主意。你 能　推荐　一个 好　中医　吗?
Zhè shì hǎo zhǔyì. Nǐ néng tuījiàn yí ge hǎo zhōngyī ma?

A: 我的 中医　林 医生　不 错。你可以去看　他。
Wǒde zhōngyī Lín Yīshēng bú cuò. Nǐ kěyǐ qù kàn tā.

Reading Passage

中国人很喜欢锻炼。他们一般起得很早，特别是老年人。很多人早上五点就起床了。大多数人喜欢在公园，或在街旁锻炼。很少有人去健身房锻炼。中国人的锻炼方式各种各样，有的慢跑，有的打太极拳，散步，还有的练气功。中国是自行车的王国，但是人们骑自行车不是为了锻炼，而是把自行车作为交通工具。你如果去中国，早上去公园或街上看别人锻炼、骑自行车上班是一件很有意思的事。

Zhōngguórén hěn xǐhuan duànliàn. Tāmen yìbān qǐ de hěn zǎo, tèbiéshì lǎoniánrén. Hěn duō rén zǎoshàng wǔ diǎn jiù qǐchuáng le. Dàduōshù rén xǐhuan zài gōngyuán, huò zài jiē shang duànliàn. Hěn shǎo yǒu rén qù jiànshēnfáng duànliàn. Zhōngguórén de duànliàn fāngshì gèzhònggèyàng, yǒude mànpǎo, yǒude dǎ tàijíquán, sànbù, hái yǒude liàn qìgōng. Zhōngguó shì zìxíngchē de wángguó, dànshì rénmen qí zìxíngchē bú shì wèile duànliàn, érshì bǎ zìxíngchē zuò wéi jiāotōng gōngjù. Nǐ rúguǒ qù Zhōngguó, zǎoshàng qù gōngyuán huò jiē shang kàn biérén duànliàn, qí zìxíngchē qù shàngbān shì yí jiàn hěn yǒuyìsi de shì.

New Words and Expressions

舒服	shūfu	feeling well; comfortable
脸色	liǎnsè	look (n); complexion
感觉	gǎnjué	feeling
头	tóu	head
疼	téng	hurt; pain (v)
感冒	gǎnmào	cold; have a cold
发烧	fāshāo	have a fever
咳嗽	késòu	cough (n & v)
检查	jiǎnchá	exam; inspect; examination; inspection
炎症	yánzhèng	infection
治	zhì	treat (a disease)
不要紧	bú yàojǐn	doesn't matter; not important
开药	kāi yào	prescribe medicine
好	hǎo	become well; recover (from a sickness)
完	wán	finish (v)
片	piàn	classifier
病	bìng	become sick; sickness
全	quán	completely; entirely
注意	zhùyì	pay attention; be mindful of
休息	xiūxi	rest; relax
身体	shēntǐ	health; body
过敏	guòmǐn	allergic

可能	kěnéng	maybe; possible
中医	zhōngyī	Chinese medicine; doctor of Chinese medicine
西医	xīyī	Western medicine; doctor of Western medicine
推荐	tuījiàn	recommend; recommendation
锻炼	duànliàn	physical exercise; workout
特别	tèbié	especially; particularly
老年人	lǎoniánrén	old people
慢跑	mànpǎo	jogging; jog
健身房	jiànshēnfáng	gym
方式	fāngshì	method; form; way
各种各样	gèzhǒnggèyàng	various; all kinds of
太极拳	tàijíquán	taiji (taichi)
散步	sànbù	take a walk
气功	qìgōng	a system of deep breathing exercises
王国	wángguó	kingdom
人们	rénmen	people
为了	wèile	for; for the sake of; in order to
把 ...... 作为	bǎ ... zuòwéi	treat ... as
交通工具	jiāotōng gōngjù	means of transportation
不是 ...... 而是	bú shì ... ér shì...	not ... but rather

Supplementary Words and Expressions

| 嗓子 | sǎngzi | throat; voice |

牙	yá	tooth
肚子	dùzi	stomach
背	bèi	back
腿	tuǐ	leg
针灸	zhēngjiǔ	acupuncture
病人	bìngrén	patient; sick person
护士	hùshì	nurse
药房	yàofáng	pharmacy
医疗保险	yīliáo bǎoxiǎn	medical insurance
游泳	yóuyǒng	swim; swimming
举重	jǔzhòng	lift weight; weight lifting
打球	dǎ qiú	play a ballgame
中年人	zhōngniánrén	middle-aged people
年轻人	niánqīngrén	young people

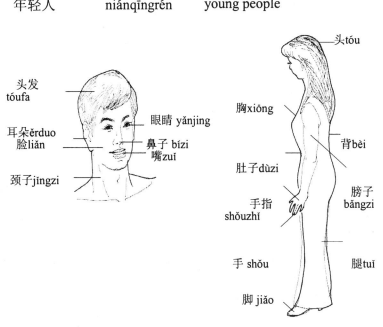

Language Points

我是有点儿不舒服 wǒ shì yǒudiǎnr bù shūfu

是 shì is used here to emphasize the following verb or the predicate adjective. It often suggests a strong assertion or strong denial:

你 是 不 应该　去 上班。
Nǐ shì bù yīnggāi qù shàngbān.
You definitely shouldn't go to work.

我　是 去 过　中国。
Wǒ shì qù guo Zhōngguó.
I definitely have been to China.

火车　是比 汽车 快。
Huǒchē shì bǐ qìchē kuài.
The train is indeed faster than the car.

他 是 不住 在　纽约。
Tā shì bú zhù zài Niǔyuē.
It is true that he does not live in New York.

This usage is similar to *do/does* or *did* in emphasizing verbs in English:

It *did* rain yesterday.
She *does* have a college degree.
We *do* accept credit card payment.

In a question, the use of 是 shì suggests that the speaker is positive about the answer and is seeking a confirmation:

你 是 不 是 不 舒服?
Nǐ shì bu shì bù shūfu?
You are not feeling well, are you?

我头疼 wǒ tóu téng

This is a typical example of the topic-comment construction in Chinese, which accounts for a large percentage of sentences in Chinese. In such a sentence, there is a binary division of two parts between *topic* and *comment*. The topic is what the speaker takes as his/her point of departure and the comment is a statement on that topic. The comment is often in the form of a sentence as in the sentence cited, where the topic is 我 wǒ (I), and 头疼 tóu téng (head hurts) is the comment. Other examples include:

象　　鼻子长。
Xiàng bízi cháng.
The elephant has a long trunk; literally *elephant trunk long*.

树　　叶子多。
Shù yèzi duō.
The tree has a lot of leaves; literally *tree leaves many*.

你哪儿不舒服 nǐ nǎr bù shūfu and 你怎么了 nǐ zěnme le

These are the two most common expressions used by doctors and other people in inquiring about someone who appears to be sick. 你哪儿不舒服 nǐ nǎr bù shūfu literally means *what part of your body troubles you* and 你怎么了 nǐ zěnme le means *what's wrong*.

舒服 shūfu in the sense of *feeling well* is only used in the negative sentence. In an affirmative sentence, 舒服 shūfu means *comfortable*.

医生说我吃一个星期的药就会好的 yīshēng shuō wǒ chī yí ge xīngqī de yào jiù huì hǎo de

就 jiù is a frequently used word in Chinese with multiple meanings. The following is the summary of the various meanings of the word that we have come across so far:

127

1. adverb used for emphasis:

银行　　就在那儿。
Yínháng jiù zài nàr.
The bank is right there.

2. adverb with the meaning of *earlier than expected* or *better than expected*.

他只上　了三年　的大学就毕业了。
Tā zhǐ shàng le sān nián de dàxué jiù bìyè le.
He graduated from college after only three years.

3. *then*, often used in conjunction with 如果 rúguǒ (if):

如果　天　不好，我　就不去野餐。
Rúguǒ tiān bù hǎo, wǒ jiù bú qù yěcān.
If the weather is not good, then I won't go to the picnic.

4. adverb indicating that an action closely follows another:

他们　下了班　就去飞机场。
Tāmen xià le bān jiù qù fēijīchǎng.
They will go to the airport as soon as they get off work.

5. *just about*, often used with 要 yào and/or 了 le:

天　就要下雨了。
Tiān jiù yào xiàyǔ le.
It is about to rain.

饭十分钟　　就好了。
Fàn shí fēnzhōng jiù hǎo le.
The meal will be ready in ten minutes.

药吃完后 yào chī wán hòu and 治好病 zhì hǎo bìng

Both 完 wán (finish) and 好 hǎo (get well; become ready) are verbs used after another verb as a complement indicating the result of an action expressed by the preceding verb. While 完 wán indicates the completion of an action, 好 hǎo suggests a satisfactory condition or readiness resulting from the action of the preceding verb. Similar examples include:

吃 完 饭
chī wán fàn
finish eating the meal

看 完 书
kàn wán shū
finish reading the book

修 好 车
xiū hǎo chē
fix the car

作 好 饭
zuò hǎo fàn
get the meal ready

Unlike past-tense verbs in English that usually indicate a result such as *the meal was cooked* and *the watch was repaired*, verbs in Chinese do not automatically indicate a result, even with a past reference. To indicate a result, a complement is needed. Compare:

车修了 chē xiū le (it only says that repair work was performed on the car, but it does not suggest that the car is now in working order), and

车修好了 chē xiū hǎo le (it says that the car has been fixed and is in working order).

饭作了 fàn zuò le (it only says that the process of cooking has started, but it does not say if the meal is ready), and

饭作好了 fàn zuò hǎo le (it says that the meal is ready).

To suggest a negative result that has already been produced, 没有 méiyou is used before the verb:

我 没有 看 完 这 本 书。
Wǒ méiyou kàn wán zhè běn shū.
I didn't finish reading the book.

你的 车 没有 修 好。
Nǐde chē méiyou xiū hǎo.
Your car has not been fixed.

To suggest a potential negative result, 不 bù is used. It is placed after the verb and before the complement:

我 今天 看 不 完 这 本 书。
Wǒ jīntiān kàn bù wán zhè běn shū.
I can't finish reading the book today.

他 修 不 好 我的 车。
Tā xiū bù hǎo wǒde chē.
He can't fix my car.

怎么 zěnme and 为什么 wèishénme

Both of them can be used to mean *why*. Whereas 怎么 zěnme usually suggests surprise or implies criticism, 为什么 wèishénme is quite neutral. Compare:

你 为什么 来 晚 了?
Nǐ wèishénme lái wǎn le?

Why are you late—an innocent question inquiring about the reason.

你 怎么 来 晚 了？
Nǐ zěnme lái wǎn le?
How come you are late—implying you shouldn't have been late.

中医能治好西医治不好的病吗 zhōngyī néng zhì hǎo xīyī zhì bù hǎo de bìng ma?

西医治不好 xīyī zhì bù hǎo is a sentence functioning as the attribute of the noun 病 bìng. Since it is a modifier, it is placed before the modified word 病 bìng. 的 de is used between them to mark the relationship. Other examples are:

这 是 我 昨天 买 的书。
Zhè shì wǒ zuótiān mǎi de shū.
This is the book I bought yesterday.

我们 住 的 地方 很 小。
Wǒmen zhù de dìfang hěn xiǎo.
The place where we live is very small.

不是 bú shì ... 而是 ér shì

They are always used in conjunction with each other to mean *not ... but rather*:

他 去 中国 不 是 工作， 而是 玩儿。
Tā qù Zhōngguó bú shì gōngzuò, ér shì wánr.
He is going to China not to work, but for pleasure.

我 不 是 美国人， 而是 英国人。
Wǒ bú shì Měiguórén, ér shì Yīngguórén.
I'm not American, rather I'm English.

Exercises

I. Answer the following questions:

1. 你 最近 身体 好 吗？有 没有 看 过 医生？
   Nǐ zuìjìn shēntǐ hǎo ma? Yǒu méiyǒu kàn guo yīshēng?

2. 你 学 中文 是 为了 去 中国 吗？
   Nǐ xué Zhōngwén shì wèile qù Zhōngguó ma?

3. 你 有 没有 看 过 中医？你 觉得 中医 怎么样？
   Nǐ yǒu méiyou kàn guo zhōngyī? Nǐ juéde zhōngyī zěnmeyàng?

4. 你 每 天 锻炼 吗？你 怎么 锻炼？
   Nǐ měi tiān duànliàn ma? Nǐ zěnme duànliàn?

5. 你 有 自行车 吗？你 把自行车 作为 锻炼 的 工具
   Nǐ yǒu zìxíngchē ma? Nǐ bǎ zìxíngchē zuòwéi duànliàn de gōngjù
   还是 交通 工具？
   háishi jiāotōng gōngjù?

6. 你 一般 在 哪儿锻炼？
   Nǐ yìbān zài nǎr duànliàn?

7. 你 过敏 吗？你 对 什么 过敏？
   Nǐ guòmǐn ma? Nǐ duì shénme guòmǐn?

8. 医生 见 到 病人 时，会 怎么 说？
   Yīshēng jiàn dào bìngrén shí, huì zěnme shuō?

9. 一个 人 如果 感冒，会 有 什么 感觉？
   Yí ge rén rúguǒ gǎnmào, huì yǒu shénme gǎnjué?

10. 在 中国，　　病人　在 医院　的 药房　拿 药。在 美国，
Zài Zhōngguó, bìngrén zài yīyuàn de yàofáng ná yào. Zài Měiguó,
病人　在 哪儿 拿 药？
bìngrén zài nǎr　ná yào?

II. How do you say the following in Chinese?

1. the doctor who works in Shanghai
2. the place where we exercise
3. the time when they begin their class
4. the teacher who teaches us English
5. things that need to be done today
6. open the door
7. turn on the TV
8. drive
9. prescribe medicine
10. attend a meeting

III. Fill in the blanks with the complements 好 hǎo or 完 wán:

1. 我 这 个 周末　很 忙，看 不 _____ 这 本 书。
Wǒ zhè ge zhōumò hěn máng, kàn bù _____ zhè běn shū.

2. 他 用 _____ 了 钱。
Tā yòng _____ le qián.

3. 西医 没有　治 _____ 我的 病，中医　治 _____ 了
Xīyī méiyou zhì _____ wǒde bìng, zhōngyī zhì _____ le
我的 病。
wǒde bìng.

4. 今天　老师　让 学生们　　写 一百 个 字，但是 他们　写
Jīntiān lǎoshī ràng xuéshengmen xiě yìbǎi ge zì,　dànshì tāmen xiě

不 _____ 。

bù _____.

5. 爸爸 没有　听 _____ 孩子 的 话　就 说　他 不 能　出 去

Bàba méiyou tīng _____ háizi de huà jiù shuō tā bù néng chū qù

玩。

wán.

IV. Rewrite the following sentences, using 是 shì to emphasize the verb and then turn them into questions:

1. 我　家 我 爸爸 做　饭。

Wǒ jiā wǒ bàba zuò fàn.

2. 他 在 北京　大学　学习。

Tā zài Běijīng Dàxué xuéxí.

3. 我　太太 不 喜欢　看　电影。

Wǒ tàitai bù xǐhuan kàn diànyǐng.

4. 大多数　中国人　　起 得 很 早。

Dàduōshù Zhōngguórén qǐ de hěn zǎo.

5. 打 太极拳　对 身体　有　帮助。

Dǎ tàijíquán duì shēntǐ yǒu bāngzhù.

V. Express the following using supplementary words:

1. I had a stomachache yesterday.
2. My husband has a toothache.
3. He has a sore throat.
4. That gentleman has a backache.
5. The patient has a pain in her leg.

VI. Decide which of the following are topic-comment sentences:

1. 那 个 老 人 身体 不 好。
   Nà ge lǎo rén shēntǐ bù hǎo.

2. 桂林 的 风景 很 美。
   Guìlín de fēngjǐng hěn měi.

3. 他的 美国 朋友 名字 叫 麦克。
   Tāde Měiguó péngyou míngzi jiào Màikè.

4. 我 觉得 英国 的 英语 比 美国 的 英语 好听。
   Wǒ juéde Yīngguó de Yīngyǔ bǐ Měiguó de Yīngyǔ hǎotīng.

5. 我们的 老师 工作 很 忙。
   Wǒmende lǎoshī gōngzuò hěn máng.

6. 公司 的经理 在 打 电话。
   Gōngsī de jīnglǐ zài dǎ diànhuà.

7. 我 头 不 疼，但是 肚子疼。
   Wǒ tóu bù téng, dànshì dùzi téng.

8. 美国 的 北边 是 加拿大。
   Měiguó de běibian shì Jiā'nádà.

9. 男 学生 数学 好，女 学生 语文 好。
   Nán xuésheng shùxué hǎo, nǚ xuésheng yǔwén hǎo.

10. 你 一定 能 找 到 老师 的 工作。
    Nǐ yídìng néng zhǎo dào lǎoshī de gōngzuò.

VII. Explain what 就 jiù in each of the following sentences means:

1. 如果 找 不 到 工作， 我 就 去 读 研究生。
   Rúguǒ zhǎo bú dào gōngzuò, wǒ jiù qù dú yánjiūshēng.

2. 前面 就 是 火车站。
   Qiánmiàn jiù shì huǒchēzhàn.

3. 他们 就 要 结婚 了。
   Tāmen jiù yào jiéhūn le.

4. 老师 打 完 电话 就 去 教室 了。
   Lǎoshī dǎ wán diànhuà jiù qù jiàoshì le.

5. 她 用 了半 个 小时 就 把 作业 作 完 了。
   Tā yòng le bàn ge xiǎoshí jiù bǎ zuòyè zuò wán le.

VIII. Translate the following into Chinese:

1. Is it true that China is in East Asia?
2. I do live in New York.
3. Please put the newspaper on the table.
4. It is Sunday today. How come you are still at work?
5. When did you begin to have a fever?
6. Many people believe in (信 xìn) Chinese medicine because they think Chinese medicine can cure some diseases that Western medicine can't.
7. The doctor said that you have to be on medication for a month.
8. It doesn't matter if you don't speak Chinese.
9. The teacher asked the students to pay attention to pronunciation.
10. I've seen many doctors, but none could cure my disease.

IX. Translate the following into English:

1. 中国　　　没　有　私人 (private) 医生。人们　　有　病　的
Zhōngguó méi yǒu sīrén　　　yīshēng. Rénmen yǒu bìng de
时候　要 去 医院　看　医生。
shíhou yào qù yīyuàn kàn yīshēng.

2. 医生　　没有　　给我 检查　　就 说　我 没　有　病。
Yīshēng méiyou gěi wǒ jiǎnchá jiù shuō wǒ méi yǒu bìng.

3. 我　妈妈　很 会 作　菜，特别 是 中国　　菜。
Wǒ māma hěn huì zuò cài, tèbié shì Zhōngguó cài.

4. 他 今天　来 上班　　了，但是　病　还 没有　全　好。
Tā jīntiān lái shàngbān le, dànshì bìng hái méiyou quán hǎo.

5. 你的 脸色 不 是 不 好，是 很　不好。
Nǐde liǎnsè bú shì bù hǎo, shì hěn bù hǎo.

6. 很　多 人 在 西医 治 不 好 他们的 病　的 时候，才 去 看
Hěn duō rén zài xīyī zhì bù hǎo tāmende bìng de shíhou, cái qù kàn
中医。
zhōngyī.

7. 发烧　是 很 多 病　的 症状 (symptom)。
Fāshāo shì hěn duō bìng de zhèngzhuàng.

8. 打 太极拳　的 人 大多数　是 中年人　　和 老年人。
Dǎ tàijíquán de rén dàduōshù shì zhōngniánrén hé lǎoniánrén.

9. 每　天 慢跑　是 很　好 的 锻炼　方式。
Měi tiān mànpǎo shì hěn hǎo de duànliàn fāngshì.

10. 我 学 中文　　不 是 为了 和 中国人　　说话，　而是
Wǒ xué Zhōngwén bú shì wèile hé Zhōngguórén shuōhuà, ér shì

为了 看 书。
wèile kàn shū.

X. Topics for discussion/writing:

1. 你 一般 是 怎么 锻炼　 的?
Nǐ yìbān shì zěnme duànliàn de?

2. 你 觉得 美国　 的 医疗 制度 好 不 好? 什么　 地方 好?
Nǐ juéde Měiguó de yīliáo zhìdù hǎo bu hǎo? Shénme dìfang hǎo

什么　 地方 不 好?
Shénme dìfang bù hǎo?

English Translation of the Text

Conversations

A: Are you feeling sick? You don't look well.
B: It's true that I'm not feeling well.
A: What bothers you?
B: I have a headache. I don't think I can go to work today.
A: You shouldn't go to work. You should go to see a doctor.

       *   *   *   *   *

A: What bothers you?
B: Doctor, I have a headache. I think that I have a cold.
A: When did you develop this headache?
B: Last night.
A: Do you have a fever?
B: I don't think so, but I cough.

A: Let me examine you.

      *   *   *   *   *

A: What did the doctor say?
B: He said that I have an infection.
A: Did he say how he is going to treat it?
B: He examined me and said that it was nothing major.
A: Did he prescribe any medicine for you?
B: Yes, he did. The doctor said that I would get well after taking the medicine for a week. He asked me to see him if I don't get well after finishing the medicine.
A: How should you take this medicine?
B: Three times a day and two tablets each time.

      *   *   *   *   *

A: Why didn't you come to class yesterday?
B: I was sick.
A: What was wrong?
B: I had a little fever.
A: Are you well now?
B: It's much better today than yesterday, but I've not completely recovered.
A: Did you go to see a doctor?
B: No. I think it is a minor thing, not a big deal.
A: You should take it easy.
B: I will.

      *   *   *   *   *

A: I heard that you have not been in good health recently. What's wrong?
B: I have an allergy.
A: What are you allergic to?
B: I don't know and the doctors don't know either. That's why no one can cure me.

A: You may want to try Chinese medicine.
B: Do you think Chinese medicine can cure what Western medicine can't?
A: It's possible.
B: This is a good idea. Can you recommend a good doctor of Chinese medicine?
A: My Chinese doctor Dr. Lin is very good. You may go to see him.

Reading Passage

Chinese people like to exercise very much. They usually get up very early, especially the old people. Many people get up as early as five o'clock in the morning. Most people like to exercise in parks or by the street side. Few people exercise at the gym. There are various types of exercises that Chinese people do. Some go jogging, others do *taiji* or take a walk and still others practice *qigong*. China is the kingdom of bicycles, but people ride bicycles not as exercise, but rather as a means of transportation. If you go to China, it would be an interesting thing to go to the parks or the streets in the morning to see people exercise and ride the bicycle to go to work.

7

HOLIDAYS & FESTIVALS

Conversations

A: 你能 不 能 给 我 介绍 一下儿中国 的节日?
Nǐ néng bu néng gěi wǒ jièshào yíxiàr Zhōngguó de jiérì?

B: 当然 能。 可是 中国 的节日很 多，我们 只 能 说
Dāngrán néng. Kěshì Zhōngguó de jiérì hěn duō, wǒmen zhǐ néng shuō
重要 的。
zhòngyào de.

A: 好。我 想 先 问问 中国人 过 不 过 元旦。
Hǎo. Wǒ xiǎng xiān wènwen Zhōngguórén guò bu guò yuándàn.

B: 过。但是 对 中国人 来 说，元旦 不是 最 重要
Guò. Dànshì duì Zhōngguórén lái shuō, yuándàn bú shì zuì zhòngyào
的节日。最 重要 的节日是 中国 新 年。
de jiérì. Zuì zhòngyào de jiérì shì Zhōngguó Xīn Nián.

A: 中国 新 年 是 几月 几号?
Zhōngguó Xīn Nián shì jǐ yuè jǐ hào?

B：每 年 不一样。有时 在 一月，有时 在 二月。
Měi nián bù yíyàng. Yǒushí zài yíyuè, yǒushí zài èryuè.

A：你 能 告诉 我 春节 是 什么 节日吗？
Nǐ néng gàosù wǒ Chūnjié shì shénme jiérì ma?

B：春节 就 是中国 新 年。有 人 说 春节， 有 人 说
Chūnjié jiù shì Zhōngguó Xīn Nián. Yǒu rén shuō Chūnjié, yǒu rén shī
新 年， 都 一样。
Xīn Nián, dōu yíyàng.

A：除了 春节， 还 有 什么 重要 的节日？
Chúle Chūn jié, hái yǒu shénme zhòngyào de jiérì?

B：五月 一号 是 劳动节。 全 国 放 一 星期 的 假。
Wǔyuè yī hào shì Láodòngjié. Quán guó fàng yì xīngqī de jià.

A：中国 有 没 有 国庆节？
Zhōngguó yǒu méi yǒu Guóqìngjié?

B：有。 中国 的国庆节 是 十月 一号。全 国 也放 一
Yǒu. Zhōngguó de Guóqìngjié shì shíyuè yī hào. Quán guó yě fàng yì
星期 的 假。
xīngqī de jià.

A：中国 有 没 有 圣诞节？
Zhōngguó yǒu méi yǒu shèngdànjié?

B：没 有。虽然 圣诞节 不 是 中国人 的节日，但是
Méi yǒu. Suīrán Shèngdànjié bú shì Zhōngguórén de jiérì, dànshì
现在 有的 人 也 过 这 个 节日。
xiànzài yǒude rén yě guò zhè ge jiérì.

我　听说　　有　一个 中秋节。　　 这　是 什么　　 节？
Wǒ tīngshuō yǒu yí ge Zhōngqiūjié. Zhè shì shénme jié?

"中"　　 的　意思 是 *middle*，"秋"　的 意思 是 *autumn*。"中秋节"
"Zhōng" de yìsi shì *middle*，"qiū" de yìsi shì *autumn*。"Zhōngqiūjié"
的意思就 是 *Mid-Autumn Festival*。这　一　天　月亮　　 最　圆。
de yìsi jiù shì *Mid-Autumn Festival*. Zhè yì tiān yuèliàng zuì yuán.
人们　　 吃 月饼，　 全　 家 团聚。
Rénmen chī yuèbǐng, quán jiā tuánjù.

中秋节　　 是 什么　　 时候？
Zhōngqiūjié shì shénme shíhou?

中秋节　　 和 新　年　一样，　每　年　不同，　　但是 一般 在
Zōngqiūjié hé Xín Nián yíyàng, měi nián bùtōng, dànshì yìbān zài
十月。
shíyuè.

*　　　　*　　　　*　　　　*　　　　*

你 知道 明年　　 的中国　　 新　年　是 哪 一 天 吗？
Nǐ zhīdào míngnián de Zhōngguó Xīn Nián shì nǎ yì tiān ma?

明年　　 的 中国　　 新　年　 是 二月 十 号。
Míngnián de Zhōngguó Xīn Nián shì èryuè shí hào.

中国人　　 一般 怎么 过 年？
Zhōngguórén yìbān zěnme guò nián?

新　年　前，中国人　　　 一般 都 要 打扫 房子, 布置 房子。
Xīn Nián qián, Zhōngguórén yìbān dōu yào dǎsǎo fángzi, bùzhì fángzi.
除夕 的 晚上，　 全　 家人 团聚，做 很　多　菜，吃 很　多
Chúxī de wǎnshang, quán jiā rén tuánjù, zuò hěn duō cài, chī hěn duō

菜。新 年 的那 天, 人们 互相 拜 年, 大人还要 给
cài. Xīn Nián de nà tiān, rénmen hùxiāng bài nián, dàrén hái yào gěi
小孩子 红包。
xiǎoháizi hóngbāo.

A: 什么 是 红包?
Shénme shì hóngbāo?

B: 红包 里装 着 钱, 是 给 小孩子 的 礼物。
Hóngbāo lǐ zhuāng zhe qián, shì gěi xiǎoháizi de lǐwù.

A: 新 年 的 时候 大家 交换 礼物吗?
Xīn Nián de shíhou dàjiā jiāohuàn lǐwù ma?

B: 中国人 没 有 这 个 习惯。
Zhōngguórén méi yǒu zhè ge xíguàn.

A: 中国人 过 年 一般 吃 些 什么?
Zhōngguórén guò Nián yìbān chī xiē shénme?

B: 各种各样 的 东西, 但 大多数 人 都 要 吃 饺子。
Gèzhǒnggèyàng de dōngxī, dàn dàduōshù rén dōu yào chī jiǎozi.

* * * * *

A: 中国 新 年 时, 我 常 听 人 说 "恭喜 发财"。这
Zhōngguó Xīn Nián shí, wǒ cháng tīng rén shuō "gōngxǐ fācái." Zhè
是 什么 意思?
shì shénme yìsī?

B: "恭喜" 的 意思是 "祝贺", "发财" 的 意思是 "好运"。 "恭喜
"Gōngxǐ" de yìsi shì "zhùhè," "fācái" de yìsi shì "hǎoyùn." "Gōngxǐ
发财" 的意思就 是 "祝 你 好 运"。
fācái" de yìsi jiù shì "zhù nǐ hǎoyùn."

: 新 年 时，我 要 对 你 说 "恭喜 发财"。
Xīn Nián shí, wǒ yào duì nǐ shuō "gōngxǐ fācái."

: 谢谢，但是 现在 大多数 人 都 说 "新 年 好"。
Xièxie, dànshì xiànzài dàduōshù rén dōu shuō "Xīn Nián hǎo."

: 那 我 也 要 说 "新 年 好"。
Nà wǒ yě yào shuō "Xīn Nián hǎo."

: 你 学 得 真 快!
Nǐ xué de zhēn kuài!

*   *   *   *   *

: 明年 是 什么 年?
Míngnián shì shénme nián?

: 明年 是 鸡年。明年 生 的 孩子 都 属 鸡。
Míngnián shì jī nián. Míngnián shēng de háizi dōu shǔ jī.

: 我 不 知道 我 属 什么。 你 能 告诉 我 吗?
Wǒ bù zhīdào wǒ shǔ shénme. Nǐ néng gàosù wǒ ma?

: 可以。你 今年 多 大?
Kěyǐ. Nǐ jīnnián duō dà?

: 我 今年 二十三 岁，我 是 一九七九 年 生 的。
Wǒ jīnnián èrshí sān suì, wǒ shì yī jiǔ qī jiǔ nián shēng de.

: 你 比 我 小 两 岁。你 是 羊 年 生 的，你 属 羊。
Nǐ bǐ wǒ xiǎo liǎng suì. Nǐ shì yáng nián shēng de, nǐ shǔ yáng.

: 我 知道 了，如果 你 知道 一个 人 属 什么，你 就 能 猜
Wǒ zhīdào le, rúguǒ nǐ zhīdào yí ge rén shǔ shénme, nǐ jiù néng cāi

145

到 他 有 多 大。
dào tā yǒu duō dà.

B: 你 说 得 不 错。一般 是 这样。
Nǐ shuō de bú cuò. Yìbān shì zhèyàng.

Reading Passage

对很多美国人来说，圣诞节是一年中最重要的节日。孩子们特别喜欢
这个节日，因为他们能得到很多礼物。圣诞节有点儿象中国的新年。
节前人们要打扫房子，布置房子。很多人在家里放圣诞树，树上摆着
各种各样的装饰品。圣诞节的除夕，全家人要团聚，做很多的菜，吃
很多的菜。美国人过圣诞节和中国人过春节有一个很大的不同，这就
是美国人要交换礼物，他们在圣诞节前要花很多时间去商店选礼物、
买礼物。

Duì hěn duō Měiguórén lái shuō, Shèngdànjié shì yì nián zhōng zuì
zhòngyào de jiérì. Háizimen tèbié xǐhuan zhè ge jiérì, yīnwéi tāmen néng
dédào hěn duō lǐwù. Shèngdànjié yǒudiǎnr xiàng Zhōngguó de Xīn Nián.
Jié qián rénmen yào dǎsǎo fángzi, bùzhì fángzi. Hěn duō rén zài jiā lǐ fàng
Shèngdànshù, shù shang bǎi zhe gèzhònggèyàng de zhuāngshìpǐn.
Shèngdànjié de chúxī, quán jiā rén yào tuánjù, zuò hěn duō de cài, chī hěn
duō de cài. Měiguórén guò Shèngdànjié hé Zhōngguórén guò Chūnjié yǒu
yí ge hěn dà de bù tóng, zhè jiù shì Měiguórén yào jiāohuàn lǐwù, tāmen zài
Shèngdànjié qián yào huā hěn duō shíjiān qù shāngdiàn xuǎn lǐwù, mǎi
lǐwù.

New Words and Expressions

| 介绍 | jièshào | say sth. about; introduce; introduction |

节日	jiérì	holiday; festival
元旦	Yuándàn	(Western) New Year
对 ...... 来说	duì ... lái shuō	as far as ... is concerned; for
一样	yíyàng	same; similar
春节	Chūnjié	Spring Festival; Chinese New Year
放假	fàngjià	have a vacation; have a day off
劳动节	Láodòngjié	Labor Day
国庆节	Guóqìngjié	National Day; Independence Day
中秋节	Zhōngqiūjié	Mid-Autumn Festival
月亮	yuèliang	moon
圆	yuán	round
月饼	yuèbǐng	moon cake
不同	bùtóng	difference; different
打扫	dǎsǎo	clean; sweep
房子	fángzi	house
除夕	chúxī	eve
团聚	tuánjù	get together
大人	dàrén	adult; grownup
包	bāo	bag
装	zhuāng	hold; load; install
着	zhe	*aspect marker*
大家	dàjiā	everyone; people
拜年	bài nián	wish happy new year
交换	jiāohuàn	exchange (v & n)
礼物	lǐwù	gift; present
习惯	xíguàn	habit; custom

147

猜	cāi	guess
恭喜发财	gōngxǐ fācái	Happy New Year
好运	hǎo yùn	good luck
属	shǔ	born in the Chinese zodiac year of
生	shēng	give birth to; be born; produce
岁	suì	(of age) year
因为	yīnwéi	because
得到	dédào	receive; obtain; acquire
象	xiàng	resemble; similar to
树	shù	tree
摆	bǎi	place (v); put; arrange
装饰品	zhuāngshìpǐn	decorative objects; decorations
花	huā	spend (time or money)

Supplementary Words and Expressions

日历	rìlì	calendar
阴历	yīnlì	lunar calendar
庆祝	qìngzhù	celebrate; celebration
情人节	Qíngrénjié	Valentine's Day
母亲节	Mǔqinjié	Mother's Day
父亲节	Fùqinjie	Father's Day
万圣节	Wànshèngjié	Halloween
感恩节	Gǎn'ēnjié	Thanksgiving Day
灯笼	dēnglong	lantern

闹	rènào	buzzing with excitement
会	wǎnhuì	evening party
会	wǔhuì	dance (n); ball
舞	tiàowǔ	dance (v)
鼠	lǎoshǔ	mouse; rat
	hǔ	tiger
	tù	rabbit
	shé	snake
	yáng	sheep
	hóu	monkey
	gǒu	dog

Language Points

日 jiérì and 假 jià

日 jiérì is equivalent to *holiday* or *festival* in English. It is often shortened to 节 jié, particularly when used with a descriptive word such as 节 Chūnjié (Chinese New Year) and 中秋节 Zhōngqiūjié (Mid-Autumn Festival). All the holidays and festivals in China and the translations of most foreign holidays and festivals end in 节 jié.

假 jià, on the other hand, refers to *vacation, days off* or *leave* such as 暑假 jià (summer vacation), 寒假 hánjià (winter vacation), 事假 shìjià (personal day), 病假 bìngjià (sick leave). The verb usually used in collocation with 假 jià in the sense of *have a vacation* is 放 fàng, which literally means *set free* or *release*:

149

你们　劳动节　放　不　放　假？
Nǐmen Láodòngjiè fàng bu fàng jià?
Are you getting days off for Labor Day?

我们　　国庆节　放　两　天　假。
Wǒmen Guóqìngjié fàng liǎng tiān jià.
We are getting two days off for National Day.

我们只能说重要的 wǒmen zhǐ néng shuō zhòngyào de

The noun that follows 的 de is often left out when its antecedent (节日 jì in this case) has appeared in the prior context or is understood. Other examples include:

A：你要　坐八点　的火车　还是　九点　的火车？
　　Nǐ yào zuò bā diǎn de huǒchē háishi jiǔ diǎn de huǒchē?

B：我　要　坐　九点　的。
　　Wǒ yào zuò jiǔ diǎn de.

A：那　是　谁的　书？
　　Nà shì shuíde shū?

B：那　是　我　朋友　　的。
　　Nà shì wǒ péngyou de.

我想先问问中国人过不过元旦 wǒ xiǎng xiān wènwen Zhōngguórén guò bu guò yuándàn

如果 rúguǒ is equivalent to *if* when used to indicate a condition, but 如果 rúguǒ can't be used where *if* indicates a form of yes/no question as in the sentence cited. The whole sentence means *I'd like to ask if the Chinese celebrate the (Western) New Year).* Similar examples include:

想 知道 你 明天 来不来。

ǒ xiǎng zhīdào nǐ míngtiān lái bu lái.

d like to know if you are coming tomorrow.

生们 问 老师 这 个 星期 有 没 有 考试。

uéshengmen wèn lǎoshī zhè ge xīngqī yǒu méi yǒu kǎoshì.

:udents ask the teacher if there is an exam this week.

both of the above sentences, 如果 rúguǒ can't be used. The question is
dicated by the yes/no question format: 来不来 lái bu lái and 有没有 yǒu
éi yǒu.

然圣诞节不是中国人的节日，但是现在有的人也过这个节日

uīrán Shèngdàn jié yě bú shì Zhōngguórén de jiérì, dànshì xiànzài yǒude
n yě guò zhè ge jiérì

is ungrammatical in English to use *although* in one clause (subordinate
ause) when *but* appears in the other clause (main clause), but it is
:rfectly grammatical to use 虽然 suīrán in conjunction with 但是 dànshì
Chinese. In fact, they are usually used in the same sentence such as:

然 大家都 很 累，但是 没 有 人 想 休息。

uīrán dàjiā dōu hěn lèi, dànshì méi yǒu rén xiǎng xiūxi.

lthough everyone was tired, no one wanted to rest.

然 情人节 不 是 中国 的 节日，但是 越来越 多 的

uīrán Qíngrénjié bú shì Zhōngguó de jiérì, dànshì yuèláiyuè duō de

:轻人 现在 过 这 个 节日。

ánqīngrén xiànzài guò zhè ge jiérì.

lthough Valentine's Day is not a Chinese festival, more and more young
:ople are now celebrating it.

'hen the 虽然 suīrán clause and the 但是 dànshì clause share the same
1bject, the subject in the 但是 dànshì clause is usually left out:

151

他们　虽然　离了婚，但是　还　是　好　朋友。
Tāmen suīrán lí le hūn, dànshì hái shì hǎo péngyou.
Although they are divorced, they remain good friends.

她虽然　只　学　了半　年　的中文，　　但是　已经　说　　得很　流利
Tā suīrán zhǐ xué le bàn nián de Zhōngwén, dànshì yǐjīng shuō de hěn liúlì
了。
le.
Although she has only studied Chinese for half a year, she already speaks
fairly fluently.

家 jiā and 房子 fángzi

家 jiā usually refers to *home* or *family*, whereas 房子 fángzi refers to the
physical structure—*house*. *Home-buying*, as often heard in English, does
not make sense to the Chinese. To them, one can only buy a 房子 fángzi,
but not 家 jiā.

祝你好运 zhù nǐ hǎo yùn

To wish someone something, Chinese usually uses the following pattern:

祝　你
Zhù nǐ _____!

For example:

祝　你 成功/　　　身体　健康！
Zhù nǐ chénggōng/shēntǐ jiànkāng!
Wish you success/good health!

红包里装着钱 hóngbāo lǐ zhuāng zhe qián

着 zhe in the sentence indicates the continuous state of an action:

152

门　开 着。

Mén kāi zhe.

The door is open.

杯子 在 桌子　上　　放　着。

Bēizi zài zhuōzi shang fàng zhe.

The cups are lying on the table.

树　上　 摆　着 各种各样　　　 的装饰品。

shù shang bǎi zhe gèzhǒnggèyàng de zhuāngshìpǐn.

On the tree decorations are displayed.

Contrast these with

门　开 了。

Mén kāi le.

The door was opened.

他 把 杯子 放　在 桌子　　上。

Tā bǎ bēizi fàng zài zhuōzi shang.

He put the cups on the table.

我太太　 把 装饰品　　　 摆 在 树　上。

Wǒ tàitai bǎ zhuāngshìpǐn bǎi zài shù shang.

My wife put decorations on the tree.

In these three sentences, the verbs indicate pure actions.

The negative form of a verb followed by 着 zhe is 没有 méiyǒu + verb:

门　没有　 开 着。

Mén méiyou kāi zhe.

The door is not open.

杯子 没有　在 桌子 上　　放 着。
Bēizi méiyou zài zhuōzi shang fàng zhe.
The cup is not lying on the table.

树　上　没有　摆 着 装饰品。
Shù shang méiyou bǎi zhe zhuāngshìpǐn.
On the tree decorations are not displayed.

Chinese zodiac signs

Each Chinese lunar year is associated with a zodiac animal. People who are born in the same year share the same animal sign. There are altogether twelve animals that form a cycle. See the graph on the following page for the twelve animals and the lunar years that are associated with them.

Another easy way to find your zodiac sign is to enter your date of birth at this website and it will tell you what your sign is:

http://astrology.yahoo.com/us/astrology/divination/chinese/index.html

Like the Western zodiac signs, Chinese zodiac animals are associated with certain attributes. For example, people who are born in the year of the horse are said to be youthful, intellectual and charming, but also impatient and reckless at times. The above website also lists the attributes for all the animal signs.

你今年多大 nǐ jīnnián duō dà?

There are a number of ways in Chinese to ask someone's age depending on who you ask. The most common and useful question form is 你多大 nǐ duō dà (how old are you) or 你今年多大 nǐ jīnnián duō dà (how old are you this year), which can be used for almost anyone. There are two other forms used when we ask the age of children and old people. For children, the question form is 你几岁 nǐ jǐ suì, and that for old people is 你多大年纪 nǐ

uō dà niánjì. Since 你多大年纪 nǐ duō dà niánjì suggests an advanced age,
is not appropriate to use for people of other age groups.

Snake	Horse	Goat	Monkey
2001 1989	2002 1990	2003 1991	2004 1992
1977 1965	1978 1966	1979 1967	1980 1968
1953 1941	1954 1942	1955 1943	1956 1944
1929 1917	1930 1918	1931 1919	1932 1920
Rooster	Dog	Pig	Rat
2005 1993	2006 1994	2007 1995	2008 1996
1981 1969	1982 1970	1983 1971	1984 1072
1957 1945	1958 1946	1959 1947	1960 1948
1933 1921	1934 1922	1935 1923	1936 1924
Ox	Tiger	Rabbit	Dragon
2009 1997	2010 1998	2011 1999	2000 1988
1985 1973	1986 1974	1987 1975	1976 1964
1961 1949	1962 1950	1963 1951	1952 1940
1937 1925	1938 1926	1939 1927	1928 1916

圣诞节有点儿象中国的新年 Shèngdànjié yǒudiǎnr xiàng hōngguó de Xīn Nián

Beginner's Chinese, we learned the word 好象 hǎoxiàng. 好象 hǎoxiàng
nd 象 xiàng are often confused. While 好象 hǎoxiàng means *seem* or *look*
ke, 象 xiàng suggests more of a physical resemblance between two things.

Compare:

你 好象　　很 忙。
Nǐ hǎoxiàng hěn máng.
You seem to be very busy.

天　好象　　要 下雨。
Tiān hǎoxiàng yào xiàyǔ.
It looks like rain.

With:

我们的　　儿子不 象　　我，象　　我 太太。
Wǒmende érzi bú xiàng wǒ, xiàng wǒ tàitai.
Our son does not resemble me. He resembles my wife.

纽约　　的 天气 很　象　　北京　　的 天气。
Niǔyuē de tiānqì hěn xiàng Běijīng de tiānqì.
The weather in New York is very similar to the weather in Beijing.

There are two additional differences between 好象 hǎoxiàng and 象 xiàng
First, 好象 hǎoxiàng cannot be modified by an adverb, whereas 象 xiàng
can. Common adverbs that modify 象 xiàng include 很 hěn (very), 非常
fēicháng (extremely), 有点儿 yǒudiǎnr (somewhat). Second, if the
sentence takes the negative form, 不 bù appears before 象 xiàng, but after
好象 hǎoxiàng. For *you don't seem to like the movie*, the Chinese is 你好
不喜欢这个电影 nǐ hǎoxiàng bù xǐhuan zhè ge diànyǐng.

Exercises

I. Answer the following questions:

1. 对 中国人 来 说，什么 节日最 重要？
   Duì Zhōngguórén lái shuō, shénme jiérì zuì zhòngyào?

2. 对 你 来说， 什么 节日最 重要？
   Duì nǐ lái shuō, shénme jiérì zuì zhòngyào?

3. 你 知道 明年 的 中国 新 年 是 几月 几号 吗？
   Nǐ zhīdào míngnián de Zhōngguó Xīn Nián shì jǐ yuè jǐ hào ma?

4. 中国人 过 年 时，一般 作 什么？
   Zhōngguórén guò nián shí, yìbān zuò shénme?

5. 你 过 不 过 圣诞节？ 怎么 过？
   Nǐ guò bu guò Shèngdànjié? Zěnme guò?

6. 中国 的 国庆节 是 什么 时候？
   Zhōnguó de Guóqìngjié shì shénme shíhou?

7. 你们 元旦 放 不 放 假？放 几天 假？
   Nǐmen Yuándàn fàng bu fàng jià? Fàng jǐ tiān jià?

8. 中秋节 时，中国人 都 要 吃 什么？ 为什么？
   Zhōngqiūjié shí, Zhōngguórén dōu yào chī shénme? Wèishénme?

9. 你 知道 明年 的 中国 新 年 是 什么 年 吗？
   Nǐ zhīdào míngnián de Zhōngguó Xīn Nián shì shénme nián ma?

10. 你 属 什么？
    Nǐ shǔ shénme?

II. How do you say the following:

1. Five characters are written on the blackboard.
2. The dinner is laid on the table.

3. Ten books are being carried in the bag.
4. A map of the world is hanging on the wall.
5. A lot of cups and plates are loaded in the car.
6. Please ask him if he is a student.
7. Could you tell me if there is a hospital here?
8. Do you know if she will be upset if we don't go?
9. If Christmas falls on a Sunday, we'll also have Monday off.
10. I want to know if I can exchange money at the hotel.

III. Fill the blanks with 好象 hǎoxiàng or 象 xiàng:

1. 你 妈妈 _____ 有点儿　不 高兴。
   Nǐ māma _____ yǒudiǎnr bù gāoxìng.

2. 旧金山　的中国城　　　　　不_____　纽约　　的
   Jiùjīnshān de Zhōngguóchéng bú _____ Niǔyuē de
   中国城。
   Zhōngguóchéng.

3. 他 _____　懂　广东话。
   Tā _____ dǒng Guǎngdōnghuà.

4. 中国　　有的　地方　的人 很 _____　俄国人。
   Zhōngguó yǒude dìfang de rén hěn _____ Éguórén.

5. 明年　　的 中国　　新年 _____　是 一 月 二十 五 号。
   Míngnián de Zhōngguó Xīnnián _____ shì yī yuè èrshí wǔ hào.

6. 澳大利亚的 英语　有点儿 _____　英国　　的 英语。
   Àodàlìyà de Yīngyǔ yǒudiǎnr _____ Yīngguó de Yīngyǔ.

158

'. In what months do the following holidays fall?

rite in Chinese in the blanks the months that the following holidays fall
. If a holiday can be in one of two months, write both months.

诞节 èngdànjié	在 zài	_____
国 国庆节 ōngguó Guóqìngjié	在 zài	_____
国 国庆节 ;iguó Guóqìngjié	在 zài	_____
旦 ándàn	在 zài	_____
人节 ınrénjié	在 zài	_____
国 新 年 ōngguó Xīn Nián	在 zài	_____
恩节 n'ēnjié	在 zài	_____
国 劳动节 ;iguó Láodòngjié	在 zài	_____
国 劳动节 ōngguó Láodòngjié	在 zài	_____
秋节 ōngqiūjié	在 zài	_____

V. Write the zodiac signs of your family members, using the following patterns:

我　太太　属鸡。
Wǒ tàitai shǔ jī.
My wife was born in the year of the chicken.

VI. Translate the following into Chinese:

1. For most people in America, Christmas is the most important holiday
2. My favorite holiday is Thanksgiving, because our whole family will together.
3. Let me say something about our company first.
4. Can you guess how old I am?
5. Can you tell me something about holidays in your country?
6. The Chinese food in the restaurants in America is not the same as tha in the restaurants in China.
7. I'm not in the habit of drinking.
8. Chinese New Year is also called Spring Festival.
9. Many people in China now celebrate Christmas, although it is not a Chinese holiday.
10. Children in China especially like the New Year, because they can receive a lot of red envelopes that day.

VII. Translate the following into English:

1. 我　弟弟比我小　十二岁，我们　都　属羊。
   Wǒ dìdi bǐ wǒ xiǎo shíèr suì, wǒmen dōu shǔ yáng.

2. 中国人　　过　年　的时候，没有　交换　礼物的习惯。
   Zhōngguórén guò nián de shíhou, méi yǒu jiāohuàn lǐwù de xíguàn.

3. 以前　中国　新　年　时，人们　都　说　"恭喜发财"。
   Yǐqián Zhōngguó Xīn Nián shí, rénmen dōu shuō "Gōngxǐ fācái."

现在　人们　常　说　"新　年　好"。它们的　意思都　一样。
Xiànzài rénmen cháng shuō "Xīn Nián hǎo." Tāmende yìsī dōu yíyàng.

4. 中国　　的劳动节　在五　月　一号。美国　　的 劳动节　　在
Zhōngguó de Láodòngjié zài wǔ yuè yī hào. Měiguó de Láodòngjié zài
九　月　的 第 一个 星期一。
jiǔ yuè de dì yī ge xīngqī yī.

5. 在　中国，　　中秋节　　不 放假。
Zài Zhōngguó, Zhōngqiūjié bú fàngjià.

6. 美国人　　庆祝　　各种各样　　　的节日。
Měiguórén qìngzhù gèzhònggèyàng de jiérì.

7. 我　最　喜欢　九月。九　月　的节日最　多。
Wǒ zuì xǐhuān jiǔ yuè. Jiǔ yuè de jiérì zuì duō.

8. 节日时，中国人　　喜欢　进　城，　美国人　　喜欢　出　城。
Jiérì shí, Zhōngguórén xǐhuan jìn chéng, Měiguórén xǐhuan chū chéng.

9. 亚洲　　的很 多　国家 也庆祝　中国　　新　年。
Yàzhōu de hěn duō guójiā yě qìngzhù Zhōngguó Xīn Nián.

10. 我　已经　用　完　了今年　的假了。
Wǒ yǐjīng yòng wán le jīnnián de jiǎ le.

III. Topics for discussion/writing:

请　介绍　一下儿你最喜欢　的节日。
Qǐng jièshào yíxiàr nǐ zuì xǐhuan de jiérì.

请　介绍　一下儿 你们　国家　最　重要　　的节日。
Qǐng jièshào yíxiàr nǐmen guójiā zuì zhòngyào de jiérì.

English Translation of the Text

Conversations

A: Can you tell me something about holidays in China?

B: Sure, but there are many holidays in China. We can only talk about important ones.

A: Okay. I'd like to first ask if Chinese people celebrate the (Western) New Year.

B: Yes, they do. But to the Chinese, the (Western) New Year is not the most important holiday. The most important holiday is the Chinese New Year.

A: When is the Chinese New Year?

B: It's different every year. Sometimes it is in January and sometimes in February.

A: Can you tell me, what is the Spring Festival?

B: The Spring Festival is the Chinese New Year. Some people call it the Spring Festival, while others call it the New Year. They are the same.

A: Besides the Spring Festival, what are some of the important holidays?

B: May 1 is the Labor Day. The entire country gets a week off.

A: Is there a National Day in China?

B: Yes, the National Day in China is October 1. The entire country gets another week off.

A: Is there Christmas in China?

B: No, but although Christmas is not a Chinese holiday, some people are now celebrating it.

A: I heard that there is a *Zhōngqiūjié*. What kind of festival is it?

B: "Zhōng" means *middle*, "qiū" means *autumn*. "Zhōngqiūjié" means *Mid-Autumn Festival*. The moon is the fullest on this day. People eat moon cake and families get together.

A: When is the Mid-Autumn Festival?

B: Like the New Year, the date for the Mid-Autumn Festival is different every year, but it usually falls in October.

*   *   *   *   *

Do you know when the Chinese New Year is next year?
The Chinese New Year next year is February 10.
How do the Chinese celebrate the Chinese New Year?
Before the New Year, Chinese people generally would clean the house
and decorate the house. On the New Year's Eve, the whole family
would get together, cooking and eating a lot of food. On New Year's
Day, people wish happy New Year to each other. Grownups will also
give children red envelopes.
What is the red envelope?
The red envelopes contain money. It is a gift for children.
Do people exchange gifts during the New Year?
Chinese people do not have this custom.
What do Chinese people eat when they celebrate the New Year?
All kinds of things, but most people eat dumplings.

*   *   *   *   *

During the Chinese New Year, I often hear people say "gōngxǐ fācái."
What does this mean?
"Gōngxǐ" means *wish*; "fācái" means *good luck*. "Gōngxǐ fācái" means
wish you good luck.
When it is New Year, I will say "gōngxǐ fācái" to you.
Thank you, but most people now say "Xīn Nián hǎo."
In that case, I'll also say "Xīn Nián hǎo".
You are learning fast!

*   *   *   *   *

What (zodiac) year is next year?
Next year is the year of the rooster. Children born next year all have
the zodiac sign of the rooster.
I don't know my sign. Could you tell me?
Sure. How old are you this year?
I'm twenty-three this year. I was born in 1979.
You are two years younger than I am. You were born in the year of the
sheep. Your sign is the sheep.

A: Now I know. If you know a person's sign, you will be able to guess
    age.
B: You are right. It is generally the case.

Reading Passage

To many Americans, Christmas is the most important holiday of the year
Children particularly like the day because they will receive a lot of gifts.
Christmas is somewhat like the Chinese New Year. Before the holiday,
people will clean the house and decorate the house. Many people place a
Christmas tree in their homes. Various kinds of decorated items will then
be displayed on the tree. On Christmas Eve, the whole family will get
together, cooking and eating a lot of food. There is a major difference in
way Americans celebrate Christmas and the Chinese celebrate the Chines
New Year. That is, Americans have the custom of exchanging gifts. They
spend a lot of time in the stores before Christmas choosing and buying
presents.

8

JOB HUNTING & INTERVIEWING

Conversations

你 今天　怎么　没有　　去上班?
Nǐ jīntiān zěnme méiyou qù shàngbān?

上　　星期 我 被 解雇了。我 没 有　工作　了。
Shàng xīngqī wǒ bèi jiěgù le.　Wǒ méi yǒu gōngzuò le.

你 被 解雇了? 这 怎么　可能?
Nǐ bèi jiěgù le? Zhè zěnme kěnéng?

我们　公司　的 生意　不 好, 所以 解雇了很 多 人。
Wǒmen gōngsī de shēngyì bù hǎo, suǒyǐ jiěgù le hěn duō rén.

你 有 没有　找　到 新 的 工作?
Nǐ yǒu méiyou zhǎo dào xīn de gōngzuò?

我 找 了一个月, 但是 还 没有　找　到。你 知道　哪儿要
Wǒ zhǎo le yí ge yuè, dànshì hái méiyou zhǎo dào.　Nǐ zhīdào nǎr　yào

165

人 吗？
rén ma?

A：你 想　　找　什么样　　的 工作？
Nǐ xiǎng zhǎo shénmeyàng de gōngzuò?

B：我 作　的 是 秘书。我 还 想　　找　秘书 的 工作。　你 能
Wǒ zuò de shì mìshū. Wǒ hái xiǎng zhǎo mìshū de gōngzuò. Nǐ néng
　帮　我的 忙　　吗？
bāng wǒde máng ma?

A：我　试试看。　我 去 问问　　我们　公司　的 人事部。我们
Wǒ shìshi kàn. Wǒ qù wènwen wǒmen gōngsī de rénshìbù. Wǒmen
公司　可能　　需要 人。
gōngsī kěnéng xūyào rén.

B：谢谢　你的 帮助。
Xièxie nǐde bāngzhù.

A：不 客气。我 一有　消息　就 给 你 打 电话。
Bú kèqì.　Wǒ yì yǒu xiāoxi jiù gěi nǐ dǎ diànhuà.

　＊　　　　＊　　　　＊　　　　＊　　　　＊

A：小　　王，　我们　学校　在 找　一 位 中文　　老师。你 有
Xiǎo Wáng, wǒmen xuéxiào zài zhǎo yí wèi Zhōngwén lǎoshī. Nǐ yǒu
兴趣　吗？
xìngqù ma?

B：你们　要 全职　　老师 还是　半职 老师？
Nǐmen yào quánzhí lǎoshī háishi bànzhí lǎoshī?

A: 我们 要 全职 老师。
Wǒmen yào quánzhí lǎoshī.

B: 我 对 教书 很 有 趣, 可是 我 只 能 作 半职 工作。
Wǒ duì jiāoshū hěn yǒu xìngqù, kěshì wǒ zhǐ néng zuò bànzhí gōngzuò.

A: 你 知道 不 知道 别人 有 没 有 兴趣 教 中文?
Nǐ zhīdào bu zhīdào biérén yǒu méi yǒu xìngqù jiāo Zhōngwén?

B: 我 可以 问问 我的 朋友们。 你 能 不 能 告诉 我
Wǒ kěyǐ wènwen wǒde péngyoumen. Nǐ néng bu néng gàosù wǒ
你们 学校 的 工资 和 福利?
nǐmen xuéxiào de gōngzī hé fúlì?

A: 工资 要看 学历 和 经验。 我们 提供 医疗 保险 和
Gōngzī yào kàn xuélì hé jīngyàn. Wǒmen tígòng yīliáo bǎoxiǎn hé
退休金。 每年 有 十 个 星期 的 假。
tuìxiūjīn. Měi nián yǒu shí ge xīngqī de jià.

B: 好, 我 一有 消息 就 给你 打 电话。 你 也可以 在 中文
Hǎo, wǒ yì yǒu xiāoxi jiù gěi nǐ dǎ diànhuà. Nǐ yě kěyǐ zài Zhōngwén
报纸 上 作 一个 广告, 一定 会 有 很 多 人 来
bàozhǐ shang zuò yí ge guǎnggào, yídìng huì yǒu hěn duō rén lái
申请。
shēnqǐng.

A: 好 主意。
Hǎo zhǔyì.

*　　　*　　　*　　　*　　　*

B: 我 是 来 申请 贵 公司 电脑 工程师 的 工作 的。
Wǒ shì lái shēnqǐng guì gōngsī diànnǎo gōngchéngshī de gōngzuò de.

167

B: 你 是 怎么 知道 我们 需要 电脑 工程师 的?
Nǐ shì zěnme zhīdào wǒmen xūyào diànnǎo gōngchéngshī de?

A: 我 是 在 报纸 上 看 到 你们的 广告 的。
Wǒ shì zài bàozhǐ shang kàn dào nǐmende guǎnggào de.

B: 谢谢 你 对 我们 公司 的 兴趣。你 能 介绍 一下儿 你
Xièxie nǐ duì wǒmen gōngsī de xìngqù. Nǐ néng jièshào yīxiàr nǐ
自己 吗?
zìjǐ ma?

A: 当然。 这 是 我的 学历。我 去年 从 大学 毕业。毕业后
Dāngrán. Zhè shì wǒde xuélì. Wǒ qùnián cóng dàxué bìyè. Bìyè hòu
在 美国 电话 公司 工作。
zài Měiguó Diànhuà Gōngsī gōngzuò.

B: 美国 电话 公司 是 个 大 公司,你 为什么 要 离开?
Měiguó Diànhuà Gōngsī shì ge dà gōngsī, nǐ wèishénme yào líkāi?

A: 不错, 美国 电话 公司 是 个 大 公司, 但是 我 作 的
Bú cuò, Měiguó Diànhuà Gōngsī shì ge dà gōngsī, dànshì wǒ zuò de
工作 和 电脑 没 有 关系。我 想 在 贵 公司 能
gōngzuò hé diànnǎo méi yǒu guānxì. Wǒ xiǎng zài guì gōngsī néng
有 更 多 的 机会。
yǒu gèng duō de jīhuì.

B: 你 在 大学 学 的 是 什么 专业?
Nǐ zài dàxué xué de shì shénme zhuānyè?

A: 我 学 的 是 电脑。 我 在 学历 上 列 了 我的 主要 成绩。
Wǒ xué de shì diànnǎo. Wǒ zài xuélì shang liè le wǒde zhǔyào chéngjī

B: 你 什么　时候　能　开始　工作?
Nǐ shénme shíhou néng kāishǐ gōngzuò?

A: 三　个 星期　以后。
Sān ge xīngqī yǐhòu.

B: 好。我们　会 考虑 你的　申请，　在 一个星期　里给你 答复。
Hǎo. Wǒmen huì kǎolǜ nǐde shēnqǐng, zài yí ge xīngqī lǐ gěi nǐ dáfù.

A: 谢谢。
Xièxie.

B: 你 有　没 有　问题　问　我?
Nǐ yǒu méi yǒu wèntí wèn wǒ?

A: 现在　　没　有。
Xiànzài méi yǒu.

Reading Passage

中国的学校，特别是大学，每年需要很多外国英语老师去教英语。他们要求外国老师有大学文凭，英语是第一语言，能认真教课。外国老师的工资不太高，但是他们不用付房租。大多数学校还提供飞机票。中国的东西很便宜，所以虽然工资不高，但是生活没有问题。很多人去中国教英语是想利用这个机会学中文和了解中国文化。外国老师一般每星期工作十五个小时。他们教的课有口语、阅读、作文，等等。你有兴趣去中国教英语吗?

Zhōngguó de xuéxiào, tèbié shì dàxué, měi nián xūyào hěn duō wàiguó Yīngyǔ lǎoshī qù jiāo Yīngyǔ. Tāmen yāoqiú wàiguó lǎoshī yǒu dàxué wénpíng, Yīngyǔ shì dìyī yǔyán, néng rènzhēn jiāo kè. Wàiguó lǎoshī de gōngzī bú tài gāo, dànshì tāmen bú yòng fù fángzū. Dàduōshù xuéxiào hái

169

tígòng fēijīpiào. Zhōngguó de dōngxi hěn piányi, suǒyǐ suīrán gōngzī bù gāo, dànshì shēnghuó méi yǒu wèntí. Hěn duō rén qù Zhōngguó jiāo Yīngyǔ shì xiǎng lìyòng zhè ge jīhuì xué Zhōngwén hé liǎojiě Zhōngguó wénhuà. Wàiguó lǎoshī yìbān měi xīngqī gōngzuò shíwǔ ge xiǎoshí. Tāmen jiāo de kè yǒu kǒuyǔ, yuèdú, zuòwén, děngděng. Nǐ yǒu xìngqù qù Zhōngguó jiāo Yīngyǔ ma?

New Words and Expressions

被	bèi	*passive marker*
解雇	jiěgù	lay off
生意	shēngyì	business
什么样	shénmeyàng	what kind of
秘书	mìshū	secretary
人事部	rénshìbù	personnel department
需要	xūyào	need
一 ... 就 ...	yí ... jiù ...	as soon as
消息	xiāoxi	news; word
问	wèn	ask
兴趣	xìngqu	interest
全职	quánzhí	full time
半职	bànzhí	part time
工资	gōngzi	salary
福利	fúlì	benefits
学历	xuélì	academic credentials; resume
经验	jīngyàn	experience
提供	tígòng	provide

退休金	tuìxiūjīn	pension
广告	guǎnggào	advertisement; commercial
申请	shēnqǐng	apply; application
工程师	gōngchéngshī	engineer
自己	zìjǐ	oneself; one's own
离开	líkāi	leave
和 ...... 有关系	hé ... yǒu guānxi	have to do with
更	gèng	even more
列	liè	list (v)
考虑	kǎolù	consider
答复	dáfù	reply (n & v)
要求	yāoqiu	requirement; require
认真	rènzhēn	conscientious; conscientiously
付	fù	pay (v)
房租	fángzū	rent
生活	shēnghuo	livelihood; life
利用	lìyòng	make use of; take advantage of
了解	liáojiě	gain understanding
文化	wénhuà	culture
文凭	wénpíng	diploma; degree
阅读	yuèdú	reading

Supplementary Words and Expressions

| 雇主 | gùzhǔ | employer |

171

雇员	gùyuán	employee
失业	shīyè	lose one's job; be out of work
辞职	cízhí	resign; resignation (from a job)
老板	lǎobǎn	boss
空缺	kòngquē	vacancy
面谈	miàntán	(job) interview
特长	tècháng	specialty; expertise
经济	jīngjì	economy; economic; economical
条件	tiáojiàn	terms; conditions
行业	hángyè	profession; trade
退休	tuìxiū	retire
省	shěng	save

Language Points

我被解雇了 wǒ bèi jiěgù le

Chinese does not make a distinction between the active voice and the passive voice. A lot depends on the context. For example, if there is no object or prior reference, 鱼吃了 yú chī le can only mean *the fish was eaten*. If there is an object, 鱼 yú would be the agent such as 大鱼吃了小鱼 dà yú chī le xiǎo yú (the big fish ate the small fish). There are, however, a number of passive markers in Chinese that are used to make the agent explicit in a sentence when the recipient of an action is expressed as the subject. The most common of these passive markers is 被 bèi:

他 被 老师 批评 了。
Tā bèi lǎoshī pīpíng le.
He was criticized by the teacher.

172

The agent can often be omitted from the sentence, but 被 bèi must be retained:

他 被 批评 了。
Tā bèi pīpíng le.
He was criticized.

汽车 被 偷 了。
Qìchē bèi tōu le.
The car was stolen.

Verbs used with 被 bèi or 被 bèi phrase tend to suggest an undesirable action, as shown in the above sentences.

帮我的忙 bāng wǒde máng

"帮 bāng" and "忙 máng" in "帮我的忙 bāng wǒde máng" are part of the word 帮忙 bāngmáng (help). A disyllabic word, 帮忙 bāngmáng belongs to a class of verbs in Chinese that internally consist of a verb and an object. In this case, the verb is 帮 bāng and the object is 忙 máng. Since there is already a built-in object in the verb, 帮忙 bāngmáng can't take an object. For example, we can't say 帮忙我 bāngmáng wǒ. To express the idea of *help me* or *do me a favor* by using 帮忙 bāngmáng, we'll need to say 帮我的忙 bāng wǒde máng. The three words are in the following relationship:

帮	我的	忙
bāng	wǒde	máng
verb	attribute	noun object

There is another word in the lesson that also means *help*: 帮助 bāngzhù. The difference between 帮忙 bāngmáng and 帮助 bāngzhù is that 帮忙 bāngmáng refers more to a physical act or an action that involves physical effort, whereas 帮助 bāngzhù is not restricted to physical acts. So for example, when a person lends you money to tide you over in a time of financial difficulty, or if he helps you move (houses), what he does is 帮忙 bāngmáng. But if a person helps you with your Chinese or gives you advice what he does is 帮助 bāngzhù. Here are some of the commonly used sentence patterns involving these two words:

你 能　帮　我　一个忙　　吗?
Nǐ néng bāng wó yí ge máng ma?
Can you do me a favor?

你 帮　　了我　一个 大忙。
Nǐ bāng le wǒ yí ge dà máng.
You did me a big favor.

我　一点儿忙　　也 没　帮。
Wǒ yìdiǎnr máng yě méi bāng.
I didn't help at all.

你 帮　　我的　忙，　我　帮　你的　忙。
Nǐ bāng wǒde máng, wǒ bāng nǐde máng.
You help me, and I will help you.

谢谢　你的帮助。
Xièxie nǐde bāngzhù.
Thank you for your help.

没　有 你的帮助，　　我　找　不　到　工作。
Méi yǒu nǐde bāngzhù, wǒ zhǎo bú dào gōngzuò.
Without your help, I can't find a job.

我的　美国　　朋友　帮助　　我 学　英语。
Wǒde Měiguó péngyou bāngzhù wǒ xué Yīngyǔ.
My American friend helps me with my English.

们　　互相　　帮助　　吧。

ǒmen hùxiāng bāngzhù ba.

t's help each other.

一有消息就给你打电话 wǒ yì yǒu xiāoxi jiù gěi nǐ dǎ diànhuà

e pattern "一 …… 就 yī … jiù" is used to indicate that one action
xpressed by 就 jiù) closely follows another action (expressed by 一 yī).

一来　我　就　走。

yì lái wǒ jiù zǒu.

soon as you come, I'll leave.

te that **a**) the main clause (in this case, 我就走 wǒ jiù zǒu) always
lows the subordinate clause; **b**) the subject of the main clause (in this
e 我 wǒ) always precedes 就 jiù instead of following it; and **c**) if the
rb in the main clause shares the subject with the verb in the subordinate
use, the subject in the main clause is always left out. The sentence cited
m the text is a case in point.

对教书很有兴趣 wǒ duì jiāoshū hěn yǒu xìngqù

th 教 jiāo and 教书 jiāoshū mean *teach*, but there is an important
ference. 教 jiāo is a transitive verb and must be followed by an object,
ereas 教书 jiāoshū (a verb + object structure) is an intransitive verb and
nnot be followed by an object. So for *he teaches at a middle school*, we
n't say 他在中学教 tā zài zhōngxué jiāo; we can only say 他在中学教书
ā zài zhōngxué jiāoshū (he teaches at a middle school). If there is an object
the sentence, it would be fine to use 教 jiāo: 他在中学教数学 tā zài
ōngxué jiāo shùxué (he teaches math at a middle school).

e Chinese structure for *to be interested in* is 对 …… 有兴趣 duì … yǒu
gqù:

你 对 什么　有　兴趣?
Nǐ duì shénme yǒu xìngqù?
What are you interested in?

我　对　中医　　有　很　大的 兴趣。
Wǒ duì zhōngyī yǒu hěn dà de xìngqù.
I'm very interested in Chinese medicine.

The negative form is 对 ……没有兴趣 duì … méi yǒu xìngqù:

我　对　音乐　没　有　兴趣。
Wǒ duì yīnyuè méi yǒu xìngqù.
I'm not interested in music.

贵公司 guì gōngsi

This 贵 guì is the same 贵 guì as in 您贵姓 nín guì xìng (what is your la
name). It is an honorific prefixed to a place name to show respect to your
addressee. Other examples include 贵校 guì xiào (your school), 贵国 guì
guó (your country), 贵店 guì diàn (your store).

你能介绍一下儿你自己吗 nǐ néng jièshào yīxiàr nǐ zìjǐ ma?

自己 zìjǐ is mainly used in the following two ways:

1. Used with a personal pronoun to mean *oneself* or *one's own*: 我自己 w
zìjǐ (myself); 你自己 nǐ zìjǐ (yourself); 他自己 tā zìjǐ (himself); 我自己的
房子 wǒ zìjǐ de fángzi (my own house).

2. Used in the sense of *by oneself* or *alone*:

你　自己去还是　和 别人　去?
Nǐ zìjǐ qù háishi hé biérén qù?
Are you going alone or with somebody else?

多人去中国教英语是想利用这个机会学中文和了解中国文化
n duō rén qù Zhōngguó jiāo Yīngyǔ shì xiǎng lìyòng zhè ge jīhuì
é Zhōngwén hé liǎojiě Zhōngguó wénhuà

;ed after a verb or a verb phrase, 是 shì indicates purpose or reason. The
ove sentence means *many people go to teach English in China because
ey would like to use the opportunity to learn Chinese and understand
iinese culture.* Other examples of this usage include:

来 是 工作 的, 不 是 玩 的。
ǒ lái shì gōngzuò de, bú shì wán de.
ame to work, not to play.

给 你 打 电话 是 想   请 你 去 吃饭。
ι gěi nǐ dǎ diànhuà shì xiǎng qǐng nǐ qù chīfàn.
: called you to invite you to go (to his place) to eat.

Exercises

Answer the following questions:

. 你 工作 吗? 你 喜欢 你 现在 的 工作   吗?
  Nǐ gōngzuò ma? Nǐ xǐhuān nǐ xiànzài de gōngzuò ma?

. 你 有 没有 被 解雇 过? 你 被 解雇 后 是 怎么 找 到
  Nǐ yǒu méiyou bèi jiěgù guò? Nǐ bèi jiěgù hòu shì zěnme zhǎo dào
  工作 的?
  gōngzuò de?

3. 你 觉得 找 什么样 的 工作 容易，什么样 的
   Nǐ juéde zhǎo shénmeyàng de gōngzuò róngyì, shénmeyàng de
   工作 不 容易?
   gōngzuò bù róngyì?

4. 你 找 工作 的 时候，有没有 去 面谈? 和 你 面谈
   Nǐ zhǎo gōngzuò de shíhou, yǒu méiyou qù miàntán? Hé nǐ miàntán
   的 人 问 了 你 什么 问题?
   de rén wèn le nǐ shénme wèntí?

5. 去 中国 教 英语 需要 有 什么 条件?
   Qù Zhōngguó jiāo Yīngyǔ xūyào yǒu shénme tiáojiàn?

6. 你 对 什么样 的电影 有 兴趣?
   Nǐ duì shénmyàng de diànyǐng yǒu xìngqù?

7. 在 美国，面谈 的 时候 雇主 不 能 问 什么 问题?
   Zài Měiguó, miàntán de shíhou, gùzhǔ bù néng wèn shénme wèntí?

8. 你 现在 的 工作 和你 在 大学 学 的 专业 有 没 有
   Nǐ xiànzài de gōngzuò hé nǐ zài dàxué xué de zhuānyè yǒu méi yǒu
   关系?
   guānxì?

9. 你们 单位 的 福利 怎么样? 你们 有 什么 福利?
   Nǐmen dānwèi de fúlì zěnmeyàng? Nǐmen yǒu shénme fúlì?

10. 学历 和 经验，你 觉得 哪 一个 更 重要?
    Xuélì hé jīngyàn, nǐ juéde nǎ yī gè gèng zhòngyào?

II. How do you say the following:

1. got laid off

look for a job
found a job
within three months
in a year
more opportunities
saw the news on TV
very interested in music
not interested in swimming
He didn't do me the favor.
I didn't ask him to do me the favor.
Where does your wife teach? She teaches fine arts at a college.
Salary is commensurate with experience.
I came here to buy, not to sell.
This matter has nothing to do with our company.

. Change the following active sentences to passive sentences:

医生　治 好 了病人。
Yīshēng zhì hǎo le bìngrén.

学生们　　把 书 带 回 家了。
Xuéshengmen bǎ shū dài huí jiā le.

他 喝了 茶。
Tā hē le chá.

我 爸爸 卖 了他的汽车。
Wǒ bàba mài le tāde qìchē.

我的 女朋友　关　掉 了她的手机。
Wǒde nǚpéngyou guān diào le tāde shǒujī.

老板　考虑 了你的申请。
Lǎobǎn kǎolǜ le nǐde shēnqǐng.

IV. Change the following passive sentences to active sentences:

1. 鱼 被 猫 吃 了。
   Yú bèi māo chī le.

2. 桌子 被 老师 拿 进 来 了。
   Zhuōzi bèi lǎoshī ná jìn lai le.

3. 词典 被 他 放 在 书架 上 了。
   Cídiǎn bèi tā fàng zài shūjià shang le.

4. 圣诞节   的礼物被 孩子们   看   到 了。
   Shèngdànjié de lǐwù bèi háizimen kàn dào le.

5. 毛衣 被 妈妈 洗了。
   Máoyī bèi māma xǐ le.

6. 这 个 问题 已经 被 很 多 人 问 过 了。
   Zhè ge wèntí yǐjīng bèi hěn duō rén wèn guo le.

V. Fill in the blanks with either 帮助 bāngzhù, 帮忙 bāngmáng o a variation of them:

1. 你 _____ 了她一个 大 _____。
   Nǐ _____ le tā yí ge dà _____.

2. 我_____ 你学 中文,   你 _____ 我 学 英文。
   Wǒ _____ nǐ xué Zhōngwén, nǐ _____ wǒ xué Yīngwén.

3. 考试 的 时候, 学生们   不 应该 互相 _____。
   Kǎoshì de shíhou, xuéshengmen bù yīnggāi hùxiāng _____.

老师　要　重新　　布置　教室。我们　　去 _____。好 不
Lǎoshī yào chóngxīn bùzhī jiàoshì. Wǒmen qù _____. Hǎo bu
好？
hǎo?

谢谢　你的_____。
Xièxie nǐde _____.

你 不 能_____　他 这 个_____。
Nǐ bù néng _____ tā zhè ge _____.

. Translate the following into Chinese:

Elementary and secondary schools in New York City need a lot of
English teachers.
I'm not interested in jobs that do not provide medical insurance.
Please list your major accomplishments on your resume.
To some employers, experience is more important than a diploma.
I only did you a small favor. You don't need to give me money.
He has changed jobs three times in the last two years.
What I'm doing now has a lot to do with what I studied at college.
I don't have a college degree. Do you think they would hire me?
When are you available to start to work and how long can you commit
to working here?
She has been looking for a job for two months, but has not found one.

I. Translate the following into English:

有的　雇主　解雇 员工　　不 是 因为　生意　不好，是 想
Yǒude gùzhǔ jiěgù yuángōng bú shì yīnwéi shēngyì bù hǎo, shì xiǎng
省　　钱。
shěng qián.

2. 这 份 工作　虽然 工资　不 高，但是　福利 很　好。
   Zhè fèn gōngzuò suīrán gōngzī bù gāo, dànshì fúlì　hěn hǎo.

3. 我们　一作 决定　就会 给 你 答复。
   Wǒmen yí zuò juédìng jiù huì gěi nǐ dáfù.

4. 三 年 前 电脑　工作　很 好 找，现在 不 好 找。
   Sān nián qián diànnǎo gōngzuò hěn hǎo zhǎo, xiànzài bù hǎo zhǎo.

5. 医生　要 你 在 家 休息 是 不 想　要 你 太 累。
   Yīshēng yào nǐ zài jiā xiūxi shì bù xiǎng yào nǐ tài lèi.

6. 我 一个 月 后 才 能　开始 给 你们　工作。
   Wǒ yí ge yuè hòu cái néng kāishǐ gěi nǐmen gōngzuò.

7. 你 没 有　大学 文凭，　英语　不 是 你的 第一 语言，所以
   Nǐ méi yǒu dàxué wénpíng, Yīngyǔ bú shì nǐde dìyī yǔyán, suǒyǐ
   我们　不 能　考虑 你的 申请。
   wǒmen bù néng kǎolǜ nǐde shēnqǐng.

8. 他 要 你 作　的 是 给 他的 秘书　写 信。
   Tā yào nǐ zuò de shì gěi tāde mìshū xiě xìn.

9. 面谈　时 请 把 你的 学历 和 文凭　带 来。
   Miàntán shí qǐng bǎ nǐde xuélì hé wénpíng dài lai.

10. 全职　雇员 有　退休金，半职 雇员 没 有。
    Quánzhí gùyuán yǒu tuìxiūjīn, bànzhí gùyuán méi yǒu.

VIII. Topics for discussion/writing:

Describe your job.
Describe a job-hunting experience of yours.

English Translation of the Text

nversations

Why didn't you go to work today?

I was laid off last week. I don't have a job anymore.

You were laid off? How could this be possible?

Business at our company is not good, so it laid off a lot of people.

Have you found a new job?

I have been looking for a month, but I have not found one yet. Do you know a place where they need people?

What kind of work would you like to find?

I worked as a secretary. I would still like to look for a secretary's job. Can you help me?

Let me try. I'll check with the personnel department of our company. Our company may need people.

Thank you for your help.

You are welcome. I'll call you as soon as I hear from them.

*   *   *   *   *

Xiao Wang, our school is looking for a Chinese teacher. Are you interested?

Are you looking for a full-time teacher or part-time teacher?

We are looking for a full-time teacher.

I'm very interested in teaching, but I can only work part-time.

Do you know someone else who might be interested in teaching Chinese?

I can ask my friends. Can you let me know your salary and benefits?

Salary is commensurate with academic credentials and experience. We provide medical insurance and pension. There is a ten-week vacation a year.

Good. I'll call you as soon as I find something. You can also put an ad in the Chinese newspapers. I'm sure there will be many people applying.

Good idea.

*	*	*	*	*

A: I'm here to apply for a computer engineer's position at your compan

B: How did you learn that we need a computer engineer?

A: I saw your ad in the newspaper.

B: Thank you for your interest in our company. Can you say a few thing about yourself?

A: Sure. This is my resume. I graduated from college last year. Since then, I have been working for American Telephone Company.

B: American Telephone is a big company. Why do you want to leave?

A: Yes, American Telephone is a big company, but the work I do there not related to computers. I think I'll have more opportunities at your company.

B: What was your major at college?

A: I studied computer science. I listed my major achievements on my resume.

B: When can you start?

A: In three weeks.

B: Good. We'll consider your application and give you a reply in a wee

A: Thank you.

B: Do you have questions for me?

A: Not for the moment.

Reading Passage

Schools in China, particularly universities, need a lot of foreign English teachers to teach English there. They require that the foreign teachers hav a college degree, English as their first language and commitment to teaching. Salary for foreign teachers is not very high, but they don't have pay rent. Additionally, most schools also provide airfare. Besides, things are very inexpensive in China. Although the salary is not high, making a living is not a problem. Many people want to teach in China in order to us this opportunity to study Chinese and understand Chinese culture. Generally, foreign teachers work fifteen hours a week. The classes that th teach include conversation, reading, writing and so on. Are you intereste in teaching in China?

9

NEWSPAPER & INTERNET

Conversations

A: 你 每 天 都 看 报 吗?
   Nǐ měi tiān dōu kàn bào ma?

B: 差不多 每 天 都 看。
   Chàbuduō měi tiān dōu kàn.

A: 你 一般 看 什么 报?
   Nǐ yìbān kàn shénme bào?

B: 我 一般 看《华尔街 时报》。报 上 的内容 跟 我的
   Wǒ yìbān kàn "Huá'ěrjiē Shíbào." Bào shang de nèiróng gēn wǒde
   工作 有 很 大 的 关系。你呢? 你看 不看《华尔街
   gōngzuò yǒu hěn dà de guānxi. Nǐ ne? Nǐ kàn bu kàn "Huá'ěrjiē
   时报》?
   Shíbào"?

A: 我 很 少 看。我 对 金融 没 有 兴趣。我 一般 看
   Wǒ hěn shǎo kàn. Wǒ duì jīnróng méi yǒu xìngqù. Wǒ yìbān kàn

《纽约　时报》。你看 不看《纽约　时报》？
"Niǔyuē Shíbào." Nǐ kàn bu kàn "Niǔyuē Shíbào"?

B：我 有时 也看。
Wǒ yǒushí yě kàn.

A：你有 没有　看 今天　的《纽约　时报》？
Nǐ yǒu méiyou kàn jīntiān de "Niǔyuē Shíbào"?

B：没有。　我 今天 很 忙，　连 标题 都 没 有 时间 看。
Méiyou. Wǒ jīntiān hěn máng, lián biāotí dōu méi yǒu shíjiān kàn.
今天　有 什么　重要　的 新闻？
Jīntiān yǒu shénme zhòngyào de xīnwén?

A：股票　市场　跌 得很 厉害。昨天　跌 了差不多　两
Gǔpiào shìchǎng diē de hěn lìhai. Zuótiān diē le chābuduō liǎng
百点。
bǎi diǎn.

B：你 担心　不 担心？
Nǐ dānxīn bù dānxīn?

A：我 很 担心。我 有 很 多 股票。
Wǒ hěn dānxīn. Wǒ yǒu hěn duō gǔpiào.

　　*　　*　　*　　*　　*

A：你喜欢 看 星期天　的 报纸　吗？
Nǐ xǐhuan kàn xīngqītiān de bàozhǐ ma?

B：喜欢。　其实 我 只看 星期天　的 报纸。平常　太 忙，
Xǐhuan. Qíshí wǒ zhǐ kàn xīngqītiān de bàozhǐ. Píngcháng tài máng,
没 有 时间 看 报。
méi yǒu shíjiān kàn bào.

186

A: 星期天　的 报纸　内容　　太 多，你 都 看　吗？
　　Xīngqītiān de bàozhǐ nèiróng tài duō, nǐ dōu kàn ma?

B: 我 不 都　看。除了 国际，国内　新闻，我　大多 看　体育
　　Wǒ bù dōu kàn. Chúle guójì, guónèi xīnwén, wǒ dàduō kàn tǐyù
　　消息。你 呢，你 喜欢　看　星期天　　的 报纸　吗？
　　xiāoxi. Nǐ ne,　nǐ xǐhuan kàn xīngqītiān de bàozhǐ ma?

A: 我 不 太 喜欢。我　只 看　标题。我　觉得 里面 的 广告
　　Wǒ bú tài xǐhuan. Wǒ zhǐ kàn biāotí. Wǒ juéde lǐmiàn de guǎnggào
　　太 多。
　　tài duō.

B: 是　这样。　我 买 了星期天　的 报纸 后 作 的 第一 件
　　Shì zhèyàng.　Wǒ mǎi le xīngqītiān de bàozhǐ hòu zuò de dì yī jiàn
　　事 就 是把 广告　　扔　掉。
　　shì jiù shì bǎ guǎnggào rēng diào.

　　　*　　　　　*　　　　　*　　　　　*　　　　　*

A: 我 想 去 中国　　学 中文。　　你 能　给 我 推荐 一个
　　Wǒ xiǎng qù Zhōngguó xué Zhōngwén. Nǐ néng gěi wǒ tuījiàn yí ge
　　学校　　吗？
　　xuéxiào ma?

B: 中国　　的很 多 大学 给 外国　学生　　开 中文　　课。
　　Zhōngguó de hěn duō dàxué gěi wàiguó xuésheng kāi Zhōngwén kè.
　　我 离开中国　　已经 很 多 年 了，对 它们 也 不 很
　　Wǒ líkāi Zhōngguó yǐjīng hěn duō nián le, duì tāmen yě bù hěn
　　熟悉。
　　shúxī.

A： 我　怎么　能　找　到　关于　这些　学校　的 资料 呢?
　　 Wǒ zěnme néng zhǎo dào guānyú zhèxiē xuéxiào de zīliào ne?

B： 你 可以上　网　去查。每 个 大学　都　有　网站。
　　 Nǐ kěyǐ shàng wǎng qù chá. Měi ge dàxué dōu yǒu wǎngzhàn.

A： 你 知道 它们的　网址　吗?
　　 Nǐ zhīdào tāmende wǎngzhǐ ma?

B： 我　知道　一些。我 回 家 查 一下，用　电子信　告诉你，
　　 Wǒ zhīdào yìxiē. Wǒ huí jiā chá yíxià, yòng diànzǐxìn gàosù nǐ,
　　 好 不 好?
　　 hǎo bù hǎo?

A： 好，谢谢　你。你 知道　我的 电子信　地址吗?
　　 Hǎo, xièxie nǐ. Nǐ zhīdào wǒde diànzǐxìn dìzhǐ ma?

B： 我　有 你的电子信　地址，但是　我　最近　给 你发 的电子
　　 Wǒ yǒu nǐde diànzǐxìn dìzhǐ, dànshì wǒ zuìjìn gěi nǐ fā de diànzǐ
　　 信 都　被 退 回 来 了。不 知 为什么?
　　 xìn dōu bèi tuì huí lai le. Bù zhī wèishénme?

A： 对不起，我 换　了地址，忘　了告诉 你。
　　 Duìbuqǐ, wǒ huàn le dìzhǐ, wàng le gàosù nǐ.

B： 你 为什么　换　地址?
　　 Nǐ wèishénme huàn dìzhǐ?

A： 我 每　天 收到　太 多 的 垃圾邮件，讨厌　极了。
　　 Wǒ měi tiān shōudào tài duō de lājī yóujiàn, tǎoyàn jíle.

B： 对 了，你打算　什么　时候 去 中国　学 中文?
　　 Duì le, nǐ dǎsuan shénme shíhou qù Zhōngguó xué Zhōngwén?

A：我 打算 放 了假就去。
Wǒ dǎsuan fàng le jià jiù qù.

*   *   *   *   *

A：你爸爸妈妈 也在美国 吗？
Nǐ bàba māma yě zài Měiguó ma?

B：不 在，他们 在 中国。
Bú zài, tāmen zài Zhōngguó.

A：你常 给他们 写信 吗？
Nǐ cháng gěi tāmen xiě xìn ma?

B：以前 常 写，我现在 一般 打电话 或 写 电子信。
Yǐqián cháng xiě, wǒ xiànzài yìbān dǎ diànhuà huò xiě diànzǐxìn.

A：你爸爸 妈妈 也会 写 电子信 吗？
Nǐ bàba māma yě huì xiě diànzǐxìn ma?

B：会，就 连 我 爷爷，奶奶 也会 写。
Huì, jiù lián wǒ yéye, nǎinai yě huì xiě.

A：你给他们 写 电子信 的 时候 用 中文 还是 英语？
Nǐ gěi tāmen xiě diànzǐxìn de shíhou yòng Zhōngwén háishi Yīngyǔ?

B：他们 不 懂 英语，我 用 中文 给 他们 写，但是
Tāmen bù dǒng Yīngyǔ, wǒ yòng Zhōngwén gěi tāmen xiě, dànshì
我 给朋友 写 的时候，用 英语。
wǒ gěi péngyou xiě de shíhou, yòng Yīngyǔ.

A：我 能 用 中文 给你 写 电子信 吗？
Wǒ néng yòng Zhōngwén gěi nǐ xiě diànzǐxìn ma?

B: 没　问题，但是　你 得 有　中文　　软件。
　　Méi wèntí,　dànshì nǐ děi yǒu Zhōngwén ruǎnjiàn.

A: 我　有　"NJStar", 可以不 可以?
　　Wǒ yǒu "NJStar",　kěyǐ bu kěyǐ?

B: 可以，你回　家 就　试试。
　　Kěyǐ,　nǐ huí jiā jiù shìshi.

Reading Passage

互联网和电子信给我们带来了很大的方便，现在我们可以在网上查
资料，买东西，看报，聊天，甚至上课。以前我们跟国外的朋友联
系的时候要写信或打电话。信在路上要走很多天，打电话又很贵。
但是现在写电子信就可以了。没有电脑的人可以去网吧。中国的每
个城市都有网吧，也很便宜，所以很方便。

Hùliánwǎng hé diànzǐxìn gěi wǒmen dài lai le hěn dà de fāngbiàn,
xiànzài wǒmen kěyǐ zài wǎng shang chá zīliào, mǎi dōngxī, kàn bào,
liáotiān, shènzhì shàng kè. Yǐqián wǒmen gēn guówài de péngyou liánxì
de shíhou yào xiě xìn huò dǎ diànhuà. Xìn zài lù shang yào zǒu hěn duō
tiān, dǎ diànhuà yòu hěn guì. Dànshì xiànzài xiě diànzǐxìn jiù kěyǐ le.
Méi yǒu diànnǎo de rén kěyǐ qù wǎngbā. Zhōngguó de měi ge chéngshì
dōu yǒu wǎngbā, yě hěn piányi, suǒyǐ hěn fāngbiàn.

New Words and Expressions

差不多	chàbuduō	more or less; approximately
华尔街	Huá'ěrjiē	Wall Street
时报	Shíbào	(newspaper title) Times

内容	nèiróng	content
很少	hěn shǎo	seldom
金融	jīnróng	finance
连	lián	even
标题	biāotí	headline
新闻	xīnwén	news
股票	gǔpiào	stock
市场	shìchǎng	market
跌	diē	fall (v)
厉害	lìhai	terrible; formidable
担心	dānxīn	worry
其实	qíshí	actually
平常	píngcháng	ordinarily; generally
国际	guójì	international
国内	guónèi	domestic; national
扔掉	rēng diào	throw away
开	kāi	offer; start (a class or a business)
熟悉	shúxi	familiar
关于	guānyú	about; regarding; concerning
查	chá	check; consult
网站	wǎngzhàn	website
网址	wǎngzhǐ	web address
电子信	diànzǐxìn	email
发	fā	send (email; telegraph, etc.)
退	tuì	reject; return; retreat
垃圾	lājī	garbage

邮件	yóujiàn	mail
爷爷	yéye	(paternal) grandfather
奶奶	nǎinai	(paternal) grandmother
得	děi	have to
软件	ruǎnjiàn	software
互联网	hùliánwǎng	internet
资料	zīliào	information; data; material
聊天	liáotiān	chat
国外	guówài	overseas; abroad
必须	bìxū	must
网吧	wǎngbā	internet café

Supplementary Words and Expressions

订	dìng	subscribe to
日报	rìbào	(newspaper title) daily
报摊	bàotān	newspaper stand
记者	jìzhě	reporter
社论	shèlùn	editorial
商业	shāngyè	business; commerce
本地	běndì	local
书评	shūpíng	book review
杂志	zázhì	magazine
经济	jīngjì	economy; economic; economical
文章	wénzhāng	article

报道	bàodǎo	report (n)
篇	piān	*classifier* (for articles, reports)
头版	tóubǎn	front page
传真	chuánzhēn	fax

Language Points

你每天都看报吗 nǐ měi tiān kàn bào ma?

As an adverb, 都 dōu is often used after such words as 每 měi (every), 全 quán (entire), 各 gè (each) and 任何 rènhé (any) to emphasize inclusiveness:

他们　全　家都　去了博物馆。
Tāmen quán jiā dōu qù le bówùguǎn.
Their whole family went to the museum.

各个大学都给外国学生　开中文　课。
Gè ge dàxué dōu gěi wàiguó xuésheng kāi Zhōngwén kè.
Each (every) university offers Chinese classes to foreign students.

任何　人都　得参加考试。
Rènhé rén dōu děi cānjiā kǎoshì.
Everyone must take the exam.

连标题都没有时间看 lián biāotí dōu méi yǒu shíjiān kàn

连 lián in the sense of *even* is usually used in conjunction with 也 yě, 都 dōu or 还 hái to form a special construction: 连 lián ......也 yě/都 dōu/还 hái to give prominence to the item following 连 lián. This item can be the subject or the object of the sentence:

连 我 都 会 做饭。
Lián wǒ dōu huì zuòfàn.
Even I can cook.

我的 美国 朋友 连 上海话 都 会 说。
Wǒde Měiguó péngyou lián Shànghǎihuà dōu huì shuō.
My American friend can even speak Shanghai dialect.

连 lián can be intensified by another adverb such as 就 jiù:

就 连 我 爷爷, 奶奶 也 会 写 电子信。
Jiù lián wǒ yéye, nǎinai yě huì xiě diànzǐxìn.
Even my grandfather and grandmother can write email.

The sentence cited is an example where the item highlighted is the object of the sentence. It means *(I) don't have time to read even the headlines.*

我不都看 wǒ bù dōu kàn

The position of the negative word in Chinese is very important. Negation extends to the section of the sentence that lies to the right of the negative word, but not the section that lies to the left of the negative word. 我不都看 wǒ bù dōu kàn means *I don't read all of them*; whereas 我都不看 wǒ dōu bù kàn would mean *I read none of them*. This explains why the following sentence for *my wife doesn't work in a school* is incorrect:

我 太太 在 学校 不 工作。
Wǒ tàitai zài xuéxiào bù gōngzuò.

What we should negate in the sentence is 在学校 zài xuéxiào, but since the phrase lies to the left of the negative word, it is not negated. What gets negated by mistake is the verb 工作 gōngzuò. If we force an interpretation, the sentence would mean *my wife is in school, but she doesn't work—implying that she does something else*. The correct sentence should therefore be:

我　太太不在 学校　　工作。
Wǒ tàitai bú zài xuéxiào gōngzuò.

This explains why in the sentence that contains a complement of result, the negative word appears before the complement instead of the verb. For example:

他 修 不 好　你的汽车。
Tā xiū bù hǎo nǐde qìchē.
He can't fix your car.

The logic is that he performed the action of repairing, but didn't produce the result.

Similarly, for the English sentence *I don't think he will come*, the Chinese is

我　想　　他 不 会 来。
Wǒ xiǎng tā bú huì lái.

Again, note the position of the negative word 不 bù. It is illogical to the Chinese to put *don't* before *think*. To do so would imply that the thinking didn't even take place. If you didn't even think, how could you know he was not coming?

In the sentence cited: 我不都看 wǒ bù dōu kàn (I don't read all), the object (newspaper) didn't appear because it appeared earlier. If it is to appear in the sentence, it cannot be placed after the verb 看 kàn. The general rule is that when 都 dōu refers to the object, the object must be placed at the beginning of the sentence:

In response to a question such as

你 喜欢　米饭 还是　面条?
Nǐ xǐhuan mǐfàn háishi miàntiáo?
Do you like rice or noodles?

The object is always left out:

我　都　喜欢。
Wǒ dōu xǐhuan.
I like both.

Or

我　都　不 喜欢。
Wǒ dōu bù xǐhuan.
I like neither.

It is ungrammatical to say

我　都　喜欢　米饭 和 面条。
Wǒ dōu xǐhuan mǐfàn hé miàntiáo.
I like both rice and noodles.

The only way to include the object in the sentence is to relocate it to the beginning of the sentence:

米饭　和面条　　我　都　喜欢。
Mǐfàn hé miàntiáo wǒ dōu xǐhuan.

However, when 都 dōu refers to the subject, the relocation of the object is not needed:

我　和 我 太太 都　喜欢　面条。
Wǒ hé wǒ tàitai dōu xǐhuan miàntiáo.
Both my wife and I like noodles.

新闻 xīnwén and 消息 xiāoxi

These two words are often used interchangeably to mean *news* as transmitted by mass media, but there are three main differences between them. First, 新闻 xīnwén is more inclusive than 消息 xiāoxi. It can be long or short, but 消息 xiāoxi usually refers to brief news dispatches, flashes or releases. Second, a news report (新闻报道 xīnwén bàodào) can not only take the forms of printed language or spoken language, but also of pictures, photos, videos, etc. 消息 xiāoxi, on the other hand, can only take the form of printed or spoken language. Third, 消息 xiāoxi can be used in the sense of *information* or *word* such as

你 有 没 有 他的消息?
Nǐ yǒu méi yǒu tāde xiāoxi?
Do you have any news about him?

新闻 xīnwén does not have this sense.

把广告扔掉 bǎ guǎnggào rēng diào

掉 diào is a verb often used as a complement after a verb to indicate the result, suggesting a clean break. It is very similar to *off* and *away* in the English expressions: *wash off the dirt, turn off the cell phone* and *throw away the garbage*. Chinese examples include:

关 掉 手机
guān diào shǒujī
turn off the cell phone

扔 掉 垃圾
rēng diào lājī
throw away the garbage

客人 走 掉 了。
Kèrén zǒu diào le.
The guest has left.

发电子信 fā diànzǐxìn

Note that the verb for *send* varies depending on what is sent. If what is sent is a regular letter, the verb is 寄 jì. If what is sent is a fax, telegraph or email, the verb is 发 fā.

爷爷，奶奶 yéye, nǎinai

Chinese kinship terminology belongs to a system where each relative is called by a different term. It is much more complicated than that in English, where different types of kin are often called by the same term. Other than the terms for the nuclear family, which we have already learned, here are a few more terms for members of the extended family. The distinction between father's family and mother's family is an important one. The terms below are grouped under these two families:

On father's side:

爷爷
yéye
grandfather

奶奶
nǎinai
grandmother

伯伯
bóbo
uncle (*older than father*)

叔叔
shūshu
uncle (*younger than father*)

On mother's side:

外公
wàigōng
grandfather

外婆
wàipó
grandmother

舅舅
jiùjiu
uncle

姨姨
yíyi
aunt

婶婶
shěnshen
aunt

Hopefully, you have noticed at least two things from the above list. First, uncles on the father's side have to be distinguished in terminology by seniority in relation to one's father, whereas no such distinction is maintained for uncles on the mother's side. Second, no seniority distinction is made for aunts on either the father's side or the mother's side. What conclusion can we draw from this observation? This reveals that in Chinese culture, relatives on the father's side are considered more important than relatives on the mother's side and male relatives are more important than female relatives. This is a phenomenon we call "cultural emphasis," where there are more terms for things considered culturally important.

对了，你打算什么时候去中国学中文 duì le, nǐ dǎsuan shénme shíhou qù Zhōngguó xué Zhōngwén?

对了 duì le is used at the beginning of a sentence in a conversation to introduce a new topic or an afterthought about a topic previously brought up.

我打算放了假就去 wǒ dǎsuan fàng le jià jiù qù.

了 le in the sentence indicates a future completion of action. The sentence of this pattern:

S + V$_1$ + 了 le + (O) + (S) + (就 jiù) V$_2$

This pattern suggests that V$_2$ will take place after V$_1$. If the connection is immediate, 就 jiù will be used. If the both verbs share the same subject, it is always left either before V$_1$ or V$_2$. Other examples include:

今天　下 了 班 我 要　去 同事　 的 家。
Jīntiān xià le bān wǒ yào qù tóngshì de jiā.
I'm going to my colleague's home after I get off work.

昨天　 晚上　　 我 看 了 电影　 就 回　家了。
Zuótiān wǎnshang wǒ kàn le diànyǐng jiù huí jiā le.
I went home right after I saw the movie last night.

This pattern is similar in meaning to the following we have learned, but it is used more frequently in colloquial speech:

S + V$_1$ + (O) + 以后 yǐhòu, (S) + (就 jiù) V$_2$

The sentence cited would be like this, using this pattern:

我 打算　 放假　 以后 就 去。
Wǒ dǎsuan fàngjià yǐhòu jiù qù.
I'm planning to go right after vacation begins.

Note that in this pattern, 了 le is often not used after V$_1$ because the completion of the action is made explicit by the time word 以后 yǐhòu.

Exercises

I. Answer the following questions:

1. 你 每 天 看 报 吗? 你 平常　　 看 什么　 报?
   Nǐ měi tiān kàn bào ma? Nǐ píngcháng kàn shénme bào?

2. 你 对 报 上　 的 什么　 内容　 有　 兴趣?
   Nǐ duì bào shang de shénme nèiróng yǒu xìngqù?

3. 你 今天 看 报 了吗? 今天 报 上 有 什么 重要
Nǐ jīntiān kàn bào le ma? Jīntiān bào shang yǒu shénme Zhòngyào
的 新闻?
de xīnwén?

4. 你 订 杂志 吗? 你 一般 喜欢 看 什么 杂志?
Nǐ dìng zázhì ma? Nǐ yìbān xǐhuan kàn shénme zázhì?

5. 你 每 天 都 收到 很 多 垃圾邮件 吗?
Nǐ měi tiān dōu shōudào hěn duō lājī yóujiàn ma?

6. 你 今天 看 电视 了吗? 今天 有 什么 新闻?
Nǐ jīntiān kàn diànshì le ma? Jīntiān yǒu shénme xīnwén?

7. 你 每 天 都 写 电子信 吗? 给 谁 写?
Nǐ měi tiān dōu xiě diànzǐxìn ma? Gěi shuí xiě?

8. 你 知道 怎么 用 中文 写电子信 吗?
Nǐ zhīdào zěnme yòng Zhōngwén xiě diànzǐxìn ma?

9. 你 在 网 上 买 过 东西 吗? 买 过 什么 东西?
Nǐ zài wǎng shang mǎi guo dōngxi ma? Mǎi guo shénme dōngxi?
你 觉得 方便 不 方便?
Nǐ juéde fāngbiàn bu fāngbiàn?

10. 在 网 上 学 外语 是不 是 一个 好 方法?
Zài wǎng shang xué wàiyǔ shì bu shì yí ge hǎo fāngfǎ?

II. How do you say the following in Chinese?

1. local news, national news, international news, front-page news
2. know about three hundred characters
3. work out almost every day
4. seldom get on the internet

5. very familiar with Beijing
6. movie about China; book about Japan
7. throw away the old newspaper
8. I actually have not heard of that place.
9. He is worried that he might be laid off.
10. The stock market rose (涨 zhǎng) dramatically yesterday.

III. Insert the negative word in the appropriate places according to translations given.

(You may need to make necessary changes after inserting the negative word.)

1. 我 在 家 吃 中饭。
   Wǒ zài jiā chī zhōngfàn.
   I don't eat lunch at home.

2. 他 中文 说 得 流利。
   Tā Zhōngwén shuō de liúlì.
   He doesn't speak fluent Chinese.

3. 医生 治好 了这 个病。
   Yīshēng zhì hǎo le zhè ge bìng.
   The doctor can't cure this disease.

4. 书 在 桌子 上 放 着。
   Shū zài zhuōzi shang fàng zhe.
   The book is not lying on the table.

5. 老师 给 我 打了电话。
   Lǎoshī gěi wǒ dǎ le diànhuà.
   The teacher didn't call me.

6. 学生们　　　都　学习　英语。
   Xuéshengmen dōu xuéxí Yīngyǔ.
   Not all the students study English.

7. 大家　都　喜欢　这　个　餐馆。
   Dàjià dōu xǐhuan zhè ge cānguǎn.
   No one likes this restaurant.

8. 我　想　　那儿有　医院。
   Wǒ xiǎng nàr yǒu yīyuàn.
   I don't think there is a hospital there.

9. 我　觉得　今天　很　冷。
   Wǒ juéde jīntiān hěn lěng.
   I don't feel it is cold today.

10. 火车　　开得快。
    Huǒchē kāi de kuài.
    The train does not travel fast.

IV. Translate the following into Chinese, using 都 dōu in each sentence and paying attention to its various uses:

1. I don't know all the foreign teachers at our school.
2. I don't know any of the foreign teachers at our school.
3. Our teacher gives us a quiz every day without fail.
4. The patient didn't eat anything today.
5. Both of my parents like Japanese food.
6. Does every company have a website?

V. Translate the following into Chinese, using the 连 lián ..... 都 dōu/也 yě structure:

1. Even children know that.
2. I didn't even ask his name.
3. He can't even drive.
4. The doctors are so busy today that they don't even have time to eat lunch.
5. My American friend can even speak Shanghai dialect.

VI. Rewrite the following with the pattern "S + V₁ + 了 le + (O) + (S) + (就 jiù) V₂":

1. 我 到 洛杉矶　 以后 就 给 你 打 电话。
   Wǒ dào Luòshānjī yǐhòu jiù gěi nǐ dǎ diànhuà.

2. 他们　 结婚 以后 要 去 香港　　 度 蜜月。
   Tāmen jiéhūn yǐhòu yào qù Xiānggǎng dù mìyuè.

3. 你下课 以后　 来 图书馆，好　 吗?
   Nǐ xiàkè yǐhòu lǎi túshūguǎn, hǎo ma?

4. 飞机到　 北京　 以后　 就 去 上海。
   Fēijī dào Běijīng yǐhòu jiù qù Shànghǎi.

5. 我们　　 下班　 以后 要 开会。
   Wǒmen xiàbān yǐhòu yào kāihuì.

VII. Translate the following into Chinese:

1. I only read the headlines because I'm too busy.
2. Is there any report in today's paper about their wedding?
3. Do you offer classes on Chinese history?
4. Nowadays, even young children can send email and use the internet.
5. I'm not familiar with the city. Can you tell me something about it?
6. You may find information about the company on the internet.

7. In order to write Chinese using the computer, you need Chinese software.
8. The email address you gave me last time is not correct.
9. My friend is now taking a Chinese class over the internet.
10. There are more internet cafés in China than in America.

VIII. Translate the following into English:

1. 互联网　　给 我们 带 来 了很 大的 方便。　 现在
   Hùliánwǎng gěi wǒmen dài lai le hěn dà de fāngbiàn. Xiànzài
   我们　 在 网　 上　 可以看 到 中国　　的 报纸。
   wǒmen zài wǎng shang kěyǐ kàn dào Zhōngguó de bàozhǐ.

2. 经济 好不 好 和 股票　 市场　　有 很 大 的 关系。
   Jīngjì hǎo bu hǎo hé gǔpiào shìchǎng yǒu hěn dà de guānxì.

3. 我 学 中文　　已经 学 了 两 个 月 了，可是 连 "大" 字
   Wǒ xué Zhōngwén yǐjīng xué le liǎng ge yuè le,　 kěshì lián "dà" zì
   都 不 会 写。
   dōu bú huì xiě.

4. 我 妈妈 买 到 报纸　 后 作 的第一 件 事 就 是 看
   Wǒ māma mǎi dào bàozhǐ hòu zuò de dì yī jiàn shì jiù shì kàn
   广告。
   guǎnggào.

5. 中国　　的 很 多 网站　 是 用　 中文　　写 的，不
   Zhōngguó de hěn duō wǎngzhàn shì yòng Zhōngwén xiě de,　 bù
   懂　 中文　　的人 看 不 懂。
   dǒng Zhōngwén de rén kàn bù dǒng.

6. 她 每 天 收到　各 种　电子信，但是 没 有　时间　全
   Tā měi tiān shōudào gè zhǒng diànzǐxìn, dànshì méi yǒu shíjiān quán
   看。
   kàn.

7. 我　给 他 发的电子信　都　被 退 回　来了，讨厌　极了。
   Wǒ gěi tā fā de diànzǐxìn dōu bèi tuì huí lai le, tǎoyàn jíle.

8. 很　多　人 工作　太 忙，　只 能　在 坐 地铁上班　　的
   Hěn duō rén gōngzuò tài máng, zhǐ néng zài zuò dìtiě shàngbān de
   时候看报。
   shíhu kàn bào.

9. 小　报 上　的 本地 新闻　比大 报 多。
   Xiǎo bào shang de běndì xīnwén bǐ dà bào duō.

10. 我 对　股票　一点儿兴趣　也 没 有。体育新闻　更
    Wǒ duì gǔpiào yìdiǎnr xìngqù yě méi yǒu. Tǐyù xīnwén gèng
    有意思。
    yǒuyìsī.

IX. Topics for discussion and writing:

1. Talk or write about a piece of news you read in today's paper or
   heard on TV.
2. Talk or write about your experience using the internet.

English Translation of the Text

Conversations

A: Do you read the newspaper every day?
B: Almost every day.
A: What paper do you usually read?

: I usually read the *Wall Street Journal*. Its contents have a lot to do with my job. How about you? Do you read the *Wall Street Journal*?
: I seldom read the *Wall Street Journal*. I'm not interested in finance and investment. I usually read the *New York Times*. Do you read the *New York Times*?
: I sometimes do.
: Did you read the *New York Times* today?
: No. I'm so busy today that I don't even have time to read the headlines. Is there any important news there today?
: The stock market has dropped sharply. It fell almost two hundred points yesterday.
: Are you worried?
: I'm very worried. I have a lot of stocks.

*   *   *   *   *

: Do you like to read Sunday's paper?
: Yes, I do. As a matter of fact, I only read Sunday's paper. I'm so busy during the week that I don't even have time to read the paper.
: There is too much stuff in Sunday's paper. Do you read everything?
: I don't read everything. Besides international and national news, I mostly read sports news. How about you? Do you like to read Sunday's paper?
: I don't. I only read headlines. I think there are too many ads there.
: That's true. The first thing that I do after I buy the Sunday paper is to throw away the ads.

*   *   *   *   *

: I'd like to go to study Chinese in China. Can you recommend a school?
: Many universities in China offer Chinese classes for foreign students. I left China many years ago and am not familiar with the schools there.
: How do I find information about these schools?
: You can check on the internet. Every university has a website.
: Do you know their web addresses?

B: I know some. I'll check when I go home. I'll let you know by email. How does that sound?

A: Great, thank you. Do you know my email address?

B: I have your email address, but the email messages that I sent you recently were all returned. I wonder why?

A: Sorry. I changed my address, but I forgot to tell you.

B: Why did you change your address?

A: Every day, I would receive too much junk mail. It was very annoying.

B: By the way, when are you planning to go to study Chinese in China?

A: I'm planning to leave as soon as vacation starts.

*   *   *   *   *

A: Are your parents also in the U.S.?

B: No, they are in China.

A: Do you often write to them?

B: I often wrote them in the past, but now I usually call them or email them.

A: Do your parents also know how to write emails?

B: Yes, even my grandparents also know how to write emails.

A: Do you use Chinese or English when you write them?

B: They don't understand English, so I write them in Chinese, but when I write to my friends, I use English.

A: Can I write emails to you in Chinese?

B: No problem, but you need to have Chinese software.

A: I have "NJStar." Is it okay?

B: Yes. Why don't you try it as soon as you go home?

Reading Passage

The internet and email have brought us a lot of convenience. We can now check information, go shopping, read newspapers, chat or even take a class on the internet. When we wanted to get in touch with our friends abroad in the past, we would need to write letters and make phone calls. It took days for letters to arrive and making phone calls was also expensive. We can do this by email now. People who do not have a

omputer can go to the internet café. Every city in China has internet
afés, which are quite inexpensive. For this reason, it is quite convenient.

10

CHINA & AMERICA

Conversations

A：麦克，好 久没 见。你最近 有 没 有 什么 新闻?
Màikè, hǎo jiǔ méi jiàn. Nǐ zuìjìn yǒu méi yǒu shénme xīnwén?

B：有， 我们 全 家去了中国。
Yǒu, wǒmen quán jiā qù le Zhōngguó.

A：真的 吗? 你们 玩儿 得 怎么样?
Zhēnde ma? Nǐmen wánr de zěnmeyàng?

B：我们 玩儿 得 非常 高兴。
Wǒmen wánr de fēicháng gāoxìng.

A：这 是 你们 第一 次去中国 吗?
Zhè shì nǐmen dìyī cì qù Zhōngguó ma?

B：这 是 我 和 我 太太 第二次去 中国， 但是 对 孩子们
Zhè shì wǒ hé wǒ tàitai dì'èr cì qù Zhōngguó, dànshì duì háizimen

来 说， 这 是 第一 次。
lái shuō, zhè shì dìyī cì.

A: 你 和 你 太太 上　 次 是 什么　 时候　 去 中国　　 的?
Nǐ hé nǐ tàitai shàng cì shì shénme shíhou qù Zhōngguó de?

B: 我们　 是 十 年　 前 去 的。
Wǒmen shì shí nián qián qù de.

A: 你 觉得 中国　　 在 这 十 年　 里 有 没 有　 变化?
Nǐ juéde Zhōngguó zài zhè shí nián lǐ yǒu méi yǒu biànhuà?

B: 变化　　 太大 了。 很　 多 我 以前 去 过 的 地 方 变　 得
Biànhuà tài dà le. Hěn duō wǒ yǐqián qù guo de dìfang biàn de
完全　 不 一样 了。
wánquán bù yíyàng le.

A: 你们　 这 次 去 了 中国　　 的 什么　 地方?
Nǐmen zhè cì qù le Zhōngguó de shénme dìfāng?

B: 我们　 去 了 香港、　 西安、北京、 上海。　 我们　 还 游
Wǒmen qù le Xiānggǎng, Xī'ān, Běijīng, Shànghǎi. Wǒmen hái yóu
了 长江。
le Chángjiāng.

A: 这些　 地方，你 最 喜欢　 哪儿?
Zhèxiē dìfang, nǐ zuì xǐhuan nǎr?

B: 我 都 喜欢。 每 一 个 地方 都 有　 自己 的 特点。
Wǒ dōu xǐhuan. Měi yí ge dìfang dōu yǒu zìjǐ de tèdiǎn.

A: 你能　 不 能　 说说　　 它们 的 特点?
Nǐ néng bu néng shuōshuo tāmende tèdiǎn?

B：当然。　香港　　跟　纽约　　一样，是　一个 国际 城市，　你
Dāngrán. Xiānggǎng gēn Niǔyuē yíyàng, shì yí ge guójì chéngshì, nǐ
能　看　到　各 个 国家　的 人。西安 是 中国　　历史 的
néng kàn dào gè ge guójiā de rén. Xī'ān shì Zhōngguó lìshǐ de
发源地，我　最 喜欢　那儿的博物馆。
fāyuándì, wǒ zuì xǐhuan nàr de bówùguǎn.

A：北京　给 你 留下 了什么　　印象？
Běijīng gěi nǐ liú xià le shénme yìnxiàng?

B：北京　给 我 留下 了很 深　的 印象。　这 是 一个 伟大
Běijīng gěi wǒ liú xià le hěn shēn de yìnxiàng. Zhè shì yí ge wěidà
的 城市。　长城　　是 个 奇迹，故宫　也是 了不起 的
de chéngshì. Chángchéng shì ge qíjī, Gùgōng yě shì liǎobuqǐ de
建筑。
jiànzhú.

A：你 觉得 上海　　怎么样？
Nǐ juéde Shànghǎi zěnmeyàng?

B：在 我们　去 的城市　　中，　上海　　是 我 最 喜欢　的
Zài wǒmen qù de chéngshì zhōng, Shànghǎi shì wǒ zuì xǐhuan de
城市。　我 觉得 上海　　比 中国　　别的 城市　　发展 得
chéngshì. Wǒ juéde Shànghǎi bǐ Zhōngguó biéde chéngshì fāzhǎn de
都　快。
dōu kuài.

A：你 能　不 能　具体说说　　上海　　有 什么　变化？
Nǐ néng bù néng jùtǐ shuōshuo Shànghǎi yǒu shénme biànhuà?

B：上海　　在过去 几 年 里建 了无数 的高 楼，建 了两
Shànghǎi zài guòqù jǐ nián lǐ jiàn le wúshù de gāo lóu, jiàn le liǎng
条 地铁，　三 座 大桥，一条 高速 公路，一个新
tiáo dìtiě xiàn, sān zuò dàqiáo, yì tiáo gāosù gōnglù, yí ge xīn

机场。 建 这么 多 的东西 在 美国 至少 也要 二十
jīcháng. Jiàn zhème duō de dōngxi zài Měiguó zhìshǎo yě yào èrshí
年。
nián.

A: 你 知道 上海 的 City Bird 是 什么 吗?
Nǐ zhīdào Shànghǎi de City Bird shì shénme ma?

B: 不 知道, 是 什么?
Bù zhīdào, shì shénme?

A: 是 crane。
Shì crane.

B: 我 怎么 没 听说 过? 为什么 是 crane?
Wǒ zěnme méi tīngshuō guo? Wèishénme shì crane?

A: 这 个 crane 不是 鸟, 是 起重机。你 知道 吗? 全 世界
Zhè ge crane bú shì niǎo, shì qǐzhòngjī. Nǐ zhīdào ma? Quán shìjiè
百分 之 三十 的 起重机 都 在上海。
bǎifēn zhī sānshí de qǐzhòngjī dōu zài Shànghǎi.

B: 真 有意思。我们 打算 明年 再去 上海 一 次。
Zhēn yǒuyìsī. Wǒmen dǎsuan míngnián zài qù Shànghǎi yí cì.
对了,你的老家 在 哪儿?
Duìle, nǐde lǎojiā zài nǎr?

A: 我的 老家 在 南京。
Wǒde lǎojiā zài Nánjīng.

B: 南京 现在 怎么样?
Nánjīng xiànzài zěnmeyàng?

213

A: 南京 发展 得 没有 上海 快，但是 也有 很 大的
Nánjīng fāzhǎn de méiyou Shànghǎi kuài, dànshì yě yǒu hěn dà de
变化。
biànhuà.

　　　*　　　*　　　*　　　*　　　*

A: 老 李，你 来 美国 多少 年 了?
Lǎo Lǐ,　nǐ lái Měiguó duōshao nián le?

B: 我 来 美国 已经 三十 多 年 了。
Wǒ lái Měiguó yǐjīng sānshí duō nián le.

A: 你 一直 住 在 西 海岸 吗?
Nǐ yìzhí zhù zài xī hǎi'àn ma?

B: 不，我 是 三 年 前 退休 时 从 东 海岸 搬 到 西
Bù, wǒ shì sān nián qián tuìxiū shí cóng dōng hǎi'àn bān dào xī
海岸 的。
hǎi'àn de.

A: 那你 一定 对 东 海岸 和西海岸 都 很 熟悉 了。
Nà nǐ yídìng duì dōng hǎi'àn hé xī hǎi'àn dōu hěn shúxi le.

B: 我 知道 一些，不能 说 很 熟悉。你有 问题 吗?
Wǒ zhīdào yìxiē,　bù néng shuō hěn shúxi.　Nǐ yǒu wèntí ma?

A: 对，你能 不能 给 我 介绍 一下儿东 海岸 有 什么
Duì, nǐ néng bu néng gěi wǒ jièshào yíxiàr dōng hǎi'àn yǒu shénme
著名 的 城市?
zhùmíng de chéngshì?

B: 可以。东 海岸 是 美国 的 发源地。著名 的 城市
Kěyǐ.　Dōng hǎi'àn shì Měiguó de fāyuándì. Zhùmíng de chéngshì

有 华盛顿， 费城， 纽约， 波士顿， 等等。
yǒu Huáshèngdùn, Fèichéng, Niǔyuē, Bōshìdùn, děngdeng.

A: 这些 城市 我 都 听说 过，特别是 华盛顿，
Zhèxiē chéngshì wǒ dōu tīngshuō guo, tèbié shì Huáshèngdùn,
美国 的首都。
Měiguó de shǒudū.

B: 美国 和中国 有 一点儿不一样。 中国 的 首都
Měiguó hé Zhōngguó yǒu yìdiǎnr bù yíyàng. Zhōngguó de shǒudū
在 最 大的 城市， 而 华盛顿 比 纽约 和 波士顿
zài zuì dà de chéngshì, ér Huáshèngdùn bǐ Niǔyuē hé Bōshìdùn
这样 的 城市 小 得 多。
zhèyàng de chéngshì xiǎo de duō.

A: 我 也 注意 到 了。西海岸 有 什么 著名 的 城市？
Wǒ yě zhùyì dào le. Xī hǎi'àn yǒu shénme zhùmíng de chéngshì?

B: 西海岸 最 著名 的 城市 有 洛杉矶，旧金山 和
Xī hǎi'àn zuì zhùmíng de chéngshì yǒu Luòshānjī, Jiùjīnshān hé
西雅图。
Xīyǎtú.

A: 旧金山 大还是 洛杉矶 大？
Jiùjīnshān dà háishi Luòshānjī dà?

B: 旧金山 大，但是 洛杉矶 更 大。
Jiùjīnshān dà, dànshì Luòshānjī gèng dà.

A: 人口 呢？
Rénkǒu ne?

B: 旧金山 的人口 也没有 洛杉矶 的 人口 多。
Jiùjīnshān de rénkǒu yě méiyou Luòshānjī de rénkǒu duō.

A: 你 是 不 是 更 喜欢 洛杉矶?
   Nǐ shì bu shì gèng xǐhuan Luòshānjī?

B: 不 是, 我 更 喜欢 旧金山。 旧金山 靠 海, 夏天
   Bú shì, wǒ gèng xǐhuan Jiùjīnshān. Jiùjīnshān kào hǎi, xiàtiān
   没有 洛杉矶 那么 热。
   méiyou Luòshānjī nàme rè.

Reading Passage

我虽然在旧金山住了十年，但是从来没有去过那儿的中国城。上个周末我跟我的中国朋友去了一次中国城，今天我们又去了一次。我们先去参观了中国城的博物馆，然后去了一家书店，那里有各种各样的中文书和词典。从书店出来后，我们又去了一家百货公司，里面有很多中国产品，价钱非常便宜。我们最后在一家餐馆里吃了Dim Sum。我从来没有见过这种吃法。我觉得很有意思。 我要介绍我的朋友们都来中国城看一看。

Wǒ suīrán zài Jiùjīnshān zhù le shí nián, dànshì cónglái méiyou qù guo nàr de Zhōngguóchéng. Shàng ge zhōumò wǒ gēn wǒde Zhōngguó péngyou qù le yí cì Zhōngguóchéng, jīntiān wǒmen yòu qù le yí cì. Wǒmen xiān qù cānguān le Zhōngguóchéng de bówùguǎn, ránhòu qù le yì jiā shūdiàn, nàlǐ yǒu gèzhònggèyàng de Zhōngwén shū hé cídiǎn. Cóng shūdiàn chū lai hòu, wǒmen yòu qù le yì jiā bǎihuògōngsī, lǐmiàn yǒu hěn duō Zhōngguó chǎnpǐn, jiàqián fēicháng piányi. Wǒmen zuìhòu zài yì jiā cānguǎn lǐ chī le Dim Sum. Wǒ cónglái méiyou jiàn guo zhè zhòng chīfǎ. Wǒ juéde hěn yǒuyìsi. Wǒ yào jièshào wǒde péngyǒumen dōu lái Zhōngguóchéng kàn yi kàn.

New Words and Expressions

久	jiǔ	long time
变化	biànhuà	change (v & n)
变	biàn	change (v)
完全	wánquán	completely; entirely
游	yóu	tour (v)
长江	Chángjiāng	Yangtze River
特点	tèdiǎn	characteristic; trait; feature
发源地	fāyuándì	place of origin
印象	yìnxiàng	impression
伟大	wěidà	great
深	shēn	deep
长城	Chángchéng	Great Wall
奇迹	qíjī	miracle
故宫	gùgōng	Palace Museum/Forbidden City
建筑	jiànzhù	architecture
发展	fāzhǎn	develop; development
具体	jùtǐ	in detail; concrete
建	jiàn	build; construct; erect
无数	wúshù	numerous
座	zuò	*classifier* (for bridge, building, mountain, monument, etc.)
桥	qiáo	bridge
高速公路	gāosù gōnglù	highway; expressway
至少	zhìshǎo	at least

鸟	niǎo	bird
起重机	qǐzhòngjī	crane (construction machinery)
百分之	bǎifēn zhī	percent
老家	lǎojiā	hometown
一直	yìzhí	all along; straight; always
海岸	hǎi'àn	coast
搬	bān	move (house or an object)
著名	zhùmíng	famous; renowned
费城	Fèichéng	Philadelphia
波士顿	Bōshìdùn	Boston
首都	shǒudū	capital (of a country)
西雅图	Xīyǎtú	Seattle
更	gèng	even more
人口	rénkǒu	population
靠	kào	next to; near
又	yòu	again
参观	cānguān	visit
先 ……然后	xiān … ránhòu	first … then
产品	chǎnpǐn	product

Language Points

好久没见 hǎo jiǔ méi jiàn

This is the expression that the English *long time no see* is derived from. It can also be expressed as 好久不见 hǎo jiǔ bú jiàn. In the expression, 好 hǎo is not an adjective meaning *good*, rather it is an adverb meaning

218

quite a few; quite some; a good number of. It is often used before words such as 几 jǐ, 些 xiē and 多 duō:

好 几本 日语 书
hǎo jǐ běn Rìyǔ shū
several Japanese books

好 些 年
hǎo xiē nián
many years

好 多 人
hǎo duō rén
many people

你最近有没有什么新闻 nǐ zuìjìn yǒu méi yǒu shénme xīnwén?

Questions may arise as to what type of interrogative sentence this is. It looks like a Yes/No question from the phrase 有没有 yǒu méi yǒu, but there is also the presence of the Wh-word 什么 shénme. This 什么 shénme is actually not an interrogative word. It is a pronoun with the meaning of *some, something, any* or *anything.* The cited sentence means *have you had any news (to share) recently.* Similar examples are:

他 在 吃 什么 东西。
Tā zài chī shénme dōngxi.
He is eating something.

我 最近 没有 看 什么 电影。
Wǒ zuìjìn méiyou kàn shénme diànyǐng.
I haven't seen any movies recently.

Ways to indicate comparisons

The following patterns and structures are commonly used to indicate comparisons in Chinese:

1. A + 和 hé/跟 gēn B + 一样 yíyàng

This is equivalent to "A is the same as B" in English. Since 和 hé/跟 gēn B modifies 一样 yíyàng, it is placed before it:

我的　电话　号码　和 传真　　号码　一样。
Wǒde diànhuà hàomǎ hé chuánzhēn hàomǎ yíyàng.
My telephone number and my fax number are the same.

In the negative sentence, 不 bù can be placed either before 和 hé/跟 gēn or before 一样 yíyàng:

我的 专业　　跟 我女朋友　　的 专业　　不 一样。
Wǒde zhuānyè gēn wǒ nǚpéngyou de zhuānyè bù yíyàng.

我的 专业　　不 跟 我 女朋友　　的 专业　　一样。
Wǒde zhuānyè bù gēn wǒ nǚpéngyou de zhuānyè yíyàng.
My major is not the same as my girlfriend's major.

2. A + 和 hé/跟 gēn B + 一样 yíyàng + Adj.

This is equivalent to "A is as Adj. as B" in English.

和 hé/跟 gēn B and 一样 yíyàng both modify the adjective and both are therefore placed before it. Examples include:

香港　　的东西 和 上海　　的 东西　一样　贵。
Xiānggǎng de dōngxi hé Shànghǎi de dōngxi yíyàng guì.
Things in Hong Kong are as expensive as things in Shanghai.

中国　　菜跟 日本 菜 一样 好吃。
Zhōngguó cài gēn Rìběn cài yíyàng hǎochī.
Chinese food tastes as good as Japanese food.

The negative form of the pattern is:
A + 没有 méiyou + B (+ 那么 nàme) + Adj.

This is equivalent to A is not as/so Adj. as B in English. Other examples include:

旧金山　 的 人口　没有　 洛杉矶　 的 人口　多。
Jiùjīnshān de rénkǒu méiyou Luòshānjī de rénkǒu duō.
The population of San Francisco is not as large as that of Los Angeles.

今天 没有　　昨天　那么　热。
Jīntiān méiyou zuótiān nàme rè.
It is not so hot today as it was yesterday.

3. A + 比 bǐ B + Adj.

This is equivalent to "A is Adj. (in comparative-degree form) than B" in English.

比 bǐ in the pattern is a preposition with the meaning of *in comparison with*. Since the prepositional phrase "比 bǐ" modifies the adjective, it is placed before it. Other examples include:

我 妈妈　 的 身体 比 我 爸爸 的 身体 好。
Wǒ māma de shēntǐ bǐ wǒ bàba de shēntǐ hǎo.
My mother's health is better than my father's health.

对 她 来 说，　法语比西班牙语　难。
Duì tā lái shuō, Fǎyǔ bǐ Xībānyáyǔ nán.
As far as she is concerned, French is more difficult than Spanish.

Note that the adjective in Chinese does not need to be further modified by words like *more* or undergo an inflectional change by affixing *–er* as in the English examples of *more beautiful*; *prettier*. The comparative meaning is indicated by the structure itself.

The adjective in A + 比 bǐ B + Adj. cannot be modified by an intensifying adverb such as 很 hěn, 非常 fēicháng or 太 tài. For example, we can't say:

北京　的 冬天　比上海　　的 冬天　　很　冷。
Běijīng de dōngtiān bǐ Shànghǎi de dōngtiān hěn lěng.
Beijing's winter is much colder than Shanghai's winter.

我们的　学校　比 他们的　学校　　太大。
Wǒmende xuéxiào bǐ tāmende xuéxiào tài dà.
Our school is much larger than their school.

However the adjective can be modified by the following two adverbs— 更 gèng and 还 hái—with additional implied meanings:

他 比我 更　高。
Tā bǐ wǒ gèng gāo.
He is even taller than I am.

The implied meaning is that both people are tall.

这　个 国家　的 人口　比那 个 国家　的 人口　还 多。
Zhè ge guójiā de rénkǒu bǐ nà ge guójiā de rénkǒu hái duō.
This country's population is even larger than that country's population.

The implied meaning is that the population in both countries is large.

The implied meaning is absent if the adverb is not used.

In the negative form, 不 bù is to be placed before 比 bǐ rather than the adjective.

here are three variations of the pattern A + 比 bǐ B + Adj.:

) A + 比 bǐ B + Adj. + 得多 de duō

Vhile the adjective cannot be modified by an intensifying adverb as
ointed above, it can be followed by a complement of degree 得多 de
uō, as in this pattern. 得多 de duō in the pattern functions to emphasize
ıe adjective with the meaning of *much more*:

〈机比火车　快　得　多。
ēijī bǐ huǒchē kuài de duo.
he plane is much faster than the train.

丰盛顿　　比 纽约　和　波士顿　这样　　的 城市　　小　得　多。
Iuáshèngdùn bǐ Niǔyuē hé Bōshìdùn zhèyàng de chéngshì xiǎo de duō.
Vashington is much smaller than cities such as New York and Boston.

) A + V. + 得 de + 比 bǐ B + Adj.

ı this case, the comparison between two things is about the verb
omplement, which is in the form of an adjective:

二海　　发展　得 比中国　　别的 城市　都　快。
hànghǎi fāzhǎn de bǐ Zhōngguó biéde chéngshì dōu kuài.
hanghai has developed faster than all the other cities in China.

ote the variation of the pattern when the verb is a transitive one. In this
ase, the verb needs to be repeated: A + V. + O. + V. + 得 de 比 bǐ B +
.dj.:

ı说　中文　　说　得比 我　好。
ā shuō Zhōngwén shuō de bǐ wǒ hǎo.
Ie speaks Chinese better than I do.

The negative form is A + V. (+ O. + V.) + 得 de + 没有 méiyou + B (+ 那么 nàme) + Adj.

我　说　　中文　　　说　　得没有　　他那么　好。
Wǒ shuō Zhōngwén shuō de méiyou tā nàme hǎo.
I don't speak Chinese as well as he does.

c) A + 比 bǐ B + Adj. + Quantifier

The quantifier specifies the difference between two items:

我　比 我　太太　大 三 岁。
Wǒ bǐ wǒ tàitai dà sān suì.
I'm three years older than my wife.

他们　公司　　比 我们　　公司　　多　五　百　个 人。
Tāmen gōngsī bǐ wǒmen gōngsī duō wǔ bǎi ge rén.
Their company has five hundred more people than our company does.

咖啡 比 茶　贵 两　毛　钱。
Kāfēi bǐ chá guì liǎng máo qián.
Coffee is twenty cents more expensive than tea.

4. A + Adj., B + 更 gèng + Adj.

更 gèng (more) is not necessary before the adjective in A + 比 bǐ B + Adj., but there is a difference when 更 gèng is used. In 洛杉矶比旧金山 大 Luòshānjī bǐ Jiùjīnshān dà (Los Angeles is larger than San Francisco) there is no implication that Los Angeles is large. It simply says that in comparison with San Francisco, Los Angeles is large. Maybe both cities are small. In 洛杉矶比旧金山更大 Luòshānjī bǐ Jiùjīnshān gèng dà (Los Angeles is even larger than San Francisco), there is clearly the implication that both cities are large.

全世界百分之三十的起重机都在上海 quán shìjiè bǎifēnzhī
sānshí de qǐzhòngjī dōu zài Shànghǎi

One of the cardinal principles mentioned in *Beginner's Chinese* that
govern the word order in Chinese is that larger units precede smaller
units and general precedes specific. This is also referred to as whole
preceding part. There are two examples in this lesson.

To indicate a percentage, Chinese places percent (whole) before the
specific number (part): 百分之十 bǎifēn zhī shí (10%), 百分之九十五
bǎifēn zhī jiǔshí wǔ (95%). 之 zhī in the expression is a remnant of
classic Chinese with the same meaning as the possessive 的 de except
that it is only used in set expressions or structures.

The way to express a fraction is similar to that for percentage:

十分 之 一
shífēn zhī yī
one-tenth

五分 之 四
wǔfēn zhī sì
four-fifths

三分 之 二
sānfēn zhī èr
two-thirds

The other example in the lesson that shows the whole-part sequence is:

这些 地方，你最 喜欢 哪儿?
Zhèxiē dìfang, nǐ zuì xǐhuan nǎr?
Of these places, which one do you like the most?

This is the only order possible in Chinese.

中国的首都在最大的城市，而华盛顿比纽约和波士顿这样的城市小得多 Zhōngguó de shǒudū zài zuì dà de chéngshì, ér Huáshèngdùn bǐ Niǔyuē hé Bōshìdùn zhèyàng de chéngshì xiǎo de duō

而 ér is a conjunction used to indicate a contrast, similar to *whereas* in English. The sentence means *the capital of China is in the largest city, whereas Washington is much smaller than cites such as New York and Boston.*

我们明年要再去上海 wǒmen míngnián yào zài qù Shànghǎi **and** 今天我们又去了一次 jīntiān wǒmen yòu qù le yí cì

Both 再 zài and 又 yòu are equivalent to *again* in English, but there is an important difference. While 再 zài indicates the intention of repeating an action in the future, 又 yòu indicates that the repletion of the action has already taken place. The first cited sentence means *we'll go to Shanghai again next year* (the intended repetition has not taken place) and the second cited sentence means *we went there again today* (the repeated action has already taken place).

我从来没有见过这种吃法 wǒ cónglái méiyou jiàn guo zhè zhǒng chīfǎ

从来 cónglái is usually used in the negative sentence with the meaning of *never*. It can be used either with 不 bù or 没有 méiyou. When used with 不 bù, it is a timeless statement of fact. When used with 没有 méiyou, it indicates a situation that never materialized in the past. As such, the verb is always followed by the aspect marker 过 guo. See for example:

我　从来　不喜欢　功夫　电影。
Wǒ cónglái bù xǐhuan gōngfu diànyǐng.
I never liked kung fu movies.

226

我　从来　没有　看　过　功夫　电影。
Wǒ cónglái méiyou kàn guo gōngfu diànyǐng.
I have never seen a kung fu movie.

法 fǎ in 吃法 chī fǎ is short for 方法 fāngfǎ (way; method). It can be used with a variety of words meaning a particular way of doing things such as 说法 shuōfǎ (way of saying things), 想法 xiǎngfǎ (way of thinking) and 做法 (zuòfǎ).

Exercises

I. Answer the following questions:

1. 你有　没有　去过　中国？　　你是什么　时候　去的？你
   Nǐ yǒu méiyou qù guo Zhōngguó? Nǐ shì shénme shíhou qù de? Nǐ
   去过　中国　　的什么　　地方？
   qù guò Zhōngguó de shénme dìfang?

2. 你去过　欧洲　吗？你去过　欧洲　的什么　　地方？
   Nǐ qù guo Ōuzhōu ma? Nǐ qù guo Ōuzhōu de shénme dìfang?

3. 你的　老家　在　哪儿？那里最近　发展　得　怎么样？
   Nǐde lǎojiā zài nǎr? Nàlǐ zuìjìn fāzhǎn de zěnmeyàng?

4. 你去过　中国城　　　吗？你对中国城　　　的印象
   Nǐ qù guo Zhōngguóchéng ma? Nǐ duì Zhōngguóchéng de yìnxiàng
   怎么样？
   zěnmeyàng?

5. 你觉得　你住　的城市　　这　十　年　里有　没　有　变化？
   Nǐ juéde nǐ zhù de chéngshì zhè shí nián lǐ yǒu méi yǒu biànhuà?

有什么变化?
Yǒu shénme biànhuà?

6. 华盛顿　　有　什么　特点?
   Huáshèngdùn yǒu shénme tèdiǎn?

7. 上海　　这 几年 有　什么　变化?
   Shànghǎi zhè jǐ nián yǒu shénme biànhuà?

8. 北京　的什么　有名?
   Běijīng de shénme yǒumíng?

9. 你 吃 过 Dim Sum 吗? 你 觉得 这 种　吃法 怎么样?
   Nǐ chī guo Dim Sum ma? Nǐ juéde zhè zhòng chīfǎ zěnmeyàng?

10. 你 最近 有 没 有 什么　新闻?
    Nǐ zuìjìn yǒu méi yǒu shénme xīnwén?

II. How do you say the following:

1. characteristics of the old architecture
2. impression of the city
3. have been to this place numerous times
4. in the world
5. at least three days
6. completely changed
7. 50%, 75%, 100%, 1/4, 3/5, 2/3
8. have never read this book
9. detailed data
10. went to the bank again today

III. Comparative sentences

A. Fill in the blanks with appropriate adjectives:

1. 咖啡 比 茶 _____。
   Kāfēi bǐ chá _____.

2. 飞机票 比 汽车 票_____。
   Fēijīpiào bǐ qìchē piào _____.

3. 今年 的 经济 比去年 的 经济 _____ 得 多。
   Jīnnián de jīngjì bǐ qùnián de jīngjì _____ de duō.

4. 法国 菜比 英国 菜 _____。
   Fǎguó cài bǐ Yīngguó cài _____.

5. 你学 开 车 比 我 学 得 _____。
   Nǐ xué kāi chē bǐ wǒ xué de _____.

B. Rewrite the following sentences using comparative structures:

1. 哥哥 十 岁，弟弟 八 岁。
   Gēge shí suì, dìdi bā suì.

2. 这 条 高速 公路 长，那 条 高速 公路 短。
   Zhè tiáo gāosù gōnglù cháng, nà tiáo gāosù gōnglù duǎn.

3. 我们 班 有 三十 个 学生， 他们 班 有 二十五 个
   Wǒmen bān yǒu sānshí ge xuésheng, tāmen bān yǒu èrshí wǔ ge
   学生。
   xuésheng.

4. 这 个 汉字 难，那 个 汉字 不 难。
   Zhè ge hànzì nán, nà ge hànzì bù nán.

5. 他 走 得 快，我 走 得慢。
   Tā zǒu de kuài, wǒ zǒu de màn.

6. 姐姐 写 字写 得 好看， 妹妹 写 字写 得 不 好看。
   Jiějie xiě zì xiě de hǎokàn, mèimei xiě zì xiě de bù hǎokàn.

7. 中国 的 产品 便宜，日本 的 产品 贵。
   Zhōngguó de chǎnpǐn piányi, Rìběn de chǎnpǐn guì.

8. 我 妈妈 做 菜 做 得 好，我 爸爸 做 菜 做 得 不 好。
   Wǒ māma zuò cài zuò de hǎo, wǒ bàba zuò cài zuò de bù hǎo.

9. 今天 的 股票 市场 跌 得 厉害，昨天 的 股票 市场
   Jīntiān de gǔpiào shìchǎng diē de lìhài, zuótiān de gǔpiào shìchǎng
   跌 得 不 厉害。
   diē de bú lìhài.

10. 我 家 有 五 口 人，他家 也有 五 口 人。
    Wǒ jiā yǒu wǔ kǒu rén, tā jiā yě yǒu wǔ kǒu rén.

IV. Fill in the blanks with 又 yòu or 再 zài as appropriate:

1. 你的话 我 不 懂， 请 你 _____ 说 一遍。
   Nǐde huà wǒ bù dǒng, qǐng nǐ _____ shuō yíbiàn.

2. 客户 昨天 打来 一个电话， 今天 _____ 打 来 一个
   Kèhù zuótiān dǎ lái yí ge diànhuà, jīntiān _____ dǎ lái yí ge
   电话。
   diànhuà.

3. 他们 今年 去 过 亚洲， 明年 要 _____ 去 一次。
   Tāmen jīnnián qù guo Yàzhōu, míngnián yào _____ qù yí cì.

4. 这 本 书 我 很 多 年 前 看 过，但 都 忘 了。

Zhè běn shū wǒ hěn duō nián qián kàn guo, dàn dōu wàng le.

我 最近 ＿＿＿ 看 了 一遍。

Wǒ zuìjìn ＿＿＿ kàn le yī biàn.

5. 我的 病 已经 好 了，不用 ＿＿＿ 去 看 医生 了。

Wǒde bìng yǐjing hǎo le, búyòng ＿＿＿ qù kàn yīshēng le.

V. Translate the following into Chinese:

1. We had a good time in Europe.

2. As far as I am concerned, Xi'an is the most interesting place in China.

3. Great changes have taken place in China in the past twenty years.

4. Of all the places we have been to, my wife likes Paris (巴黎 Bālí) the most.

5. I didn't like the restaurant we went to last night.

6. It takes at least fifteen hours to go to Hong Kong from Shanghai by train.

7. One-fourth of the people in the world are Chinese.

8. My wife and I moved to Florida (佛罗里达 Fúluólǐdá) five years ago when I retired.

9. He has lived in Japan all his life and is very familiar with the country.

10. Some people don't like changes. They don't think new things are as good as old things.

VI. Translate the following into English:

1. 中文 的特点 是 语法 简单，但是 发音 难。

Zhōngwén de tèdiǎn shì yǔfǎ jiǎndān, dànshì fāyīn nán.

2. 北京　现在　有　五　条　环城 (beltway) 高速　公路。
   Běijīng xiànzài yǒu wǔ tiáo huánchéng　　gāosù gōnglù.

3. 二十　年　前，上海　　的浦东　是农村 (countryside)，但
   Èrshí nián qián, Shànghǎi de Pǔdōng shì nóngcūn,　　　　dàn
   现在　那儿有　无数　的高　楼，是一个全　新的地方。
   xiànzài nàr yǒu wúshù de gāo lóu, shì yí ge quán xīn de dìfang.

4. 如果　要看　中文　　报纸，至少　要认识　两　千　个
   Rúguǒ yàokàn Zhōngwén bàozhǐ, zhìshǎo yào rènshì liǎng qiān gè
   中国　　字。
   Zhōngguó zì.

5. 很　多　西方 (Western) 人喜欢 Dim Sum，　因为　他们　虽然
   Hěn duō Xīfāng　　　　rén xǐhuan Dim Sum, yīnwéi tāmen suīrán
   不知道　菜的名字，但是　可以选　自己喜欢　的菜。
   bù zhīdào cài de míngzì, dànshì kěyǐ xuǎn zìjǐ xǐhuan de cài.

6. 我很　喜欢　纽约。在纽约　你能　见到从　各个
   Wǒ hěn xǐhuan Niǔyuē. Zài Niǔyuē nǐ néng jiàn dào cóng gè ge
   国家　来的人。你能　听　到各种　语言。
   guójiā lái de rén. Nǐ néng tīng dào gè zhòng yǔyán.

7. 中国　　学生　　是这个学校　外国　学生　　的百分
   Zhōngguó xuésheng shì zhè ge xuéxiào wàiguó xuésheng de bǎifēn
   之二十。
   zhī èrshí.

8. 我　先生　　对金融　没　有　兴趣，从来　不看《华尔街
   Wǒ xiānsheng duì jīnróng méi yǒu xìngqù, cónglái bú kàn Huá'ěrjiē
   日报》。
   Rìbào.

9. 我 有 十年 没有 见 到 他 了。他 变 得 跟 以前
   Wǒ yǒu shí nián méiyou jiàn dào tā le.　Tā biàn de gēn yǐqián
   完全 不 一样 了。
   wánquán bù yíyàng le.

10. 他们 结婚 后 一直 住 在 波士顿。
    Tāmen jiéhūn hòu yìzhí zhù zài Bōshìdùn.

VII. Topics for discussion and writing:

1. 在 你 去 过 的 国家 和 城市 中， 哪 一个 给 你 留 下 了
   Zài nǐ qù guo de guójiā hé chéngshì zhōng, nǎ yí ge gěi nǐ liú xià le
   最 深 的 印象?
   zuì shēn de yìnxiàng?

2. 你 去 过 中国城 吗? 请 谈谈 你 对 中国城
   Nǐ qù guo Zhōngguóchéng ma? Qǐng tántan nǐ duì Zhōngguóchéng
   的 印象。
   de yìnxiàng.

English Translation of the Text

Conversations

A: Mike, long time no see. Any news recently?
B: Sure. Our whole family went to China.
A: Really? Did you have a good time?
B: We had a wonderful time.
A: Was this your first visit to China?
B: This was the second time for me and my wife to visit China, but it was the first time for the children.
A: When did you and your wife go to China last time?
B: We went there ten years ago.

A: Did you notice any changes in China during these ten years?

B: The changes are tremendous. Many places I had been to before have completely changed.

A: Where in China did you go this time?

B: We went to Hong Kong, Xi'an, Beijing and Shanghai. We also went on a Yangtze River cruise.

A: Which of these places do you like the most?

B: I like them all. Each place has its own characteristics.

A: Can you say something about their characteristics?

B: Of course. Hong Kong, like New York, is a cosmopolitan city, where you can see people from various countries. Xi'an is the origin of Chinese history. I like the museums there the most.

A: What impression did Beijing leave you with?

B: Beijing left a deep impression on me. It is a great city. The Great Wall is a miracle and the Forbidden City is also an amazing work of architecture.

A: How did you like Shanghai?

B: Of the cities we went to, I like Shanghai the most. I find that Shanghai has developed faster than any other city in China.

A: Can you be specific about the changes in Shanghai?

B: In the last few years, Shanghai built numerous high-rise buildings, two subway lines, three bridges, a highway, and a new airport. It would take at least twenty years in the U.S. to build so many things.

A: Do you know what the city bird is for Shanghai?

B: No, I don't. What is it?

A: It is the crane.

B: How come I have never heard of it? Why is it the crane?

A: This crane is not a bird. It is the mechanical crane. Do you know 30% of the cranes in the world are in Shanghai?

B: That is so interesting! We are planning to go to Shanghai again next year. By the way, what's your hometown?

A: My hometown is Nanjing.

B: How is Nanjing now?

A: Although Nanjing didn't develop as fast as Shanghai, there are also major changes there.

*   *   *   *   *

A: Lao Li, how long have you been in the U.S.?

B: I have been in the U.S. for more than thirty years.

A: Have you always lived on the West Coast?

B: No, it was only three years ago when I retired that I moved from the East Coast to the West Coast.

A: You must be familiar with both the East Coast and the West Coast.

B: I know a few things, but I can't say I'm very familiar with them. Do you have any questions?

A: Yes. Can you tell me something about the famous cities on the East Coast?

B: Sure. The East Coast is the origin of the United States. Famous cities include Washington, Philadelphia, New York, Boston and so on.

A: I have heard of all these cities, particularly Washington, capital of the United States.

B: There is a little difference between the United States and China. China's capital is in the largest city, but Washington is much smaller than cities like New York and Boston.

A: I've also noticed that. What are the famous cities on the West Coast?

B: The most famous cities on the West Coast are Los Angeles, San Francisco and Seattle.

A: Which is larger, San Francisco or Los Angeles?

B: San Francisco is large, but Los Angeles is larger.

A: How about the population?

B: The population in San Francisco is not as large as that in Los Angeles.

A: Is it true that you like Los Angeles better?

B: No, I actually like San Francisco better. It is on the sea and not as hot as Los Angeles during the summer.

Reading Passage

Although I have lived in San Francisco for ten years, I had never been to its Chinatown. I went with my Chinese friend last weekend and we went there again today. First we went to visit the museum in Chinatown and then we went to a bookstore, where there are all kinds of Chinese books and dictionaries. After we came out of the bookstore, we went to a department store. There are many Chinese products there, which are very cheap. Finally, we ate Dim Sum in a restaurant. I have never seen such a way of eating. I find it very interesting. I'll ask all of my friends to come for a visit to Chinatown.

Glossary for *Beginner's Chinese*

Character	Pinyin	English	Lesson
澳州	Àozhōu	Australia	9
八	bā	eight	4
爸爸	bàba	father	1
百	bǎi	hundred	4
百货公司	bǎi huò gōngsi	department store	7
白酒	báijiǔ	liquor	8
半	bàn	half	5
办公室	bàngōngshì	office	3
报纸	bàozhǐ	newspaper	6
包子	bāozi	steamed stuffed bun	8
杯	bēi	cup	7
北	běi	north	10
北京	Běijīng	Beijing	3
本	běn	*classifier*	4
比	bǐ	than	10
冰	bīng	ice	10
博物馆	bówùguǎn	museum	3
不	bù	not	1
不一定	bù yídìng	not necessarily	7
菜	cài	dishes	8
菜单	càidān	menu	8
餐馆	cānguǎn	restaurant	2
餐巾	cānjīn	napkin	8
厕所	cèsuǒ	restroom	3
叉	chā	fork	8
茶	chá	tea	8

长	cháng	long	7
常	cháng	often	9
常常	chángchang	often	10
炒	chǎo	fry	8
车	chē	vehicle	9
城	chéng	town; city	3
衬衫	chènshān	shirt; blouse	7
吃	chī	eat	2
出	chū	go out	10
穿	chuān	wear; put on	7
船	chuán	boat; ship	9
春天	chūntiān	spring	10
出租汽车	chūzū qìchē	taxi	9
次	cì	time (occurrence)	8
从	cóng	from	6
从...到...	cóng .... dào ...	from ... to ...	9
错	cuò	wrong; bad	1
大	dà	big	10
大概	dàgài	probably	9
带	dài	carry	10
当然	dāngrán	of course	7
但是	dànshì	but	6
单位	dānwèi	workplace	3
刀	dāo	knife	8
导游	dǎoyóu	guide	9
大学	dàxué	university	3
大学生	dàxuésheng	college student	4
大衣	dàyī	coat	7
的	de	*possessive marker*	2
德国	Déguó	Germany	6
等	děng	wait	7
第	dì	*ordinal number indicator*	7

点	diǎn	o'clock	5
电车	diànchē	trolley-bus	9
电话	diànhuà	telephone	3
电视	diànshì	television	6
电影	diànyǐng	movie	8
电影院	diànyǐngyuàn	movie theater	3
弟弟	dìdi	younger brother	1
地方	dìfang	place	9
地铁	dìtiě	subway	9
东	dōng	east	10
懂	dǒng	understand	6
冬天	dōngtiān	winter	10
东西	dōngxi	things; stuff	7
都	dōu	both; all	2
度	dù	degree	10
短	duǎn	short	7
对	duì	right; correct	8
对不起	duìbuqǐ	sorry	5
度假	dùjià	go on vacation	10
多	duō	many; much	7
多少	duōshao	*question word about numbers*	4
二	èr	two	4
儿子	érzi	son	2
法国	Fǎguó	France	6
饭店	fàndiàn	hotel	3
翻译	fānyì	translate	6
法语	Fǎyǔ	French language	6
肥	féi	loose	7
飞机	fēijī	airplane	9
飞机场	fēijīchǎng	airport	3
非洲	Fēizhōu	Africa	9

239

分	fēn	minute	5
分	fēn	monetary unit	7
风	fēng	wind	10
分钟	fēnzhōng	minute	9
付	fù	pay	7
服装店	fúzhuāngdiàn	clothing store	7
告诉	gàosu	tell	7
高兴	gāoxìng	happy	1
个	gè	*classifier*	4
哥哥	gēge	older brother	1
给	gěi	give	8
公安局	gōng'ānjú	police station	3
工人	gōngrén	factory worker	2
公司	gōngsi	company	2
工艺品	gōngyìpǐn	handicraft product	7
公园	gōngyuán	park	3
工作	gōngzuò	work	3
广东	Guǎngdōng	Canton (the province)	6
广州	Guǎngzhōu	Canton (the city)	6
关门	guān mén	close; closed (for business)	7
贵	guì	distinguished; expensive	2
顾客	gùkè	customer	7
过	guo	*aspect marker*	8
过	guò	celebrate	9
国	guó	country	6
国语	guóyǔ	Mandarin	6
海关	hǎiguān	customs	9
海滩	hǎitān	beach	10
海鲜	hǎixiān	seafood	8
杭州	Hángzhōu	Hangzhou	9
好	hǎo	good	1

号	hào	number	5
好象	hǎoxiàng	seem	8
喝	hē	drink	8
和	hé	and	4
很	hěn	very	1
合适	héshì	suitable	7
红	hóng	red	8
红酒	hóngjiǔ	wine	8
话	huà	speech; dialect	6
换	huàn	change; exchange	7
欢迎	huānyíng	welcome	8
华盛顿	Huáshèngdùn	Washington	9
华氏	huáshì	Fahrenheit	10
滑雪	huáxuě	ski	10
会	huì	know how to	6
回答	huídá	answer	6
会话	huìhuà	conversation	6
火车站	huǒchēzhàn	train station	3
护照	hùzhào	passport	9
几	jǐ	*question word about numbers*	4
鸡	jī	chicken	8
家	jiā	home; family	3
价格	jiàgé	price	7
件	jiàn	*classifier*	7
教	jiāo	teach	6
叫	jiào	call	2
教堂	jiàotáng	church	3
饺子	jiǎozi	dumpling	8
加州	Jiāzhōu	California	3
街	jiē	street	9
姐姐	jiějie	older sister	1
结束	jiéshù	end	5

鸡蛋	jīdàn	egg	8
季节	jìjié	season	10
极了	jíle	extremely	8
近	jìn	close	9
警察	jǐngchá	police; policeman	9
经理	jīnglǐ	manager	2
纪念品	jìniànpǐn	souvenir	7
今年	jīnnián	this year	5
今天	jīntiān	today	5
九	jiǔ	nine	4
旧金山	Jiùjīnshān	San Francisco	3
觉得	juéde	feel; think	7
句子	jùzi	sentence	6
咖啡	kāfēi	coffee	7
开	kāi	operate; drive	9
开门	kāi mén	open (for business)	7
开始	kāishǐ	begin	5
看	kàn	read; see	2
看书	kànshū	read	5
烤鸭	kǎoyā	roast duck	8
课	kè	class; lesson	5
可能	kěnéng	maybe	9
客气	kèqi	polite; formal	2
课文	kèwén	text	6
可以	kěyǐ	may	7
空调	kōngtiáo	air conditioning	10
口	kǒu	*classifier*	4
块	kuài	*monetary unit*	7
筷子	kuàizi	chopsticks	8
裤子	kùzi	pants	7
辣	là	spicy	8

来	lái	come	1
老板	lǎobǎn	boss	2
老师	lǎoshī	teacher	1
雷	léi	thunder	10
累	lèi	tired	1
冷	lěng	cold	10
离	lí	away from	9
凉	liáng	cool	10
练习	liànxí	exercise	6
零	líng	zero	4
历史	lìshǐ	history	4
六	liù	six	4
溜冰	liūbīng	ice skate	10
楼	lóu	floor; building	6
路	lù	road; route	9
洛杉矶	Luòshānjī	Los Angeles	3
绿	lǜ	green	8
旅馆	lǚguǎn	hotel	9
律师	lǜshī	lawyer	1
旅行	lǚxíng	travel	9
旅行社	lǚxíngshè	travel agency	9
吗	ma	*particle*	1
买	mǎi	buy	7
卖	mài	sell	7
妈妈	māma	mother	1
马马虎虎	mǎma hūhu	so-so	1
慢	màn	slowly	6
忙	máng	busy	1
曼哈顿	Mànhādūn	Manhattan	3
毛	máo	*monetary unit*	7
毛衣	máoyī	sweater	7
帽子	màozi	hat	7

每	měi	every; each	5
没	méi	not	2
没关系	méi guānxii	That's all right.	5
美国	Měiguó	United States	1
妹妹	mèimei	younger sister	1
美元	Měiyuán	U.S. dollars	7
美洲	Měizhōu	America	9
们	men	*plural suffix*	2
面包	miànbāo	bread	8
面条	miàntiáo	noodle	2
米饭	mǐfàn	cooked rice	8
明年	míngnián	next year	5
明天	míngtiān	tomorrow	5
名字	míngzi	name	2
哪	nǎ	which	4
那	nà	that	5
奶奶	nǎinai	paternal grandmother	4
哪儿	nǎr	what place	3
那儿	nàr	there	3
南	nán	south	10
男	nán	male	2
男孩	nánhái	boy	4
南京	Nánjīng	Nanjing	3
呢	ne	*particle*	1
能	néng	can	7
你	nǐ	you	1
年	nián	year	9
您	nín	you (*polite form*)	2
牛奶	niúnǎi	milk	8
牛肉	niúròu	beef	8
纽约	Niǔ Yuē	New York	3
暖	nuǎn	warm	10

暖气	nuǎnqì	heat; heating	10
女	nǔ	female	2
女儿	nǚ'er	daughter	2
女孩	nǚhái	girl	4
欧洲	Ōuzhōu	Europe	9
盘子	pánzi	plate	8
朋友	péngyou	friend	2
便宜	piányi	cheap	7
票	piào	ticket	9
啤酒	píjiǔ	beer	8
瓶	píng	bottle	8
普通话	pǔtōnghuà	Mandarin	6
七	qī	seven	4
骑	qí	ride	9
汽车站	qìchēzhàn	bus stop	3
起床	qǐchuáng	get up	5
千	qiān	thousand	4
钱	qián	money	7
签证	qiānzhèng	visa	9
晴	qíng	sunny	10
请 ...... 吃饭	qǐng ... chīfàn	invite sb. to dinner	8
青岛	Qīngdǎo	Qingdao	8
请问	qǐng wèn	May I ask ...	3
秋天	qiūtiān	fall	10
去	qù	go	1
去年	qùnián	last year	5
热	rè	hot	10
人	rén	person; people	2
人民币	Rénmínbì	Renminbi (*Chinese currency*)	7

认识	rènshi	know	1
日本	Rìběn	Japan	1
日语	Rìyǔ	Japanese	5
肉	ròu	meat	8
三	sān	three	4
伞	sǎn	umbrella	10
闪电	shǎndiàn	lightning	10
上	shàng	up	9
上班	shàngbān	go to work	5
商店	shāngdiàn	store	3
上海	Shànghǎi	Shanghai	3
上午	shàngwǔ	morning	5
上学	shàng xué	go to school	9
生词	shēngcí	new word	6
圣诞节	Shèngdànjié	Christmas	9
生日	shēngrì	birthday	5
什么	shénme	what	2
摄氏	shèshì	Centigrade	10
十	shí	ten	4
是	shì	be	1
试	shì	try	7
市场	shìchǎng	market	7
时候	shíhou	time	5
时间	shíjiān	time	5
市长	shìzhǎng	mayor	2
市中心	shì zhōngxīn	city center; downtown	9
收	shōu	accept	7
瘦	shòu	tight	7
手表	shǒubiǎo	watch	5
售货员	shòuhuòyuán	sales clerk	7
书	shū	book	2
双	shuāng	pair	7

书店	shūdiàn	bookstore	7
书法	shūfǎ	calligraphy	6
谁	shuí	who	4
水果	shuǐguǒ	fruit	8
睡觉	shuìjiào	sleep	5
说	shuō	speak; say	6
四	sì	four	4
四川	Sìchuān	Sichuan	6
酸	suān	sour	8
素菜	sùcài	vegetable dish	8
苏州	Sūzhōu	Suzhou	9
他	tā	he	1
她	tā	she	1
它	tā	it	1
太	tài	too	3
台风	táifēng	typhoon	10
汤	tāng	soup	8
糖	táng	sugar	8
甜	tián	sweet	8
天	tiān	day; weather	5
天气	tiānqì	weather	10
天堂	tiāntáng	paradise	9
条	tiáo	*classifier*	7
听	tīng	listen	6
听说	tīngshuō	it is said	7
同事	tóngshì	colleague	2
图书馆	túshūguǎn	library	3
外国	wàigōng	maternal grandfather	4
外国	wàiguó	foreign country	6
外国人	wàiguórén	foreigner	6
外婆	wàipó	maternal grandmother	4

247

外语	wàiyǔ	foreign language	6
碗	wǎn	bowl	8
玩	wán	play	9
万	wàn	ten thousand	4
晚饭	wǎnfàn	dinner	5
晚上	wǎnshang	evening	5
袜子	wàzi	socks	7
位	wèi	*classifier*	8
味道	wèidào	taste	8
为什么	wèishénme	why	10
问题	wèntí	question	2
我	wǒ	I	1
五	wǔ	five	4
雾	wù	fog	10
西	xī	west	10
下	xià	down; fall	9
下班	xiàbān	get off work	5
咸	xián	salty	8
想	xiǎng	would like; think	9
香港	Xiānggǎng	Hong Kong	6
先生	xiānsheng	Mr.; husband	1
现在	xiànzài	now	5
小	xiǎo	small	10
小费	xiǎofèi	tip	8
小姐	xiǎojiě	Miss	1
小时	xiǎoshí	hour	9
小学生	xiǎoxuésheng	elementary school student	4
校长	xiàozhǎng	school principal/president	2
夏天	xiàtiān	summer	10
下午	xiàwǔ	afternoon	5
西班牙语	Xībānyáyǔ	Spanish language	6
写	xiě	write	6

鞋店	xiédiàn	shoe store	7
谢谢	xièxie	thank (you)	2
鞋子	xiézi	shoes	7
喜欢	xǐhuan	like	1
新	xīn	new	9
姓	xìng	family name	2
行李	xíngli	luggage	9
星期	xīngqī	week	5
新闻	xīnwén	news	6
信用卡	xìnyòngkǎ	credit card	7
学	xué	study	3
雪	xuě	snow	10
学生	xuésheng	student	1
学习	xuéxí	study	4
学校	xuéxiào	school	2
盐	yán	salt	8
羊肉	yángròu	lamb	8
颜色	yánsè	color	7
要	yào	want; take (time; etc.)	7
要看	yào kàn	It depends	7
亚洲	Yàzhōu	Asia	9
也	yě	also	1
夜里	yèlǐ	night	5
爷爷	yéye	paternal grandfather	4
一	yī	one	4
一般	yìbān	generally; usually	5
一遍	yíbiàn	once	6
一点儿	yìdiánr	a little	6
一定	yídìng	certainly; definitely	8
衣服	yīfu	clothes	7
一共	yígòng	altogether	7
阴	yīn	cloudy	10

249

英国	Yīngguó	England	6
英语	Yīngyǔ	English language	6
银行	yínháng	bank	2
医生	yīshēng	doctor	1
意思	yìsi	meaning	6
医院	yīyuàn	hospital	3
用	yòng	use	6
有	yǒu	have; there is/are	2
有的	yǒu de ... yǒude		
有的		some ... others ...	7
有点儿	yǒu diǎnr	a little	8
邮局	yóujú	post office	3
有名	yǒumíng	famous	8
邮票	yóupiào	stamps	7
有时	yǒushí ... yǒushí		
有时		sometimes ... sometimes	5
鱼	yú	fish	8
雨	yǔ	rain	10
远	yuǎn	far	3
预报	yùbào	forecast	10
月	yuè	month	5
语法	yǔfǎ	grammar	6
云	yún	cloud	10
语言	yǔyán	language	6
雨衣	yǔyī	raincoat	10
在	zài	in; at	3
再	zài	again	6
再见	zàijiàn	good-bye	2
早饭	zǎofàn	breakfast	5
早上	zǎoshang	early morning	5
杂志	zázhì	magazine	6
怎么	zěnme	how	6

怎么样	zěnmeyàng	how is ...?	1
炸	zhà	deep fry	8
张	zhāng	*classifier*	7
帐单	zhàngdàn	check; bill	8
找	zhǎo	look for; find	9
这	zhè	this	1
这儿	zhèr	here	3
只	zhǐ	only	6
知道	zhīdao	know	2
支票	zhìpiào	check	7
种	zhǒng	kind; variety	6
中饭	zhōngfàn	lunch	5
中国	Zhōngguó	China	1
中文	Zhōngwén	Chinese language	2
中午	zhōngwǔ	noon	5
中学生	zhōngxuésheng	secondary school student	4
周末	zhōumò	weekend	5
住	zhù	live	3
猪肉	zhūròu	pork	8
字	zì	Chinese character	6
字典	zìdiǎn	dictionary	6
自行车	zìxíngchē	bicycle	9
走	zǒu	walk	9
最	zuì	most	7
最好	zuìhǎo	best; had better	10
作	zuò	do	4
坐	zuò	sit; take (the bus; etc)	8
做饭	zuòfàn	cook	8
昨天	zuótiān	yesterday	5

Glossary for *Intermediate Chinese*

Character	Pinyin	English	Lesson
安全	ānquán	safe	3
澳门	Àomén	Macao	1
把	bǎ	*preposition*	4
把 …… 作为	bǎ … zuòwéi	treat … as	6
摆	bǎi	place (v); put; arrange	7
百分之	bǎifēn zhī	percent	10
拜年	bài nián	wish happy new year	7
搬	bān	move (houses)	10
班	bān	class	2
半岛	bàndǎo	peninsula	1
办法	bànfǎ	way; means; method	2
帮助	bāngzhù	help; assist	2
半职	bànzhí	part time	8
包	bāo	bag	7
被	bèi	*passive marker*	8
弊	bì	drawback; disadvantage	3
变	biàn	change (v)	10
变化	biànhuà	change (v & n)	10
标题	biāotí	headline	9
别人	biérén	other people	3
病	bìng	become sick; sickness	6
比如说	bǐrúshuō	for example	2
必须	bìxū	must	5
毕业	bìyè	graduate (v)	5
毕业生	bìyèshēng	graduate (n)	5
博士	bóshì	Ph.D.; doctoral degree (holder)	5
波士顿	Bōshìdùn	Boston	10

部	bù	*classifier*	3
部	bù	part; section	4
不是…… 而是	bú shì ... ér shì	not ... but rather	6
不同	bùtóng	difference; different	7
不要紧	bú yàojǐn	doesn't matter; not important	6
布置	bùzhì	arrange (furniture); decorate	4
猜	cāi	guess	7
才	cái	as late as; not until	2
参观	cānguān	visit	10
参加	cānjiā	participate (in); join; take part (in)	1
查	chá	check; consult	9
差	chà	poor	2
差不多	chàbuduō	more or less; approximately	9
长城	Chángchéng	Great Wall	10
长江	Chángjiāng	Yangtze River	4
产品	chǎnpǐn	product	10
炒饭	chǎofàn	fried rice	3
成绩	chéngjī	grade; result; achievement	5
城市	chéngshì	city	2
重新	chóngxīn	again; anew	4
出	chū	go out; exit	5
窗子	chuāngzi	window	4
除了	chúle	besides; in addition to	1
春节	Chūnjié	Spring Festival; Chinese New Year	7
除夕	chúxī	eve	7
打	dǎ	make (a phone call); hit	3
大道	dàdào	avenue	3
大多数	dàduōshù	majority; most of	5
答复	dáfù	reply (n & v)	8
带	dài	bring; take; carry	3
大家	dàjiā	everyone; people	7

当	dāng	become; act as	1
当时	dāngshí	at that time	1
担心	dānxīn	worry	9
但愿如此	dànyuàn rú cǐ	hope so	5
到	dào	arrive; reach	2
到时	dàoshí	at that (future) time	1
大人	dàrén	adult; grownup	7
打扫	dǎsǎo	clean; sweep	7
打算	dǎsuan	plan (v & n)	1
得	de	*verb complement marker*	2
得到	dédào	receive; obtain; acquire	7
得	děi	have to	9
等等	děngděng	so on	5
电脑	diànnǎo	computer	3
电子信	diànzǐxìn	email	9
跌	diē	fall (v)	9
地图	dìtú	map	4
地址	dìzhǐ	address	3
豆腐	dòufu	tofu	3
读	dú	study; read aloud	5
锻炼	duànliàn	physical exercise; workout	6
对	duì	to; for, regarding	3
对 ...... 来说	duì ... lái shuō	as far as ... is concerned; for	7
俄国	Éguó	Russia	4
发	fā	send (email, etc.)	9
放	fàng	put; lay	4
方便	fāngbiàn	convenient; convenience	3
放假	fàngjià	have a vacation; have a day off	7
方式	fāngshì	method; form; way	6
房子	fángzi	house	7
房租	fángzū	rent	8

发烧	fāshāo	have a fever	6
发音	fāyīn	pronounce; pronunciation	2
发源地	fāyuándì	place of origin	10
发展	fāzhǎn	develop; development	10
费城	Fèichéng	Philadelphia	10
分	fēn	divide; separate; distinguish	5
分	fèn	*classifier*	3
风景	fēngjǐng	scenery	1
付	fù	pay (v)	8
福利	fúlì	benefits	8
感觉	gǎnjué	feeling	6
感冒	gǎnmào	cold; have a cold	6
高	gāo	high; tall	5
高速公路	gāosù gōnglù	highway; expressway	10
给	gěi	to; give	3
跟	gēn	with; and	2
更	gèng	even more	8
各种各样	gèzhǒnggèyàng	various; all kinds of	6
工程师	gōngchéngshī	engineer	8
恭喜发财	gōngxǐ fācái	Happy New Year	7
工资	gōngzī	salary	8
够	gòu	enough	2
挂	guà	hang	4
关掉	guān diào	turn off (a device)	3
广告	guǎnggào	advertisement; commercial	8
关于	guānyú	about; regarding; concerning	9
故宫	gùgōng	Palace Museum/Forbidden City	10
国际	guójì	international	9
国家	guójiā	country	4
过敏	guòmǐn	allergic	6
国内	guónèi	domestic; national	9
国庆节	Guóqìngjié	National Day; Independence Day	7

国外	guówài	overseas; abroad	9
股票	gǔpiào	stock	9
还	hái	also; additionally	1
还	hái	fairly; passably; still	2
海岸	hǎi'àn	coast	10
韩国	Hánguó	(South) Korea	4
汉字	hànzì	Chinese characters	2
好	hǎo	become well; recover	6
号码	hàomǎ	(telephone) number	3
好运	hǎo yùn	good luck	7
和 …… 有关系	hé...yǒu guānxi	have to do with	8
很少	hěn shǎo	seldom	9
后边	hòubian	behind; at the back of	4
花	huā	spend (time or money)	7
华尔街	Huá'ěrjiē	Wall Street	9
环境	huánjìng	environment	2
回	huí	return (to a place); reply	1
会	huì	will (modal verb)	1
互联网	hùliánwǎng	internet	9
婚礼	hūnlǐ	wedding	1
或	huò	or	5
互相	hùxiāng	each other; mutually	2
建	jiàn	build; construct; erect	10
检查	jiǎnchá	exam; examination	6
健身房	jiànshēnfáng	gym	6
建筑	jiànzhù	architecture	10
教	jiāo	teach	1
交换	jiāohuàn	exchange (v & n)	7
教室	jiàoshì	classroom	4
交谈	jiāotán	converse; chat	1
交通工具	jiāotōnggōngjù	means of transportation	6

接	jiē	pick up; answer (a phone call)	3
节	jié	period (of a class)	5
解雇	jiěgù	lay off	8
结婚	jiéhūn	get married	1
节日	jiérì	holiday; festival	7
介绍	jièshào	introduce; introduction	7
介意	jièyì	mind (v)	1
机会	jīhuì	opportunity	2
进	jìn	enter; come in	3
进步	jìnbù	progress (n & v)	2
经验	jīngyàn	experience	8
尽快	jìnkuài	as soon as possible	3
金融	jīnróng	finance	9
久	jiǔ	long time	10
就	jiù	right away	1
就	jiù	as early as; already; then	2
继续	jìxù	continue	5
决定	juédìng	decide; decision	5
具体	jùtǐ	in detail; concrete	10
举行	jǔxíng	hold	1
开	kāi	offer; start (a class or a business)	9
开会	kāi huì	attend a meeting	3
开药	kāi yào	prescribe medicine	6
靠	kào	next to; near	10
考虑	kǎolǜ	consider	8
考试	kǎoshì	exam (v); examination	5
客户	kèhù	client	1
可能	kěnéng	maybe; possible	6
咳嗽	késòu	cough (n & v)	6
可以	kěyǐ	pretty good; not bad	2
口语	kǒuyǔ	spoken language	2
快 ...... 了	kuài ... le	about to	1

垃圾	lājī	garbage	9
劳动节	Láodòngjié	Labor Day	7
老家	lǎojiā	hometown	10
老年人	lǎoniánrén	old people	6
利	lì	benefit; advantage	3
连	lián	even	9
练	liàn	practice (v)	2
脸色	liǎnsè	look (n); complexion	6
联系	liánxì	contact (v & n)	3
练习	liànxí	practice (n & v)	2
聊	liáo	chat	3
了不起	liǎobuqǐ	amazing; remarkable; extraordinary	2
了解	liáojiě	gain understanding	8
聊天	liáotiān	chat	9
里边	lǐbian	in; inside	4
列	liè	list (v)	8
厉害	lìhai	terrible; formidable	9
离开	líkāi	leave	8
留	liú	leave (a message)	3
流利	liúlì	fluent	2
礼物	lǐwù	gift; present	7
利用	lìyòng	make use of; take advantage of	8
慢跑	mànpǎo	jogging; jog	6
美	měi	pretty; beautiful	1
美术	měishù	fine art	5
门	mén	door; gate	4
蒙古	Měnggǔ	Mongolia	4
秘书	mìshū	secretary	8
蜜月	mìyuè	honeymoon	1
拿	ná	take, hold	4
奶奶	nǎinai	(paternal) grandmother	9

哪里	nǎlǐ	*polite response to a compliment*	2
那么	nàme	in that case; like that	5
难	nán	hard; difficult	2
内容	nèiróng	content	9
年级	niánjí	(of school) grade	5
鸟	niǎo	bird	10
宁静	níngjìn	quiet; tranquil	4
旁边	pángbiān	beside; next to	4
片	piàn	*classifier*	6
平常	píngcháng	ordinarily; generally	9
普遍	pǔbiàn	popular	3
普通	pǔtōng	common; ordinary	3
前边	qiánbian	in front of; ahead of	4
墙	qiáng	wall	4
桥	qiáo	bridge	10
气功	qìgōng	system of deep breathing exercises	6
奇迹	qíjī	miracle	10
请帖	qǐngtiě	invitation card/letter	1
其实	qíshí	actually	9
起重机	qǐzhòngjī	crane (construction machinery)	10
全	quán	completely; entirely	6
全职	quánzhí	full time	8
让	ràng	ask (sb. to do sth.); let	3
认	rèn	recognize	2
扔掉	rēng diào	throw away	9
人口	rénkǒu	population	10
人们	rénmen	people	6
人事部	rénshìbù	personnel department	8
认真	rènzhēn	conscientious; conscientiously	8
容易	róngyì	easy	5

软件	ruǎnjiàn	software	9
如果	rúguǒ	if	2
散步	sànbù	take a walk	6
沙发	shāfā	sofa	4
上边	shàngbian	on; over; above	4
上网	shàng wǎng	get on the internet	2
上学	shàngxué	attend school; go to school	2
深	shēn	deep	10
生	shēng	give birth to; be born; produce	7
生活	shēnghuo	livelihood; life	8
生意	shēngyì	business	8
什么样	shénmeyàng	what kind of	8
申请	shēnqǐng	apply; application	8
身体	shēntǐ	health; body	6
甚至	shènzhì	even	3
室	shì	room; suite	3
事	shì	matter; thing (to do)	1
时报	Shíbào	(newspaper title) Times	9
市场	shìchǎng	market	9
世界	shìjiè	world	4
收到	shōudào	receive	1
首都	shǒudū	capital (of a country)	10
手机	shǒujī	cell phone	3
属	shǔ	born in the Chinese zodiac year of	7
树	shù	tree	7
书包	shūbāo	book bag	4
舒服	shūfu	feeling well; comfortable	6
书架	shūjià	bookshelf	4
硕士	shuòshì	master's degree (holder)	5
暑期	shǔqī	summertime; summer vacation	2
熟悉	shúxi	familiar	9
数学	shùxué	mathematics	5

私	sī	private	1
送	sòng	deliver; take sb. or sth. to	3
岁	suì	(of age) year	7
随时	suíshí	any time	3
所以	suǒyǐ	therefore	5
太极拳	tàijíquán	taiji (tai chi)	6
讨厌	tǎoyàn	annoying; be annoyed by	3
特别	tèbié	especially; particularly	6
特点	tèdiǎn	characteristic; trait; feature	10
疼	téng	hurt; pain (v)	6
提供	tígòng	provide	8
体育	tǐyù	physical education	5
通过	tōngguò	pass	5
头	tóu	head	6
团聚	tuánjù	get together	7
退	tuì	reject; return; retreat	9
推荐	tuījiàn	recommend; recommendation	6
退休金	tuìxiūjīn	pension	8
外语	wàiyǔ	foreign language	5
完	wán	finish (v)	6
网吧	wǎngba	internet café	9
王国	wángguó	kingdom	6
网站	wǎngzhàn	website	9
网址	wǎngzhǐ	web address	9
完全	wánquán	completely; entirely	10
喂	wéi	hello	3
伟大	wěidà	great	10
为了	wèile	for; for the sake of; in order to	6
问	wèn	ask	8
文化	wénhuà	culture	8
文凭	wénpíng	diploma; degree	8

文学	wénxué	literature	5
无数	wúshù	numerous	10
下边	xiàbian	under; below; underneath	4
先	xiān	first	4
先 ……然后	xiān … ránhòu	first … then	10
先 …… 再	xiān … zài	first … then	5
象	xiàng	resemble; similar to	7
消息	xiāoxi	news; word	8
习惯	xíguàn	habit; custom	7
兴趣	xìngqu	interest	8
辛苦	xīnkǔ	hard (adj); toilsome	5
新郎	xīnláng	bridegroom	1
新娘	xīnniáng	bride	1
新闻	xīnwén	news	9
休息	xiūxi	rest; relax	6
西雅图	Xīyǎtú	Seattle	10
西医	xīyī	Western medicine	6
选	xuǎn	select; choose	5
学历	xuélì	academic credential; resume	8
学期	xuéqī	semester	4
需要	xūyào	need	8
严格	yángé	rigorous; strict; tough	5
研究生	yánjiūshēng	graduate student	5
炎症	yánzhèng	infection	6
要求	yāoqiú	requirement; require	8
爷爷	yéye	(paternal) grandfather	9
一边 ... 一边	yìbiān…yìbiān	simultaneously; at the same time	3
以后	yǐhòu	after; later; in the future	1
一会儿	yíhuìr	a little while	3
已经	yǐjīng	already	2
一 ... 就 ...	yí ... jiù ...	as soon as	8

应该	yīnggāi	should; ought to	2
因为	yīnwéi	because	7
印象	yìnxiàng	impression	10
以前	yǐqián	before; previously; in the past; ago	1
一些	yìxiē	somewhat; a little	2
一样	yíyàng	same; similar	7
一直	yìzhí	all along; straight; always	10
椅子	yǐzi	chair	4
游	yóu	tour (v)	10
又	yòu	further	5
又	yòu	again	10
邮件	yóujiàn	mail	9
有意思	yǒuyìsi	interesting	1
圆	yuán	round	7
元旦	Yuándàn	(Western) New Year	7
月饼	yuèbǐng	moon cake	7
阅读	yuèdú	reading	8
越来越	yuèláiyuè	more and more; increasingly	3
月亮	yuèliang	moon	7
语文	yǔwén	language arts	5
在	zài	*progressive aspect marker*	2
着	zhe	*aspect marker*	7
真	zhēn	really; truly	2
这样	zhèyàng	so; like this	1
治	zhì	treat (a disease)	6
至少	zhìshǎo	at least	10
只是	zhǐshì	merely; only; just	3
职员	zhíyuán	clerk	1
中秋节	Zhōngqiūjié	Mid-Autumn Festival	7
重要	zhòngyào	important	2
中医	zhōngyī	Chinese medicine	6
装	zhuāng	hold; load; install	7

装饰品	zhuāngshìpǐn	decorative objects; decorations	7
专业	zhuānyè	major; profession; specialty	5
祝贺	zhùhè	congratulate; congratulations	1
著名	zhùmíng	famous; renowned	10
桌子	zhuōzi	table; desk	4
主要	zhǔyào	main; primary; mainly; primarily	2
主意	zhǔyì	idea	2
注意	zhùyì	pay attention; be mindful of	6
自己	zìjǐ	oneself; one's own	8
资料	zīliào	information; data; material	9
自然科学	zìrán kēxué	natural science	5
足够	zúgòu	enough; adequate	5
最近	zuìjìn	recently; shortly; these days	1
尊重	zūnzhòng	respect	3
座	zuò	*classifier*	10

Key to the Exercises

Lesson 1

II.

1. 结婚三十年了 jiéhūn sānshí nián le
2. 离婚五年了 líhūn wǔ nián le
3. 参加朋友的婚礼 cānjiā péngyou de hūnlǐ
4. 去夏威夷渡假 qù Xiàwēiyí dù jià
5. 我们去吧 wǒmen qù ba
6. 新娘和新郎 xīnniáng hé xīnláng
7. 十年前 shí nián qián；十年后 shí nián hòu
8. 上班前 shàngbān qián; 下班后 xiàbān hòu
9. 他们结婚的时候 tāmen jiéhūn de shíhou
10. 从美国回来 cóng Měiguó huí lái

III.

1. 以后 yǐhòu
2. 是 ...... 的 shì … de
3. 最近 zuìjìn
4. 的时候 de shíhou
5. 以前 yǐqián
6. 要 yào
7. 以前 yǐqián
8. 以后 yǐhòu
9. 的时候 de shíhou
10. 是 ...... 的 shì … de

IV.

1. 老师们每天七点上班。 Lǎoshīmen měi tiān qī diǎn shàngbān.

2. 老师们每天工作七个小时。Lǎoshīmen měi tiān gōngzuò qī ge xiǎoshí.

3. 我的美国朋友在广州住了三年。Wǒde Měiguó péngyou zài Guǎngzhōu zhù le sān nián.

4. 大卫 和 玛丽下个月结婚。Dàwèi hé Mǎlì xià ge yuè jiéhūn.

5. 你在澳门玩儿了几天? Nǐ zài Àomén wánr le jǐ tiān?

V.

1. 好吃 hǎochī
2. 好听 hǎotīng
3. 好喝 hǎohē
4. 好看 hǎokàn
5. 好玩儿 hǎowánr

VI.

新 _____ 汽车	好吃 的 菜	短 _____ 大衣
xīn _____ qīchē	hǎochī de cài	duǎn _____ dàyī

不 老 的 人	高兴 的 事	热 _____ 茶
bù lǎo de rén	gāoxìng de shì	rè _____ chá

VII.

1. 我今天没有去银行。Wǒ jīntiān méiyou qù yínháng.

2. 她来美国以前是老师。她来美国后是学生。Tā lái Měiguó yǐqián shì lǎoshī. Tā lái Měiguó hòu shì xuésheng.

3. 我爸爸妈妈十天前不在家。Wǒ bàba māma shí tiān qián bú zài jiā.

4. 你今天是几点吃的中饭? Nǐ jīntiān shì jǐ diǎn chī de zhōngfàn?

5. 他们为这个公司工作了二十年。Tāmen wèi zhè ge gōngsī gōngzuò le èrshí nián.

6. 你今天晚上打算作什么? Nǐ jīntiān wǎnshang dǎsuan zuò shénme?

7. 我妹妹快结婚了。Wǒ mèimei kuài jiéhūn le.

8. 除了法国，我们还去了英国和德国。Chúle Fǎguó, wǒmen hái qùle Yīngguó hé Déguó.

9. 孩子们看电影的时候喜欢问很多问题。Háizimen kàn diànyǐng de shíhòu xǐhuān wèn hěn duō wèntí.
10. 她说她以后告诉我。Tā shuō tā yǐhòu gàosù wǒ.

III.

1. My older sister lived in California before she got married.
2. There was no subway in Shanghai in the past.
3. Nowadays many people are not planning to get married.
4. It's about to rain.
5. She came back from China three weeks ago.
6. Besides English, my teacher can speak French and Spanish.
7. I have been busy recently and don't have time to study Chinese, but I will do it in the future.
8. They went to Washington by plane.
9. What do you like to do when you are not working?
10. It has snowed for two days.

Lesson 2

I.

1. 他正在看书。Tā zhèng zài kàn shū.
2. 他们在看电视。Tāmen zài kàn diànshì.
3. 她在打电话呢。Tā zài dǎ diànhuà ne.
4. 她正做饭呢。Tā zhèng zuò fàn ne.
5. 他在开车。Tā zài kāi chē.
6. 老师在上课。Lǎoshī zài shàng kè.

II.

1. 很流利 hěn liúlì
2. 太快 tài kuài
3. 很晚 hěn wǎn
4. 怎么样 zěnmeyàng
5. 大不大 dà bu dà

IV.

1. 老师来得不早。Lǎoshī lái de bù zǎo.

2. 我妈妈做饭做得不很好。Wǒ māma zuò fàn zuò de bù hěn hǎo.

3. 他开车开得不快。Tā kāi chē kāi de bú kuài.

4. 那个老人走得不慢。Nà ge lǎo rén zǒu de bú màn.

5. 他们在北京玩儿得不很高兴。Tāmen zài Běijīng wánr de bù hěn gāoxìng.

V.

1. 五天多 wǔ tiān duō；二十多个人 èrshí duō ge rén

2. 够长gòu cháng；不够高 bú gòu gāo

3. 有的地方容易，有的地方难 yǒude dìfang róngyì, yǒude dìfang nán

4. 学习外语的最好的办法 xuéxí wàiyǔ de zuì hǎo de bànfǎ

5. 练习口语的机会 liànxí kǒuyǔ de jīhuì

6. 互相学习 hùxiāng xuéxí

7. 跟中国朋友学习中文 gēn Zhōngguó péngyǒu xuéxí Zhōngwén

8. 认识一些汉字 rènshí yìxiē hànzì

9. 了不起的进步 liǎobùqǐ de jìnbù

10. 用英语和外国客户交谈 yòng Yīngyǔ hé wàiguó kèhù jiāotán

VI.

1. 就 jiù

2. 才 cài

3. 就 jiù

4. 才 cài

5. 才 cài

6. 就 jiù

VII.

1. 我们吃了两个小时。Wǒmen chī le liǎng ge xiǎoshí.

2. 他开车开了五个多小时。Tā kāi chē kāi le wǔ ge duō xiǎoshí.

3. 学生们正在上课。Xuéshēngmen zhèng zài shàng kè.

4. 你昨天回家的时候你妈妈在作什么？Nǐ zuótiān huí jiā de shíhòu nǐ māma zài zuò shénme?
5. 美国老师给美国打了三十分钟的电话。Měiguó lǎoshī gěi Měiguó dǎ le sānshí fēnzhōng de diànhuà.
6. 你昨天晚上睡得好吗？Nǐ zuótiān wǎnshang shuì de hǎo ma?
7. 我的美国朋友会说很多语言，比如说西班牙语、法语和德语。Wǒde Měiguó péngyǒu huì shuō hěn duō yǔyán, bǐrúshuō Xībānyáyǔ, Fǎyǔ hé Déyǔ.
8. 我学英语学了十年多了，可是我的英语还不够好。Wǒ xué Yīngyǔ xué le shí nián duō le, kěshì wǒde Yīngyǔ hái bú gòu hǎo.
9. 雪下得很大。Xuě xià de hěn dà.
10. 她睡得晚，起得早。Tā shuì de wǎn, qǐ de zǎo.

VIII.

1. You can only read the book for three days.
2. My wife worked in a middle school for twenty years.
3. He drove more than thirty hours before he got to California.
4. It takes me an hour by bus to get to work every day.
5. The students wrote the characters for thirty minutes.
6. The teacher speaks slowly.
7. The American friends had a good time in Beijing.
8. The children watched TV for two hours.
9. No one practices Chinese with me.
10. It only took us an hour to go from Shanghai to Suzhou by train.

Lesson 3

II.

1. 她对我很好。Tā duì wǒ hěn hǎo.
2. 他对你说了什么？Tā duì nǐ shuō le shénme?
3. 七点对我不好。Qī diǎn duì wǒ bù hǎo.
4. 我能不能给她留个话？Wǒ néng bu néng gěi tā liú ge huà?
5. 她想尽快开始工作。Tā xiǎng jìnkuài kāishǐ gōngzuò.
6. 我今天下午送人去机场。Wǒ jīntiān xiàwǔ sòng rén qù jīchǎng.

7. 昨天晚上我们全家都在家。Zuótiān wǎnshang wǒmen quán jiā dōu zài jiā.
8. 我们的经理在开会。Wǒmende jīnglǐ zài kāi huì.
9. 你如果有问题，请来我这儿。Nǐ rúguǒ yǒu wèntí, qǐng lái wǒ zhèr.
10. 越来越多的人学中文。Yuèláiyuè duō de rén xué Zhōngwén.

III.

1. 一会儿 yíhuìr
2. 一下儿 yíxiàr
3. 一点儿 yìdiǎnr
4. 一点儿 yìdiǎnr
5. 一会儿 yíhuìr
6. 一下儿 yíxiàr

V.

1. 你在什么商店都能买电话卡。Nǐ zài shénme shāngdiàn dōu néng mǎi diànhuà kǎ.
2. 我今年什么电影也没有看。Wǒ jīnnián shénme diànyǐng yě méiyou kàn.
3. 她昨天什么东西也没有吃，今天她什么东西也不想吃。Tā zuótiān shénme dōngxi yě méiyou chī, jīntiān tā shénme dōngxi yě bù xiǎng chī.
4. 我什么时候给她打电话，她的电话都忙。Wǒ shénme shíhòu gěi tā dǎ diànhuà, tāde diànhuà dōu máng.
5. 这个孩子的爸爸怎么跟她说，她都不听。Zhè ge háizi de bàba zěnme gēn tā shuō, tā dōu bù tīng.

VI.

1. 一边开车，一边用手机不安全。Yìbiān kāi chē, yìbiān yòng shǒujī bù ānquán.
2. 对不起，我们的经理还没有来。你要不要给他留个话？Duìbuqǐ, wǒmende jīnglǐ hái méiyou lái. Nǐ yào bu yào gěi tā liú ge huà?

. 如果你明天不能来学校，请给我打个电话。Rúguǒ nǐ míngtiān bù
néng lái xuéxiào, qǐng gěi wǒ dǎ ge diànhuà.

. 今天下午有人从北京大学给你打电话。她留了一个话，要你给她
回话。Jīntiān xiàwǔ yǒu rén cóng Běijīng Dàxué gěi nǐ dǎ diànhuà.
Tā liú le yí ge huà, yào nǐ gěi tā huí huà.

. 如果有重要的事，请打我的手机。Rúguǒ yǒu zhòngyào de shì,
qǐng dǎ wǒde shǒujī.

. 老师让我告诉你明天没有课。Lǎoshī ràng wǒ gàosù nǐ míngtiān
méi yǒu kè.

. 我请老师看看我的作业。Wǒ qǐng lǎoshī kàn kan wǒde zuòyè.

. 一边看电视一边学习不好。Yìbiān kàn diànshì yìbiān xuéxí bù hǎo.

. 请问，你能告诉我哪儿有公用电话吗？Qǐngwèn, nǐ néng gàosù
wǒ nǎr yǒu gōngyòng diànhuà ma?

. 你能过一会儿给我打电话吗？Nǐ néng guò yīhuìr gěi wǒ dǎ
diànhuà ma?

II.

. She asked me to call her, but she forgot to tell me her number.

. I hate people calling me at my dinnertime.

. Nowadays it is difficult to get through when I call people. I believe
that they are using the internet on their computer.

. In the past, college students in China only studied and never worked.
Now more and more college students work while they study.

. Twenty years ago, most Chinese didn't have phones in their homes,
which was very inconvenient. For example, you couldn't make an
appointment when you wanted to visit your friends. Sometimes you
traveled very far to see a friend only to find that he was not home.
Today, most people in China have a phone in their homes and many
have pagers and cell phones, which are very convenient.

esson 4

. 狗在桌子的下边。Gǒu zài zhuōzi de xiàbian.

. 刀在盘子的右边。Dāo zài pánzi de yòubian.

3. 盘子在刀和叉子的中间。Pánzi zài dāo hé chāzi de zhōngjiān.
4. 电脑在桌子的上边。Diànnǎo zài zhuōzi de shàngbian.
5. 教室里有老师和学生。Jiàoshì lǐ yǒu lǎoshī hé xuésheng.
6. 餐馆不在银行的左边。Cānguǎn bú zài yínháng de zuǒbian.

II.

东亚 dōng yà	南亚 nán yà	南美 nán měi
北美 běi měi	北非 běi fēi	南非 nán fēi
中非 zhōng fēi	中亚 zhōng yà	西欧 xī ōu
东欧 dōng ōu	北欧 běi ōu	南欧 nán ōu

III.

1. 医院在我们公司的对面。Yīyuàn zài wǒmen gōngsī de duìmiàn.
2. 学校里有老师和学生。Xuéxiào lǐ yǒu lǎoshī hé xuésheng.
3. 我家的东边是中国银行。Wǒ jiā de dōngbian shì Zhōngguó Yínháng.
4. 加拿大在美国的北边。Jiā'nádà zài Měiguó de běibian.
5. 中国的北边是俄国和蒙古。Zhōngguó de běibian shì Éguó hé Ménggǔ.
6. 电影院在学校和银行的中间。Diànyǐngyuàn zài xuéxiào hé yínháng de zhōngjiān.
7. 桌子上有书和词典。Zhuōzi shang yǒu shū hé cídiǎn.
8. 南边是北京火车站。Nánbian shì Běijīng Huǒchēzhàn.
9. 他的女朋友坐在他左边。Tāde nǚpéngyou zuò zài tā zuǒbian.
10. 冰箱里有很多菜。Bīngxiāng lǐ yǒu hěn duō cài.

IV.

behind the car	car in the back
in front of the school	the school in the front

n the book   the book on top

ast of the store   the store in the east

cross from the bank   the bank across

.

英国在法国的北边   印度在中国的西南

Yīngguó zài Fǎguó de běibian Yìndù zài Zhōngguó de xīnán

墨西哥在美国的南边   日本在韩国的东北

Mòxīgē zài Měiguó de nánbian Rìběn zài Hánguó de dōngběi

波兰在俄国的西边   埃及在苏丹的北边

Bōlán zà Éguó de xībian   Āijí zài Sūdān de běibian

I.

A.

1. 他把他的汽车卖了。Tā bǎ tāde qìchē mài le.
2. 我把我的手机关掉了。Wǒ bǎ wǒde shǒujī guān diào le.
3. 他们把茶喝了。Tāmen bǎ chá hē le.
4. 妈妈把那件毛衣洗了。Māma bǎ nà jiàn máoyī xǐ le.
5. 公司把我的工作换了。Gōngsī bǎ wǒde gōngzuò huàn le.

B.

1. 把书放在书包里 bǎ shū fàng zài shūbāo lǐ
2. 把钱包忘在家里 bǎ qiánbāo wàng zài jiālǐ
3. 把饭送到学校 bǎ fàn sòng dào xuéxiào
4. 把朋友带回家 bǎ péngyou dài huí jiā
5. 把你的名字写在纸上 bǎ nǐde míngzì xiě zài zhǐ shang

VII.

1. 猫在床的下面。Māo zài chuáng de xiàmiàn.
2. 大西洋在美国的东边。Dàxīyáng zài Měiguó de dōngbian.
3. 我们的学校在医院和银行的中间。Wǒmende xuéxiào zài yīyuàn hé yínháng de zhōngjiān.

4. 地图在门的后面。Dìtú zài mén de hòumiàn.
5. 我家在一家商店的旁边。Wǒ jiā zài yì jiā shāngdiàn de pángbiān.
6. 教室里有三个书架。Jiàoshì lǐ yǒu sān ge shūjià.
7. 孩子们在楼的外面玩儿。Háizimen zài lóu de wàimiàn wánr.
8. 酒店在餐馆的对面。Jiǔdiàn zài cānguǎn de duìmiàn.
9. 中国的北边有两个国家。Zhōngguó de běibian yǒu liǎng ge guójiā.
10. 加州在美国的西部。Jiāzhōu zài Měiguó de xībù.

VIII.

The United States is in North America. It is the fourth-largest country in
the world (the largest being Russia, followed by Canada and China).
North of the United States is Canada and south of it is Mexico. There are
no countries to its east and west. To its east is the Atlantic Ocean and to
its west is the Pacific Ocean.

Lesson 5

II.

1. 我们现在是老师了。Wǒmen xiànzài shì lǎoshī le.
2. 天冷了。Tiān lěng le.
3. 我现在会开车了。Wo xiànzài huì kā chē le.
4. 我爸爸不工作了。Wǒ bàba bù gōngzuò le.
5. 这个班的学生们现在有电脑了。Zhè ge bān de xuéshengmen
   xiànzài yǒu diànnǎo le.

III.

1. 我们老师说的 wǒmén lǎoshī shuō de
2. 我们看的 wǒmén kàn de
3. 公司作的 gōngsī zuò de
4. 你要的 nǐ yào de
5. 他们不能作的 tāmen bù néng zuò de

V.

1. 看到 kàn dào
2. 买到 mǎi dào
3. 吃到 chī dào
4. 找到 zhǎo dào
5. 买到 mǎi dào

√.

1. 还是 háishi
2. 或 (者) huò (zhě)
3. 或 (者) huò (zhě)
4. 还是 háishi
5. 还是 háishi

√I.

1. 这五本书都是我的。Zhè wǔ běn shū dōu shì wǒde.
2. 我想星期六或星期天去看电影。Wǒ xiǎng xīngqīliù huò xīngqītiān qù kàn diànyǐng.
3. 今年夏天很多人去中国旅行，我买不到飞机票。Jīnnián xiàtiān hěn duō rén qù Zhōngguó lǚxíng, wǒ mǎi bú dào fēijīpiào.
4. 如果不能去英国，我们就去法国。Rúguǒ bù néng qù Yīngguó, wǒmen jiù qù Fǎguó.
5. 我爸爸妈妈结婚四十年了。Wǒ bàba māma jiéhūn sìshí nián le.
6. 汽车在房子的前面。Qìchē zài fángzi de qiánmiàn.
7. 老师对我们很好。Lǎoshī duì wǒmen hěn hǎo.
8. 你的美国朋友说中文说得很好。Nǐde Měiguó péngyou shuō Zhōngwén shuō de hěn hǎo.
9. 你昨天是怎么来学校的？Nǐ zuótiān shì zěnme lái xuéxiào de?
10. 他学中文学了两年多了。Tā xué Zhōngwén xué le liǎng nián duō le.

√II.

1. 我高中毕业以后没有上大学。Wǒ gāozhōng bìyè yǐhòu méiyou shàng dàxué.

2. 我儿子的班上有二十八个学生。Wǒ érzi de bān shang yǒu èrshí bā ge xuésheng.

3. 学生们很高兴，因为老师说没有作业。Xuéshengmen hěn gāoxìng yīnwèi lǎoshī shuō méi yǒu zuòyè.

4. 对不起我今天晚上不能跟你去看电影。明天有一个考试，我要学习。Duìbuqǐ wǒ jīntiān wǎnshang bù néng gēn nǐ qù kàn diànyǐng. Míngtiān yǒu yí ge kǎoshì, wǒ yào xuéxí.

5. 很多家长要他们的孩子毕业后当律师和医生。Hěn duō jiāzhǎng yào tāmende háizi bìyè hòu dāng lǜshī hé yīshēng.

6. 我们七月初开始放暑假。Wǒmen qī yuè chū kāishǐ fàng shǔjià.

7. 老师让学生们下星期一交作业。Lǎoshī ràng xuéshengmen xià xīngqíyī jiāo zuòyè.

8. 学生们必须通过这些考试才能进大学。Xuéshengmen bìxū tōngguò zhèxiē kǎoshì cái néng jìn dàxué.

9. 很多大学生不想上研究生院。Hěn duō dàxuésheng bù xiǎng shàng yánjiūshēngyuàn.

10. 你有没有找到工作？Nǐ yǒu méiyou zhǎo dào gōngzuò?

VIII.

1. There are twelve grades at this school from elementary to high schoo.

2. Graduate students are required to take four or five classes each term.

3. High school graduates must pass the foreign languge exam before they can go to college.

4. More and more secondary schools in America are now offering Chinese language classes.

5. He can find a job, but he didn't look for one.

6. The English major is further divided into English language and English literature.

7. In China, students must first earn an master's degree before they can study for a Ph.D., but in America, students do not need to study for a master's first before they can study for a Ph.D.

8. Many college graduates go on to graduate school when they can't find a job.

9. I believe that in America, neither getting into college nor getting out of college is easy.

). Most foreign students must pass an English exam first before they are admitted into college or graduate school.

esson 6

.

. 在上海工作的医生 zài Shànghǎi gōngzuò de yīshēng

?. 我们工作的地方 wǒmen gōngzuò de dìfang

}. 他们开始上课的时间 tāmen kāishǐ shàng kè de shíjiān

). 教我们英语的老师 jiāo wǒmen Yīngyǔ de lǎoshī

). 今天要作的事 jīntiān yào zuò de shì

). 开门 kāi mén

'. 开电视 kāi diànshì

}. 开车 kāi chē

). 开药 kāi yào

). 开会 kāi huì

I.

. 完 wán

?. 完 wán

}. 好 hǎo, 好 hǎo

}. 完 wán

). 完 wán

'.

1. 我家是我爸爸做饭。Wǒ jiā shì wǒ bàba zuò fàn.
   你家是不是你爸爸做饭? Nǐ jiā shì bu shì nǐ bàba zuò fàn?

2. 他是在北京大学学习。Tā shì zài Běijīng Dàxué xuéxí.
   他是不是在北京大学学习? Tā shì bu shì zài Běijīng Dàxué xuéxí?

3. 我太太是不喜欢看电影。Wǒ tàitai shì bù xǐhuan kàn diànyǐng.
   你太太是不是喜欢看电影? Nǐ tàitai shì bu shì xǐhuan kàn diànyǐng?

4. 大多数中国人是起得很早。Dàduōshù Zhōngguórén shì qǐ de hěn zǎo.

大多数中国人是不是起得很早？Dàduōshù Zhōngguórén shì bu shì
qǐ de hěn zǎo?

5. 打太极拳是对身体有帮助。Dǎ tàijíquán shì duì shēntǐ yǒu bāngzhù.
打太极拳是不是对身体有帮助？Dǎ tàijíquán shì bu shì duì shēntǐ
yǒu bāngzhù?

V.
1. 我昨天肚子疼。Wǒ zuótiān dùzi téng.
2. 我先生牙疼。Wǒ xiānshēng yá téng.
3. 他嗓子疼。Tā sǎngzi téng.
4. 那位先生背疼。Nà wèi xiānshēng bèi téng.
5. 病人腿疼。Bìngrén tuǐ téng.

VI.
1, 3, 5, 7 and 9 are topic-comment sentences and 2, 4, 6, 8 and 10 are not

VII.
1. then (result)
2. just (for emphasis)
3. soon (for emphasis)
4. then (one action immediately follows the other)
5. only (referring to the previous action: earlier or better than expected)

VIII.
1. 中国是不是在东亚？Zhōngguó shì bu shì zài Dōngyà?
2. 我是住在纽约。Wǒ shì zhù ài Niǔyuē.
3. 请把报纸放在桌子上。Qǐng bǎ bàozhǐ fàng zài zhuōzi shang.
4. 今天是星期天。你怎么还上班？Jīntiān shì xīngqí tiān. Nǐ zěnme
hái shàngbān?
5. 你是什么时候开始发烧的？Nǐ shì shénme shíhòu kāishǐ fāshāo de?
6. 很多人信中药，因为他们觉得中医能治好西医治不好的一些病。
Hěn duō rén xìn zhōngyào, yīnwèi tāmen juédé zhōngyī néng zhì hǎo
xīyī zhì bù hǎo de yìxiē bìng.

7. 医生说你要吃一个月的药。Yīshēng shuō nǐ yào chī yí ge yuè de yào.

8. 你不会说中文没有关系。Nǐ bú huì shuō Zhōngwén méi yǒu guānxì.

9. 老师让学生注意发音。Lǎoshī ràng xuésheng zhùyì fāyīn.

10. 我看过很多医生，但是他们谁都治不好我的病。Wǒ kàn guo hěn duō yīshēng, dànshì tāmen shuí dōu zhì bù hǎo wǒde bìng.

IX.

1. There are no private doctors in China. When people are sick, they go to the hospital to see a doctor.

2. Without examining me, the doctor said that I didn't have any problems.

3. My mother is very good at cooking, especially at cooking Chinese food.

4. Although he came to work today, he was not completely recovered.

5. You don't just look sick. You look very sick.

6. Many people only go to see a Chinese doctor when a Western doctor can cure their disease.

7. Fever is the symptom of many diseases.

8. Most people who do *taiji* are middle-aged and old people.

9. Daily jogging is a very good way to exercise.

10. I study Chinese not to speak to the Chinese people, but rather to read books.

Lesson 7

I.

1. 黑板上写着五个字。Hēibǎn shang xiě zhe wǔ ge zì.

2. 桌上摆着晚饭。Zhuō shang bǎi zhe wǎnfàn.

3. 包里放着十本书。Bāo lǐ fàng zhe shí běn shū.

4. 墙上挂着世界地图。Qiáng shang guà zhe shìjiè dìtú.

5. 汽车里装着很多杯子和盘子。Qìchē lǐ zhuāng zhe hěn duō bēizi hé pánzi.

6. 请问他是不是学生。Qǐngwèn tā shì bu shì xuésheng.

7. 你能告诉我这儿有医院吗？Nǐ néng gàosù wǒ zhèr yǒu yīyuàn ma?

8. 你知道不知道我们如果不去他会不会不高兴？Nǐ zhī bù zhīdào wǒmen rúguǒ bú qù tā huì bú huì bù gāoxìng?

9. 圣诞节如果在星期天，我们星期一也放假。Shèngdànjié rúguǒ zài xīngqītiān, wǒmen xīngqī yī yě fàngjià.

10. 我想知道能不能在饭店换钱。Wǒ xiǎng zhīdào néng bu néng zài fàndiàn huàn qián.

III.

1. 好象 hǎoxiàng
2. 象 xiàng
3. 好象 hǎoxiàng
4. 象 xiàng
5. 好象 hǎoxiàng
6. 象 xiàng

IV.

1. 十二月 shíèr yuè
2. 十月 shí yuè
3. 七月 qī yuè
4. 一月 yī yuè
5. 二月 èr yuè
6. 一月或二月 yī yuè huò èr yuè
7. 十一月 shíyī yuè
8. 五月 wǔ yuè
9. 五月 wǔ yuè
10. 九月或十月 jiǔ yuè huò shí yuè

VI.

1. 对大多数美国人来说，圣诞节是最重要的节日。Duì dàduōshù Měiguórén lái shuō, Shèngdànjié shì zuì zhòngyào de jiérì.

2. 我最喜欢的节日是感恩节，因为我们全家要团聚。Wǒ zuì yǐhuan de jiérì shì Gǎnēnjié, yīnwèi wǒmen quán jiā yào tuánjù.

3. 我先来介绍一下我们的公司。Wǒ xiān lái jièshào yíxià wǒmende gōngsī.
4. 你能猜一猜我有多大吗？Nǐ néng cāi yi cāi wǒ yǒu duó dà ma?
5. 你能介绍一下你们国家的节日吗？Nǐ néng jièshào yíxià nǐmen guójiā de jiérì ma?
6. 美国餐馆里的中国菜和中国餐馆里的中国菜不一样。Měiguó cānguǎn lǐ de Zhōngguó cài hé Zhōngguó cānguǎn lǐ de Zhōngguó cài bù yíyàng.
7. 我没有喝酒的习惯。Wǒ méi yǒu hē jiǔ de xíguàn.
8. 中国新年又叫春节。Zhōngguó Xīnnián yòu jiào Chūnjié.
9. 圣诞节虽然不是中国的节日，但是现在很多中国人也过。Shèngdànjié suīrán bú shì Zhōngguó de jiérì, dànshì xiànzài hěn duō Zhōngguórén yě guò.
10. 在中国，孩子们最喜欢新年，因为他们那天能得到很多红包。Zài Zhōngguó, háizimen zuì xǐhuan Xīnnián, yīnwèi tāmen nà tiān néng dédào hěn duō hóngbāo.

VII.

1. My younger brother is twelve years younger than I am. We were both born in the year of the sheep.
2. Chinese people are not in the habit of exchanging gifts on Chinese New Year.
3. In the past, people would say "Gōngxǐ fācái" on New Year's Day, but now people often say "Xīn Nián hǎo." They mean the same thing.
4. Labor Day in China is May 1, whereas in America, Labor Day is the first Monday in September.
5. In China, people don't get a day off on the Mid-Autumn Festival.
6. American people celebrate all kinds of holidays and festivals.
7. I like September the most, when there are the most festivals.
8. During holidays, people in China like to go to the cities, but people in America like to get out of the city.
9. Many countries in Asia also celebrate Chinese New Year.
10. I've used up my vacation days for this year.

Lesson 8

II.
1. 被解雇了 bèi jiěgù le
2. 找工作 zhǎo gōngzuò
3. 找到了工作 zhǎo dào le gōngzuò
4. 三个月里 sān ge yuè lǐ
5. 一年后 yì nián hòu
6. 更多的机会 gèng duō de jīhuì
7. 看了电视里的新闻 kàn le diànshì lǐ de xīnwén
8. 对音乐很有兴趣 duì yīnyuè hěn yǒu xìngqù
9. 对游泳没有兴趣 duì yóuyǒng méi yǒu xìngqù
10. 他没有帮我这个忙。 Tā méiyou bāng wǒ zhè ge máng.
11. 我没有请他帮我这个忙。 Wǒ méiyou qǐng tā bāng wǒ zhè ge máng.
12. 你太太在哪儿教书？她在大学教美术。Nǐ tàitai zài nǎr jiāoshū? Tā zài dàxué jiāo měishù.
13. 工资多少要看经验。Gōngzī duōshao yào kàn jīngyàn.
14. 我来这儿是买东西，不是卖东西的。Wǒ lái zhèr shì mǎi dōngxi, bú shì mài dōngxi de.
15. 这件事和我们公司没有关系。Zhè jiàn shì hé wǒmen gōngsī méi yǒu guānxì.

III.
1. 病人被医生治好了。Bìngrén bèi yīshēng zhì hǎo le.
2. 书被学生们带回家了。Shū bèi xuéshengmen dài huí jiā le.
3. 茶被他喝了茶。Chá bèi tā hē le.
4. 我爸爸的汽车被他卖了。Wǒ bàba de qìchē bèi tā mài le.
5. 我女朋友的手机被她关掉了。Wǒ nǚpéngyou de shuǒjī bèi tā guān diào le.
6. 你的申请被老板考虑了。Nǐde shēnqǐng bèi lǎobǎn kǎolǜ le.

IV.
1. 猫吃了鱼。Māo chī le yú.

2. 老师 把桌子拿进来了。Lǎoshī bǎ zhuōzi ná jìn lai le.

3. 他把字典放在书架上了。Tā bǎ zìdiǎn fàng zài shūjià shang le.

4. 孩子们看到了圣诞节的礼物。Háizimen kàn dào le Shèngdànjié de lǐwù.

5. 妈妈洗了毛衣。Māma xǐ le máoyī.

6. 很多人已经问过了这个问题。Hěn duō rén yǐjīng wèn guò le zhè ge wèntí.

Ⅴ.

1. 帮 _____ 忙 bāngmáng

2. 帮助 bāngzhù, 帮助 bāngzhù

3. 帮助 bāngzhù

4. 帮忙 bāngmáng

5. 帮助 bāngzhù

6. 帮 bāng, 忙 máng

Ⅵ.

1. 纽约的中小学需要很多英语老师。Niǔyuē de zhōng xiǎoxué xūyào hěn duō de Yīngyǔ lǎoshī.

2. 我对不提供医疗保险的工作没有兴趣。Wǒ duì bù tígòng yīliáo bǎoxiǎn de gōngzuò méi yǒu xìngqù.

3. 请把你的主要成绩列在你的简历上。Qǐng bǎ nǐde zhǔyào chéngji liè zài nǐde jiǎnlì shang.

4. 对有的雇主来说，经验比学位更重要。Duì yǒude gùzhǔ lái shuō, jīngyàn bǐ xuéwèi gèng zhòngyào.

5. 我只帮了你一个小忙。你不用给我钱。Wǒ zhǐ bāng le nǐ yí ge xiǎo máng. Nǐ búyòng gěi wǒ qián.

6. 在过去两年里，他换了三次工作。Zài guòqù de liǎngnián lǐ, tā huàn le sān cì gōngzuò.

7. 我现在作的和我在大学学的有很大的关系。Wǒ xiànzài zuò de hé wǒ zài dàxué xué de yǒu hěn dà de guānxì.

8. 我没有大学文凭。你想他们会雇我吗？Wǒ méi yǒu dàxué wénpíng. Nǐ xiǎng tāmen huì gù wǒ ma?

9. 你什么时候能开始工作？你能工作多久？Nǐ shénme shíhòu néng kāishǐ gōngzuò? Nǐ néng gōngzuò duō jiǔ?

10. 她找工作找了两个月，但是还没有找到。Tā zhǎo gōngzuò zhǎo l｀ liǎngge yuè, dànshì hái méiyou zhǎo dào.

VII.

1. Some employers lay off workers not because their business is not good, but because they want to save money.
2. Although the pay is not good, the work provides good benefits.
3. We'll reply to you as soon as we make the decision.
4. Computer jobs were easy to find three years ago, but not now.
5. The doctor wanted you to rest at home because he didn't want you to be too tired.
6. I can't start working for you until after a month.
7. Since you don't have a college degree and English is not your first language, we can't consider your application.
8. What he wants you to do is to write to his secretary.
9. Please bring your resume and degree when you come to the interview
10. Full-time employees have pensions, but part-time employees don't.

Lesson 9

II.

1. 地方新闻 dìfang xīnwén, 国内新闻 guónèi xīnwén, 国际新闻 guójì xīnwén, 头版新闻 tóubán xīnwén
2. 大概认识三百个字 dàgài rènshi sānbǎi ge zì
3. 差不多每天都锻炼 chàbùduō měi tiān duō duànliàn
4. 很少上网 hěn shǎo shàng wǎng
5. 对北京很熟悉 duì Běijīng hěn shúxi
6. 关于中国的电影 guānyú Zhōngguó de diànyǐng；关于日本的书 guānyú Rìběn de shū
7. 把旧报纸扔掉 bǎ jiù bàozhǐ rēng diào
8. 实际上我没有听说过那个地方。Shíjìshang wǒ méiyou tīngshuō guo nà ge dìfang.
9. 他很担心他会被解雇。Tā hěn dānxīn tā huì bèi jiěgù.
10. 股票市场昨天涨得很厉害。Gǔpiào shìchǎng zuótiān zhǎng de hěn lìhài.

III.
1. 我不在家吃中饭。Wǒ bú zài jiā chī zhōngfàn.
2. 他中文说得不流利。Tā Zhōngwén shuō de bù liúlì.
3. 医生治不好这个病。Yīshēng zhì bù hǎo zhè ge bìng.
4. 书没有在桌子上放着。Shū méiyou zài zhuōzi shang fàng zhe.
5. 老师没有给我打电话。Lǎoshī méiyou gěi wǒ dǎ diànhuà.
6. 学生们不都学习英语。Xuéshengmen bù dōu xuéxí Yīngyǔ.
7. 大家都不喜欢这个餐馆。Dàjià dōu bù xǐhuan zhè ge cānguǎn.
8. 我想那儿没有医院。Wǒ xiǎng nàr méi yǒu yīyuàn.
9. 我觉得今天不冷。Wǒ juéde jīntiān bù lěng.
10. 火车开得不快。Huǒchē kāi de bú kuài.

IV.
1. 我们学校的外国老师我不都认识。Wǒmen xuéxiào de wàiguó lǎoshī wǒ bù dōu rènshi.
2. 我们学校的外国老师我都不认识。Wǒmen xuéxiào de wàiguó lǎoshī wǒ dōu bú rènshi.
3. 我们的老师每天都给我们测验。Wǒmende lǎoshī měi tiān dōu gěi wǒméncèyàn.
4. 病人今天什么都没有吃。Bìngrén jīntiān shénme dōu méiyou chī.
5. 我的爸爸妈妈都喜欢日本菜。Wǒ bàba māma dōu xǐhuan Rìběn cài.
6. 每个公司都有网站吗？Měi ge gōngsī dōu yǒu wángzhàn ma?

V.
1. 连孩子都知道。Lián háizi dōu zhīdào.
2. 我连他的名字也没有问。Wǒ lián tāde míngzì yě méiyou wèn.
3. 他连开车都不会。Tā lián kāi chē dōu bú huì.
4. 医生们今天忙得连吃饭的时间也没有。Yīshéngmen jīntiān máng de lián chīfàn de shíjiān yě méi yǒu.
5. 我的美国朋友连上海话都会说。Wǒde Měiguó péngyǒu lián Shànghǎihuà dōu huì shuō.

VI.

1. 我到了洛杉矶就给你打电话。Wǒ dào le Luòshānjī jiù gěi nǐ dǎ diànhuà.
2. 他们结了婚就要去香港度 蜜月。Tāmen jié le hūn jiù yào qù Xiānggǎng dù mìyuè.

3. 你下了课就来图书馆，好吗？Nǐ xià le kè jiù lǎi túshūguǎn, hǎo ma
4. 飞机到了北京就去上海。Fēijī dào le Běijīng jiù qù Shànghǎi.
5. 我们下了班要开会。Wǒmen xià le bān yào kāihuì.

VII.

1. 我太忙，没有时间，所以我只读标题。Wǒ tài máng, méi yǒu shíjiān, suǒyǐ wǒ zhǐ dú biāotí.
2. 今天的报上有关于他们婚礼的报道吗？Jīntiānde bào shang yǒu guānyú tāmen hūnlǐde bàodào ma?
3. 你们有关于中国历史的课吗？Nǐmen yǒu guānyú Zhōngguó lìshǐ de kè ma?
4. 现在连小孩子都能发电子信，用互联网。Xiànzài lián xiǎoháizi dōu néng fā diànzǐxìn, yòng hùliánwǎng.
5. 我对这城市不熟悉。你能给我介绍一下儿吗？Wǒ duì zhè ge chéngshì bù shúxi. Nǐ néng gěi wǒ jièshào yīxiàr ma?
6. 你可以在网上找到关于这个公司的资料。Nǐ kěyǐ zài wǎng shang zhǎo dào guānyú zhè ge gōngsī de zīliào.
7. 用电脑写中文，你需要有中文软件。Yòng diànnǎo xiě zhōngwén, nǐ xūyào yǒu Zhōngwén ruǎnjiàn.
8. 你上次给我的电子信地址不对。Nǐ shàng cì gěi wǒ de diànzǐxìn dìzhǐ bú duì.
9. 我的朋友在网上上中文课。Wǒde péngyou zài wǎng shang shàng Zhōngwénkè.
10. 中国的网吧比美国的多。Zhōngguó de wǎngbā bǐ Měiguóde duō.

VIII.

1. The internet brought us a lot of convenience. We can now read newspapers from China on the internet.

2. The status of the economy has a lot to do with the stock market.
3. I have been learning Chinese for two months, but I can't even write the character for "big."
4. The first thing that my mother does after she buys the newspaper is to read the ads.
5. Many websites in China are written in Chinese. Those who don't read Chinese don't understand them.
6. She receives all kinds of emails every day, but she does not have time to read them all.
7. The emails that I sent him were all returned, which is extremely annoying.
8. Many people are so busy that they can only read newspapers when they are on their way to work in the subway.
9. There is more local news in the tabloids than in big papers.
10. I have no interest in stocks at all. Sports news is more interesting.

esson 10

I.

1. 旧建筑的特点 jiù jiànzhù de tèdiǎn
2. 对这个城市的印象 duì zhè ge chéngshì de yìnxiàng
3. 到过这个地方无数次 dào guo zhè ge dìfang wúshù cì
4. 世界上 shìjiè shang
5. 至少三天 zhìshǎo sān tiān
6. 完全变了 wánquán biàn le
7. 百分之五十 bǎifēnzhī wǔshí, 百分之七十五 bǎifēnzhī qīshí wǔ, 百分之百 bǎifēnzhī bǎi, 四分之一 sìfēnzhī yī, 五分之三 wǔfēnzhī sān, 三分之二 sānfēnzhī èr
8. 从来没有读过这本书 cónglái méiyou dú guo zhè běn shū
9. 具体的资料 jùtǐde zīliào
10. 今天又去了银行 jīntiān yòu qù le yínháng

II.

1. 好喝 hǎo hē

2. 贵 guì
3. 好 hǎo
4. 好吃 hǎo chī
5. 快 kuài

B.
1. 哥哥比弟弟大两岁。Gēge bǐ dìdi dà liǎng suì.
2. 这条公路比那条公路长。Zhè tiáo gōnglù bǐ nà tiáo gōnglù cháng.
3. 我们班比他们班多五个学生。Wǒmen bān bǐ tāmen bān duō wǔ ge xuésheng.
4. 这个汉字比那个汉字难。Zhè ge hànzì bǐ nà ge hànzì nán.
5. 他走得比我快。Tā zǒu de bǐ wǒ kuài.
6. 姐姐写字写得比妹妹写得好看。Jiějie xiě zì xiěde bǐ mèimei xiě de hǎokàn.
7. 中国的产品比日本的产品便宜。Zhōngguó de chǎnpǐn bǐ Rìběn de chǎnpǐn piányi.
8. 我妈妈作菜比我爸爸作得好。Wǒ māma zuò cài bǐ wǒ bàba zuò de hǎo.
9. 今天的股票市场跌得比昨天的股票市场跌得厉害。Jīntiān de gǔpiào shìchǎng diē dé bǐ zuótiānde gǔpiào shìchǎng diē dé lìhài.
10. 我家的人和他家的人一样多。Wǒ jiā de rén hé tājiā de rén yíyàng duō.

IV.
1. 再 zài
2. 又 yòu
3. 再 zài
4. 又 yòu
5. 再 zài

V.
1. 我们在欧洲玩儿得很高兴。Wǒmen zài Ōuzhōu wánr dé hěn gāoxìng.

2. 对我来说，西安是中国最有意思的地方。Duì wǒ lái shuō, Xī'ān shì Zhōngguó zuì yǒuyìsī de dìfang.
3. 在最近二十年里，中国变化很大。Zài zuìjìn èrshí nián lǐ, Zhōngguó biànhuà hěn dà.
4. 在我们去的地方中，我太太最喜欢巴黎。Zài wǒmen qù de dìfang zhōng, wǒ tàitai zuì xǐhuan Bālí.
5. 我不喜欢我们昨天晚上去的餐馆。Wǒ bù xǐhuan wǒmen zuótiān wǎnshang qù de cānguǎn.
6. 从上海坐火车去香港至少要十五个小时。Cóng Shànghǎi zuò huǒchē qù Xiānggǎng zhìshǎo yào shíwǔ ge xiǎoshí.
7. 世界上四分之一的人是中国人。Shìjiè shang sìfēnzhī yī de rén shì Zhōngguórén.
8. 我和我太太五年前在我退休的时候搬到弗罗里达。Wǒ hé wǒ tàitai wǔ nián qián zài wǒ tuìxiū de shíhou bān dào Fóluólǐdá.
9. 他一直 (or 一生都)住在日本，对这个国家很熟悉。Tā yìzhí (or yìshēng dōu) zhù zài Rìběn, duì zhè ge guójiā hěn shúxi.
10. 有的人不喜欢变化。他们觉得新的东西没有老的东西好。Yǒude rén bù xǐhuan biànhuà. Tāmen juédé xīn de dōngxi méiyou lǎo de dōngxi hǎo.

VI.

1. The characteristic of Chinese is that its grammar is simple, but its pronunciation is difficult.
2. There are five beltways in Beijing.
3. Twenty years ago in Shanghai, Pudong was countryside, but now there are numerous highrises there and it is a completely new place.
4. In order to read Chinese newspapers, you need to know at least two thousand characters.
5. Many people in the West like Dim Sum because, although they don't know the name of the food, they can choose what they like.
6. I like New York, where you can meet people from various countries and hear various languages.
7. Chinese students make up 20% of all the foreign students at this school.

8. My husband has no interest in finance. He never reads the *Wall Street Journal*.
9. I haven't seen him for ten years. He has changed so much that he looks completely different than before.
10. They have always lived in Boston since they got married.

Computing in Chinese

The advancement of computer technology is a great boon for language learners, and particularly for students of Chinese in their dealing with Chinese characters. A complex character consisting of twenty to thirty strokes can be easily produced by tapping a couple of keystrokes on the computer. It is so effective and fun at the same time that there are teachers of Chinese who are advocating a penless approach to writing characters, using the computer.

For our purposes, computing in Chinese refers to two things: viewing or reading characters on the internet or in emails, and producing characters using the computer.

Viewing Chinese

There are two ways to view characters. First, you need an add-on or a helper Chinese program that comes with a package of Chinese fonts. Such programs work in conjunction with regular word processors and internet browsers. When it comes to inputting (more on that later), most of them are resident in that they reside in the computer's memory and within whatever applications you use, but some are stand-alone. Popular Chinese programs include TwinBridge (http://www.twinbridge.com), Chinese Star (http://www.suntendyusa.com), RichWin (http://www.richwinusa.com) and NJ Star (http://www.njstar.com). Macintosh users can use Chinese Language Kit for the Macintosh.

Second, the most up-to-date operating systems, typically Microsoft Windows 2000 Professional and Windows XP, are now equipped with features that allow Chinese text to be displayed without the assistance of a helper program as mentioned above. In order to make use of this built-in feature, you would need to change some computer configurations in your computer's "Control Panel." If you use Windows 2000 or XP: from the Start button, select Settings and then the Control Panel. From the options on the Control Panel select "Regional Options." The default selection under the General tab is English. Do not change it unless you want to work exclusively in the Chinese environment. On the lower half of the window, select simplified or traditional Chinese. It is a good idea to select both because some characters you will need to view use the simplified form, whereas others take the traditional form. At this point, you will be asked to insert the Windows 2000 Install CD and copy over the files it needs. You will then need to reboot for the new settings to take effect. If you need a step-by-step guide on how to install the program, check this site:

http://californiadream.com/workshops/info/winXPLang/winXPlangInstall Config.html

The latest version of two major browsers (Netscape and Internet Explorer) can also support Chinese without having to resort to any other add-on programs. Some Chinese web pages are so smart that they can trigger the browser for it to automatically apply Chinese fonts to display the characters. Other web pages do not have this feature, such that Chinese characters will not be automatically displayed correctly. When this happens, you need to adjust the settings under View in your browser. If you use Netscape, select View, Character Set, and then either simplified Chinese or traditional Chinese. If you use Internet Explorer, select View, Encoding, and then simplified or traditional Chinese.

If your internet browser does not display Chinese correctly, the simplest thing for you to do is to upgrade your internet browser to a newer version or to install the free language support packs when you are prompted by your computer system. If you use Windows 95, 98 or NT, you can download free Chinese language support packages at the following website:

http://www.microsoft.com/windows/ie/downloads/recommended/ime/inst all.asp

"Writing" Chinese

The software needed to write Chinese characters is basically the same as that for viewing Chinese characters. That is, use an add-on Chinese program or use the built-in input device that comes with certain operating systems.

Each of the popular add-on programs mentioned earlier (TwinBridge, Chinese Star, RichWin and NJStar) can do the job very well. Of the four, TwinBridge, Chinese Star, and RichWin are resident programs, and NJ Star is a stand-alone program. There are a variety of input methods, but for students of Chinese, I suggest the *pinyin* method, which is not only easy, but also helpful in enhancing your awareness of *pinyin* and consequently the correct pronunciation of words. When you activate one of these add-on programs, whether inside or outside a word-processing application, a panel will appear on the screen. When you type *pinyin* for a particular character, word or even phrase, it will appear in the panel. Since Chinese is famous for the proliferation of homophones, you will get a list of characters that are pronounced the same when you type *pinyin* for a character. All the homophones are numbered. If the character you intend to produce happens to be the first choice, you can simply press the space bar and the character will go on the screen where the cursor is. If the intended character is not the first item on the list, you will then need to select it by pressing the corresponding number. This undoubtedly is quite slow and time-consuming. The right way to input is to type by word rather than individual characters. Since most words in Chinese today are dissyllabic, there are far fewer homophones for dissyllabic or polysyllabic words. For example, if you want to produce the word 中文 zhōngwén, which consists of two characters 中 zhōng and 文 wén, you can do it in one of the two ways. First, you can first type 中 and then 文. If you do that, you will get seventeen characters for zhong and fifteen characters for wen (on NJStar). You will then need to pick the right character from the list. The second way is to enter the word in its entirety: zhongwen. When you do this, only one word appears on the panel because there is no other word in Chinese that is also pronounced zhongwen. Before long, you will find that you don't even have to type an entire *pinyin* before you can get a word of your choice. Some representations will suffice. For example, when you type *zhongw*, the characters for *zhongwen* already appear. If you become sufficiently familiar with the process, you will further find that you can get 中文 if you simply type *zhw*. It takes seven key strokes to type the word *Chinese* in English, but it only take three strokes to produce the equivalent in Chinese. So it is not a myth that people can type Chinese characters as fast as they type English words or even faster.

Alternatively, you can use built-in input devices that come with certain operating systems, also configured under the Language or Regional settings within your computer's Control Panel. If you do this, you won't then need an add-on Chinese program. This is how you can do it on Windows XP:

First, install East Asian language files on your computer. The files include Chinese, Japanese, and Korean. The following are steps to do this:

- Click Control Panel to open Regional and Language Options.
- On the Languages tab, under Supplemental Language Support, select Install Files for East Asian Languages. Check the box and then click OK or Apply. You will then be prompted to insert the Windows CD-ROM or point to a network location where the files are located.
- After the files are installed, you must restart your computer.

After you have installed the East Asian language files on your computer's hard disk, you must add the individual languages for which you want to input and display text. For us, Chinese is what we need:

- Open Regional and Language Options in Control Panel.
- On the Advanced tab, under Language for non-Unicode programs click Chinese (Chinese-PRC for simplified Chinese; Chinese-Taiwan for traditional Chinese)

The last step will be to choose an appropriate Chinese input method. We recommend *pinyin* to Chinese language learners:

- Open Regional and Language Options in Control Panel.
- On the Languages tab, under Text Services and Input Languages, click Details.
- Under Installed services, click Add.

- On the Input Language list, click the language for the keyboard layout or Input Method Editor (IME) you want to add. For us, we should choose "Chinese (Chinese-PRC for simplified Chinese; Chinese-Taiwan for traditional Chinese)."
- Select the Keyboard Layout/IME check box, click Chinese-simplified, Microsoft Pinyin IME3.0 on the list. If you choose Chinese-Taiwan in the second step above, you may click Microsoft phonetic IME2000 here for traditional Chinese input.

Internet Resources for Students of Chinese

Guides, Indexes & Links

Chinese home page
http://www.uni.edu/becker/chinese.html
A complete reference to China/Chinese-related websites.

Chinese language
http://bubl.ac.uk/link/c/chineselanguage.htm
A catalog of internet resources.

Chinese language & linguistics
http://www.cohums.ohio-state.edu/deall/chan.9/c-links3.htm
Annotated links compiled by Marjorie Chan to more than two hundred China and Chinese language- and linguistics-related websites.

Chinese language study
http://www.nerdworld.com/nw1800.html
Large index of Chinese language study-related internet resources.

Chinese language & writing
http://acc6.its.brooklyn.cuny.edu/~phalsall/texts/chinlng2.html
Includes the history of the Sino-Tibetan family of languages.

Chinese language-related information
http://www.webcom.com/~bamboo/chinese/chinese.html
A comprehensive subject guide to Chinese-language-related resources on the internet.

Chinese software-related homepage
http://www.gy.com/www/chlist.htm
A web of webs.

Online Chinese resources
http://www.lsa.umich.edu/asian/chinese/online/index3.html
University of Michigan's links to resources to aid in the learning of the Chinese language and culture.

Teaching and learning Chinese
http://www2.kenyon.edu/depts/mll/chinese/
A collection of resources for teaching and learning Chinese.

Dictionaries

Chinese characters dictionary web
http://zhongwen.com/zi.htm

Chinese-English dictionary
http://www.mandarintools.com/

English-Chinese dictionary
http://www.ok88.com/go/svc/ecdict.html

Online Chinese dictionaries
http://www.chinalanguage.com/Language/Dictionaries/index.html

Top Chinese dictionaries
http://www.amazon.com/exec/obidos/tg/browse/-/11520/zipubooks/102-3394847-7978527

Online Tutorials, Courses & Programs

Chinese multimedia tutorial
http://www.inform.umd.edu/EdRes/Topic/Humanities/.C-tut/C-tut.html
A tutorial on greetings, expressing thanks and food terms, including characters and sounds.

Conversational Mandarin Chinese online
http://philo.ucdavis.edu/zope/home/txie/azi/online.html
A fifteen-unit course on everyday topics.

Internet-based Chinese teaching & learning
http://chinese.bendigo.latrobe.edu.au/index.htm
La Trobe University's eight-level online Chinese language courses.

Learn Chinese
http://pasture.ecn.purdue.edu/~agenhtml/agenmc/china/ctutor.html
An audio tutorial of survival Chinese.

Learn Chinese online
http://www.csulb.edu/~txie/online.htm
Large index of links for learning, studying, or practicing Chinese online.
Links include pronunciation, conversation, grammar and characters,
literature, dictionaries, software, and more.

Speaking Chinese
http://www.speakingchinese.com/
You are learning from the best teachers with experience in teaching
Chinese to international students. They are professional, innovative and
easygoing.

Teaching and learning Chinese
http://www2.kenyon.edu/depts/mll/chinese/other.htm
Jianhua Bai's website for online language resources.

Chinese characters

A is for love
http://www.chinapage.com/flash/love.html
This is a set of flash cards for learning Chinese. The face card shows a
Chinese word. Click on the word and the card will flip over, where the
pronunciation and meaning are given.

Animated Chinese characters
http://www.ocrat.com/ocrat/chargif/
Click on any Chinese character to see how to draw it.

Character flashcards
http://www.mandarintools.com/

Chinese character flashcards
http://www.mandarintools.com/flashcard.html
A Java applet to assist in the learning of Chinese characters.

Chinese character genealogy
http://www.zhongwen.com
An etymological Chinese-English dictionary.

Chinese character pronunciations
http://www.ocrat.com/ocrat/reaf/
Input (copy-and-paste) any Chinese text and obtain the transliterated pronunciation of each Chinese character. Follow links to online Chinese magazines and use this application to look up pronunciations of unfamiliar words.

Chinese character test
http://www.clavisinica.com/chartest.html
At this site, you can test yourself to see how many Chinese characters you know.

Chinese character tutor
http://www.worldlanguage.com/chintut.htm
A Chinese dictionary and learning tool that includes one hundred predefined lessons.

Chinese character tutor V4.0
http://www.bridgetochina.com
An online dictionary and learning tool with audio and testing facilities.

Chinese characters
http://www.usc.edu/dept/ealc/chinese/newweb/character_page.html
This site animates characters that appeared in the textbook Integrated Chinese, *but can also be used by beginning students of other textbooks as there is an alphabetical order of all the characters used in* Integrated Chinese.

Chinese radical exam
http://execpc.com/~mbosley/
A study aid and test for beginners, covering one hundred and eight of the most common radicals that are also characters in their own right.

Fascinating Chinese characters
http://www.china-guide.com/characte.htm#Characters
CD program teaching how to write Chinese characters.

Flashcards
http://www.wfu.edu/~moran/flashcards.html
With a week-by-week schedule.

Flashcard wizard
http://www.foolsworkshop.com/fw.html
Besides the ability to practice flashcards with two or three fields of information, these fields may include pictures and non-roman text for language study.

Four-sided flashcards
http://www.wfu.edu/~moran/flshcrds.html
Printable flashcards for learning characters.

Learn to read and write Chinese characters
http://www.csulb.edu/~txie/character.htm
A list of resources.

Simplified characters
http://zhongwen.com/jian.htm
Click on any character to see its simplified form (and its definition and etymology).

Vocabulary

A Chinese-English database
http://zinnia.umfacad.maine.edu/~mshea/China/database.html
Chinese-English vocabulary database.

New words
http://www.sinologic.com/language.html
Here are some cool and useful words that are being used every day in China, Taiwan, and Hong Kong. Some of them have been coined only recently. These and many more words of a similar nature will be incorporated into the upcoming CD-ROM version of HyperChina.

Pronunciation

Chinese pronunciation guide
http://www.courses.fas.harvard.edu/~pinyin/
Includes a tool, pinyin sheets and courses.

Learn Mandarin pronounciation
http://www.csulb.edu/~txie/online.htm
A list of resources.

Pinyin font converter
http://www.foolsworkshop.com/pfc.html
In order to input romanized Chinese in Pinyin using the four tones of Mandarin Chinese, special fonts are used to mark vowels with tones. A variety of these fonts is available online. The Pinyin Font Converter converts texts between some of the most popular Pinyin fonts that are available for Windows and Macintosh.

Pinyin practice
http://www.uiowa.edu/~chinese/pinyin/index.html
Welcome to the world of Pinyin and Chinese sounds. Before you begin to work on the exercises contained in this site, check out some sites that explain the fundamentals of the Pinyin system. Take advantage of the many examples given. When you have a basic understanding of Pinyin, return here to try these activities.

Speech wizard
http://www.catalog.com/inforg01/software.htm
English and Chinese text-to-speech system that lets you listen to the reading of English and Chinese words, sentences or even an entire text through your multimedia speakers.

Grammar

Learn Chinese grammar
http://www.csulb.edu/~txie/grammar.htm

Chinese Study Programs

Chinese Programs
http://www.webcom.com/~bamboo/chinese/courses.html
Links to websites with information on Chinese language study courses offered by various institutions.

Scholarships for Study of Chinese Abroad
http://www.wfu.edu/~moran/schol.html

Study Chinese in China
http://www.csulb.edu/~txie/abroad.htm

Chinese-Language Radio Broadcasts

http://www.webcom.com/~bamboo/chinese/radio.html
This page collects, in one place, information on radio or other broadcasts in Mandarin, Cantonese, and other Chinese languages. The emphasis is on broadcasts that are globally available, either via short-wave radio, cable, or in recorded form over the internet.

http://broadcast-live.com/chinese.html
At this site, you can watch Chinese television and listen to radio broadcasts in the Chinese language. A wide selection of streaming audio and video broadcasts is available from Canada, France, Germany, Singapore, Britain, China and the U.S. in both Mandarin and Cantonese. Transmissions are provided in RealAudio formats.

Software Programs

Chinese Star
http://www.suntendy.com/

NJStar
http://www.njstar.com

RichWin 4.2 Plus for Windows
http://www.richwinUSA.com

Twinbridge
http://www.twinbridge.com/

Chinese Bookstores

Asia for Kids
http://www.afk.com

Cheng & Tsui
http://www.cheng-tsui.com

China Books & Periodicals
http://www.chinabooks.com

China Sprout
http://www.chinasprout.com

Chinese Book & Supply Company
http://www.chinesebookco.com

Chinese Bookstores
http://www.csulb.edu/~txie/online2.htm#book
A list of resources.

Other Hippocrene Titles by Yong Ho

Beginner's Chinese

This introduction to Mandarin Chinese is designed for those with little or no prior experience in the language. Beginning with an in-depth look at the language's prominent features, including Chinese phonetics and the written language, it provides the most basic and crucial words and patterns to enable the student to immediately communicate in Chinese. Each lesson includes basic sentence patterns, dialogues to illustrate the use of these patterns, vocabulary and expressions, language points, exercises, and cultural insights. On completion of this course, the student will have learned ninety basic sentence patterns and three hundred characters.

174 pages • 5 1/2 x 8 1/2 • 0-7818-0566-X • $14.95pb • W • (690)

Chinese-English Frequency Dictionary:
A Study Guide to Mandarin Chinese's 500 Most Frequently Used Words

Functioning as both a traditional dictionary and a study guide, this list of the 500 most frequently used words (characters) of Mandarin Chinese offers the English-speaking student of Chinese an essential source of vocabulary and a detailed reference to the world's most widely spoken language. Presented in order of frequency, each entry includes the Chinese character with pinyin transcription, meaning, explanations of usage with examples, and a selection of words and expressions that have the entry word as the first element. Two indices also list the 500 words according to frequency and alphabetical order.

500 entries • 240 pages • 5 1/2 x 8 1/2 • 0-7818-0842-1 • $16.95pb • W • (277)

China: An Illustrated History

This concise, illustrated volume offers the reader a panoramic view of this remarkable land, from antiquity to the twenty-first century. Among other topics, it explores sources of Chinese thought, cornerstones of Chinese political, religious and economic institutions, and the cohesive ties that have bound China as a nation for thousands of years.

142 pages • 50 photos/illus./maps • 5 x 7 • 0-7818-0821-9 • $14.95hc • W • (542)

Hippocrene Children's Illustrated Chinese (Mandarin) Dictionary

English-Chinese/Chinese-English

Designed to be a child's first foreign language dictionary, for ages 5-10, each entry is accompanied by a large illustration, the English word and its equivalent, along with commonsense phonetic pronunciation. Entries include people, animals, colors, numbers and objects that children encounter and use every day.

500 entries • 94 pages • 8 1/2 x 11 • 0-7818-0848-0 • $11.95pb • W • (662)

Other Chinese Language guides from Hippocrene Books

Treasury of Chinese Love Poems

in Chinese and English

Edited and Translated by Qiu Xiaolong

This groundbreaking effort is the first translation of classic Chinese poems intended for contemporary English-speaking readers. It offers 74 poems by authors such as Li Bai, Guan Daoshen, Zhang Jiuling, and Li Shangyin. All works appear in Chinese with facing English translation.

150 pages • 5 x 7 • b/w illus. • 0-7818-0968-1 • $11.95hc • W • (515)

Dictionary of 1000 Chinese Idioms

Edited and Translated by Marjorie Lin and Schalk Leonard

The authors have selected 1000 of the most frequently used idioms, listing them in alphabetical order with Pinyin transcription, while providing the English translation and the original Chinese characters.

168 pages • 6 x 9 • 0-7818-0820-0 • $14.95pb • W • (598)

Dictionary of 1000 Chinese Proverbs

Edited by Marjorie Lin and Schalk Leonard

This wonderful reference collection offers students insight into both the language and culture of China. A comparable or literal translation is provided for 1000 commonly used proverbs. The book is organized alphabetically by key word. Proverbs are arranged side-by-side with their English counterparts/translations and marked to identify literal or free translation.

208 pages • 5 1/2 x 8 1/2 • 0-7818-0682-8 • $11.95pb • W • (773)

English-Chinese Pinyin Dictionary

10,000 entries • 500 pages • 4 x 6 • 0-7818-0427-2 • $19.95pb • US • (509)

Emergency Chinese Phrasebook

Designed to give travelers key words and essential phrases when they need them most.

80 pages • 7 1/2 x 4 1/8 • 0-7818-0975-4 • $5.95pb • NA • (461)

Other Asian language titles from Hippocrene Books

Cambodian-English/English-Cambodian Standard Dictionary
15,000 entries • 355 pages • 0-87052-818-1 • $16.95pb •W • (143)

Ilocano-English/English-Ilocano Dictionary and Phrasebook
7,000 entries • 269 pages • 5 1/2 x 8 1/2 • 0-7818-0642-9 • $14.95pb •
W • (718)

Indonesian-English/English-Indonesian Practical Dictionary
17,000 entries • 289 pages • 4 1/4 x 7 • 0-87052-810-6 • $11.95pb • NA
• (127)

Speak Standard Indonesian
285 pages • 4 x 6 • 0-7818-0186-9 • $11.95pb • W • (159)

Japanese-English/English-Japanese Concise Dictionary, Romanized
8,000 entries • 235 pages • 4 x 6 • 0-7818-0162-1 • $11.95pb • W •
(474)

Japanese-English/English-Japanese Dictionary & Phrasebook
2,300 entries • 220 pages • 3 3/4 x 7 1/2 • 0-7818-0814-6 • $12.95pb •
W • (205)

Beginner's Japanese
290 pages • 5 x 8 • 0-7818-0234-2 • $11.95pb • W • (53)

Mastering Japanese
368 pages • 5 1/2 x 8 1/2 • 0-87052-923-4 • $14.95pb • US • (523)
2 cassettes: 0-87052-983-8 • $12.95 • US • (524)

Korean-English/English-Korean Practical Dictionary
8,500 entries • 365 pages • 4 x 7 1/4 • 0-87052-092-X • $14.95pb • Asia
and NA • (399)

Lao-English/English-Lao Dictionary & Phrasebook
2,000 entries • 206 pages • 3 3/4 x 7 1/2 • 0-7818-0858-8 • $12.95pb • W • (179)

Lao Basic Course
350 pages • 5 x 8 • 0-7818-0410-8 • $19.95pb • W • (470)

Pilipino-English/English-Pilipino Concise Dictionary
5,000 entries • 389 pages • 4 x 6 0-87052-491-7 • $9.95pb • W • (393)

Pilipino-English/English-Pilipino (Tagalog) Dictionary & Phrasebook
2,000 entries • 186 pages • 3 3/4 x 7 1/2 • 0-7818-0451-5 • $11.95pb • W • (295)

Thai-English/English-Thai Dictionary & Phrasebook
1,800 entries •197 pages • 3 3/4 x 7 1/2 • 0-7818-0774-3 • $12.95pb • W • (330)

Beginner's Vietnamese
517 pages • 7 x 10 • 0-7818-0411-6 • $19.95pb • W • (253)

Vietnamese-English/English-Vietnamese Standard Dictionary
12,000 entries • 501 pages • 5 x 7 • 0-87052-924-2 • $19.95pb • W • (529)

Vietnamese-English/English-Vietnamese Dictionary & Phrasebook
3,000 entries • 200 pages • 3 3/4 x 7 1/2 • 0-7818-0991-6 • $11.95 • W • (104)

All prices are subject to change without prior notice. To order **Hippocrene Books**, contact your local bookstore, call (718) 454-2366, visit www.hippocrenebooks.com, or write to: Hippocrene Books, 171 Madison Avenue, New York, NY 10016. Please enclose check or money order adding $5.00 shipping (UPS) for the first book and $.50 for each additional title.